A RESEARCH MANUAL FOR THE PERFORMANCE
COURSE IN SPEECH

3.95

A Research Manual for the Performance Course in Speech

ORAL COMMUNICATION / FUNDAMENTALS
OF SPEECH / PUBLIC SPEAKING / ARGUMENTATION
AND DEBATE / DISCUSSION / PERSUASION

PAUL D. BRANDES
UNIVERSITY OF NORTH CAROLINA

THEODORE J. WALWIK
BUTLER UNIVERSITY

Harper & Row, Publishers

NEW YORK · EVANSTON · LONDON

This book is respectfully dedicated to
Lawrence and *Sybilla Hetsch*
and to
Nicholas Cripe,
without whose assistance the authors might never
have entered the teaching profession

A Research Manual for the Performance Course in Speech

COPYRIGHT © 1967 by *Paul D. Brandes and Theodore J. Walwik.*

Printed in the United States of America. All rights reserved. No
part of this book may be used or reproduced in any manner what-
soever without written permission except in the case of brief quo-
tations embodied in critical articles and reviews. For information
address Harper & Row, Publishers, Incorporated, 49 East 33rd
Street, New York, N.Y. 10016.

Library of Congress Catalog Card Number: 67-10199

IV. THE REVOLT ON THE CAMPUS

PREFACE

———————▸◂◆▸◂———————

THE UNIQUE FEATURE of the performance course in speech is that so much of the classroom time is consumed by student performance. If the content of this performance is inferior, the class must necessarily be inferior. This situation does not exist for most other disciplines, for a superior history teacher may maintain a high-caliber performance even to an uninteresting and uninspired class. But the speech teacher in the performance class consumes less than 50 percent of the time. The majority of the class hour is devoted to student performance. If the excellence of the speech class is to be improved, the level of student performance must be improved. This *Research Manual* is dedicated to an effort to raise the content of class performance.

We propose to raise the level of content by following three philosophies:
1. The content will improve if all speeches are delivered around a central theme of significant stature.
2. The content will improve if the student is guided toward the more advanced sources for research.
3. The content will improve if the student shows individual initiative in gaining the content for his communication.

A CENTRAL THEME

Not only will the content of speeches be improved if they are delivered around one theme, but the effect will be accelerated if the theme is of a significant nature. By listening to the communications of others, students will be able to gain considerable knowledge on an important subject, and they will enjoy supplementing and contrasting the knowledge they have acquired from their own research. The class will demand a more accurate and higher caliber speech, because it will be in a better position to challenge the material presented. Moreover, the instructor will feel more competent to evaluate content, because he can gain a knowledge of the subject himself and will have the *Research Manual* to guide students toward content sources.

The four themes used in this *Manual* were chosen from a list of 23 which were ranked by more than 80 speech professors. "Population Control" ranked highest among the international themes and was selected because of its vitality and comprehensive nature. Many students in business and education are required to complete a course in speech; therefore, the themes "Business Ethics" and "Teacher Education" were chosen as appropriate to these areas of study. Of the speech-oriented themes, the professors sampled ranked highest "Attitudes Toward the Concept of Freedom of Speech." We modified this choice somewhat to meet contemporary trends and selected the theme, "The Revolt on the Campus."

For each theme, a few key sources have been reprinted. These sources are intended to give the class an introduction to the subject and a common denominator for discussion. They also allow the instructor to gain a basic command of each theme, and, with repeated use of a theme, the instructor will increase his proficiency in the subject to a point where he will gain a new security in evaluating content.

SOURCES OF CONTENT

The *Research Manual* should guide the student toward more sophisticated sources for his research. Once the student senses the power of the more scholarly periodicals and the more up-to-date books, he will no longer be satisfied with encyclopedias, the "slick" magazines, and hearsay. The purpose of this *Research Manual* is not to do the student's work for him, but to guide and inspire the student to do more and better work. Therefore, preference is given to periodicals of a scholarly nature with which the average student is likely to be unacquainted. Documents are emphasized. The readings are often taken from pamphlet material which the student might not ordinarily run across. The lists of addresses are intended to lead the researcher further on in this new realm of pamphlets and newsletters which he might otherwise overlook.

Naturally, the student may become discouraged when certain sources listed are not in his library. He should realize that he will need to supplement the *Manual* with his own research, particularly in seeking the most recent books and periodicals. Although it is not within the scope of this *Manual* to provide a course in library science, we recommend the following research techniques.

It is suggested that each student record his information on a card similar to the one shown. Such cards keep the student from forgetting bibliographical details that he may need later. The back of the card may be used for notes.

In addition to the library card catalog, the student should learn to use

Subject		Sources Where Citation Gained

Author: _____

Title: _____

_____

Editor or Translator: _____

Publication: _____ _____ _____
          (place)   (publisher)   (date)

Periodical: _____
                   (name)

_____ _____ _____
(vol.)   (no.)   (date)

       This vol._____
Detail: Tot. vols._____ _____ _____ _____
               (series) (edition) (inclusive pages)

Special Locations ( ) microfilm ( ) microcard ( ) interlibrary loan ( ) photostat	Status of Research

the indexes available to him. *The Readers' Guide to Periodical Literature* and *The Education Index* are old stand-bys, but the student should also become acquainted with the following indexes:

The Applied Science and Technology Index. The subhead, "population," is productive here.

The Bulletin of the Public Affairs Information Service. This index does not limit itself to public affairs. It lists pamphlets, government documents, books, periodicals, labor publications. There are large listings under "population."

The Business Periodicals Index. It is pointed out under the informative speeches on business ethics how certain headings may be of use in this index.

Congressional Record, Index. Both the *Record* itself and its appendixes contain vast sources of information which are painstakingly catalogued in the index. This source is particularly good for finding articles from newspapers which have no indexes of their own.

Index to the Christian Science Monitor.

The Index to Legal Periodicals. The subhead, "advertising," in this index is helpful in the unit on business ethics.

Index to the Times. The London *Times*, when used in conjunction with the New York *Times*, forms a vital source on national and international subjects.

Monthly Catalog of United States Government Publications. In the 1964 issues, for example, the headings, "population," "students," and "ethics" are all productive.

The New York Times Index. For current materials, this index is inval-
uable.

Psychological Abstracts. "Student/college," "population," and "teaching
method" are useful subject headings for this index.

The Social Sciences and Humanities Index (formerly *The International
Index to Periodicals*). Many headings are productive on all four themes,
including "advertising," "population," and "students."

INDIVIDUAL INITIATIVE

The third way to raise the content level of student speaking is to encourage the speaker to secure assistance by letter-writing and by interviewing. Students are proud of knowledge they have gained by their own initiative. Each unit includes addresses of organizations which can furnish
valuable information. Students should, preferably, visit these offices themselves. There are enough offices of the Better Business Bureau, for example,
to make this feasible for many speakers. But, when a visit is not possible,
the student should write to the address provided, asking for one of the
items listed in the *Manual* or requesting a list of releases. Releases issued
by these organizations often go out of print and are replaced by other publications; specific releases are listed here merely to give the researcher an
idea of what may be available, often free of charge.

The lists of speech subjects are offered as suggestions. Students whose
instructors approve may wish to vary from these subjects. For the persuasive speech, we feel that the student should be privileged to support or
to reject the proposition. We attempted to avoid any bias in stating the
subjects. If the persuasive speech subjects are worded in favor of a given
course of action, we assume that the student is free to propose the subject
and then argue against its adoption.

Students and instructors should expect and demand an improved content of the communications in performance courses. We hope this *Research Manual* will make a contribution toward that goal.

PAUL D. BRANDES
THEODORE J. WALWIK

June, 1966

ACKNOWLEDGMENTS

MANY PERSONS have been of assistance in producing this *Manual*. Our thanks go to Victoria Emmert, our chief research assistant; to our graduate assistants, Robert Allbritten, Roy Ambrester, Raymond Beaty, and Harvey Henderson, and to Bonnie Conaway, our typist. Acknowledgment is made to the Library of Congress and to the libraries of Hiram College, Ohio University, Ohio State University, and Marietta College for their assistance in locating materials. Of particular help were Clarence Edwards McGhee, Senior Reference Librarian of the Library of Congress, and Catherine Nelson, June Marie Coughlin, Mildred E. Dugas, and William M. Betcher of The Chubb Library of Ohio University.

Our particular thanks go to our students, who have permitted us to test the effectiveness of this *Research Manual* and its commitment to controlled research.

I

POPULATION CONTROL

SELECTED READINGS

STUDENTS USING the unit on population control will rejoice in the quality and specificity of the materials available. Their speeches should be challenging and vigorous, for the sources bear these qualities. These specific suggestions seem in order:

1. There is much about sex in this unit. The editors have not hesitated to include material on all phases of birth control. Students are expected to present such materials in a manner befitting the college classroom.

2. All viewpoints have been included. Materials favoring birth control and those opposed are given adequate coverage. Every effort has been made to make the positions of all the churches clear.

3. The preponderance of statistical materials in this unit should be handled skillfully by the communicator. Statistics are not boring, but statisticians may be. Visual support, repetition, and comparison should be used to make the figures presented meaningful.

There are many vital sources on population control in the several communities with which each student is familiar. Speakers are encouraged to consult with their clergy, with members of the sociology department, and with physicians in their area. Visits to institutions concerned, such as hospitals, offices of organizations involved with planned parenthood, and with public health officials can help to make the unit vital. Interviews with foreign students can also be helpful in explaining the differences in mores among countries.

The speaker should avoid sentimental or pretentious discussions. The subject of birth control deserves a higher consideration than the glittering generality. The world must and can find a solution to its population problems, and each student of this unit should consider that he can make a contribution.

THE POPULATION BOOM

Can it be controlled?

————————•◄••►◄————————

HUNGER AND WORLD POLITICS

*Can peace be preserved when mankind is divided into
a majority of increasingly resentful "have-nots" and
a minority of increasingly uneasy "haves"?*

Hunger, man's oldest enemy, came out of hiding in an unexpected part of the world in 1964, and the American people were shocked by what they saw. In a great mountain range winding down the eastern half of the richest nation in history, newsmen found frail, undernourished children getting their only decent meal a day under the federally supported school lunch program. The grim faces of these Appalachian children provided strong testimony to an age-old problem demanding renewed attention on U.S. shores, and "poverty in America" quickly became a major political issue in the 1964 presidential election campaigns.

Yet hunger, so strangely out of place in "affluent America," is far from a stranger to millions of the earth's inhabitants. It probably represents the oldest, most persistent, and in many ways most volatile political issue ever dealt with by the governments of men. The cry for bread helped spark two of the most profound political upheavals in modern history—the French and Russian revolutions. In our own time, that cry continues to be heard periodically, from the crowded slums of northeastern Brazil to the peasant communes of mainland China.

The Food and Agriculture Organization of the United Nations estimates that up to one-half of the world's population suffers from chronic hunger or malnutrition. Some 300–500 million people may actually feel hunger

Great Decisions, 1965, Norman Jacobs (ed.), The Foreign Policy Association, 1965, pp. 82–91. Reprinted by permission.

pangs due to insufficient calorie intake, says the UN, while another 1 billion are undernourished as a result of poor diets heavily weighted toward cheap, starchy foods. Moreover, the situation may get worse before it gets better. Many authorities fear that rapidly burgeoning populations in the world's poorest countries will, if unchecked, eventually prompt a savage struggle for the means of survival among hundreds of millions of starving people.

120 MORE A MINUTE

In the fleeting minute it may have taken you to read the above paragraphs, more than 240 babies were born and approximately 120 people died. The net increase in the world's population during that minute was more than 120, or over two new mouths to feed every second. This adds up to a total of about 64 million *additional* human beings a year. And, as though nature were deliberately flaunting its indifference to mankind's woes, the bulk of this increase is occurring in precisely those areas of Asia, Africa and Latin America which can least afford to support it, given the world's current division of income and resources.

India offers a prime example. With an area less than half the size of the U.S., India already teems with more that 460 million people—many millions more than its resources can properly feed. Experts estimate that the per capita intake of calories on this thronging subcontinent falls more than 10 percent below *minimum* nutritional levels. Almost 60 percent of the population is said to suffer from deficiencies in diet.

Yet India's population is growing so fast that it will double in approximately 29 years if its current growth rate of 2.4 percent a year holds steady. In 1965, India is expected to add over 10 million people to its crowded cities and rural communities. The quest for more food to feed these expanding multitudes will be only a part of the problems that India must confront in the years ahead.

If India is to educate its rapidly increasing population of children, says Eugene R. Black, former president of the International Bank for Reconstruction and Development, it will have to provide a three- to fourfold increase in educational expenditure by 1976. If India is to shelter the 200 million additional people who will have flooded into its cities in the three decades prior to 1986, it must invest $25 billion in new housing—a "barebones" figure which fails to account for rural housing needs, for the improvement of existing housing, or for the cost of roads, sewage systems, water supplies and other services. To understand the magnitude of this challenge, it should be noted that $25 billion represents well over four times the total development funds lent by the World Bank *to all countries* during its first 15 years of operations!

"HAVES" AND "HAVE-NOTS"

India's problems are reflected in varying degrees of severity throughout the underdeveloped world, where populations have been increasing by as much as 2.8 percent annually in Latin America as a whole, and 2.1 percent annually in Africa. UN experts have estimated that 1 billion people in Asia, Africa and Latin America (half the population) are homeless or living in unsafe, unhealthful and overcrowded dwellings. Some 700 million adults are illiterate.

In this setting of poverty the world's underdeveloped countries are struggling to pull themselves forward, to modernize and industrialize, to alleviate existing hunger and offer their peoples, if not affluence, at least progress toward fulfillment of their rising expectations. In the face of rapidly expanding populations, what chance do their efforts have? Are their plans for advancement to be washed away in a rising tide of humanity?

"I must be blunt," says Eugene Black. "Population growth threatens to nullify all our efforts to raise living standards in many of the poorer countries. We are coming to a situation in which the optimist will be the man who thinks that present living standards can be maintained. The pessimist will not look even for that."

Says British historian Arnold Toynbee: "As a result of the failure to reduce the birth rate in the indigent countries . . . the gap between the respective standards of the indigent majority of the human race and the affluent minority is at present widening. This is politically dangerous. It threatens to divide mankind into two camps: a majority camp of increasingly resentful 'have-nots' and a minority camp of increasingly uneasy 'haves.'"

These views are echoed by former Secretary of State Christian Herter. "So long as there is great disparity in living standards," he has said, "today's world will not be a peaceful place in which to live."

MEANING FOR AMERICANS

In the opinion of men such as these, the present upsurge in world population has become a matter of serious concern for U.S. foreign policy. Involved in that upsurge is not solely our traditional regard for the fate of millions of hungry people living in far-off corners of the globe. Involved are the paramount issues of war and peace, of a world in upheaval or a world of relative stability.

For more than 15 years the U.S. has been committed to a foreign aid program designed to help underdeveloped nations cast off their poverty and emerge into the modern world. Billions of dollars have thus far been allocated to this task. Economic development aid for emerging countries is currently costing the U.S. taxpayer approximately $1.5 billion a year. Can this effort succeed, however, in the face of rapid population growth in the areas we are trying to help?

As with all questions that have arisen from the debate on population trends in recent years, this one offers no easy answer. While some experts view the so-called population explosion of our time as second only to nuclear war in the threat it poses to man's welfare, others contend that humanity is threatened little more or less today by population pressures than it has ever been in the past. While some maintain that population growth will obliterate economic progress in underdeveloped areas, others suggest that population growth may be merely an inevitable reflection of that progress.

In the following sections you will have a chance to consider the salient issues of the population debate today, and their implications for U.S. foreign policy. What is causing the current increase in the world's population and what will the future bring? Are man's productive capacities and the earth's resources sufficient to meet man's growing needs? Can population growth be controlled? Indeed, should it be? What policies, if any, should the U.S. government adopt with regard to the population boom in underdeveloped countries?

TOO MANY PEOPLE?

What is the cause of the population boom? How serious is it?

Demographers estimate that during all the years of prehistory population grew so slowly that no more than about 5 million people inhabited the earth by 6000 B.C. By the dawn of the Christian era the world population had multiplied to a number roughly estimated at between 200 million and 300 million, and during the next 1,000 years appears to have moved but slightly beyond those figures. A gradual upward climb then ensued (abruptly reversed during the 14th century when the Black Death, bubonic plague, swept Europe), bringing the world total to approximately half a billion people around 1650, at the inception of the Industrial Revolution.

A SUDDEN EXPLOSION

From 1650 on there begins a population upsurge so rapid and striking that it resembles the action of a tightly bound coil suddenly springing loose. It is this uncoiling of human numbers which has, in recent years, been popularly dubbed "the population explosion."

In 200 years, from 1650 to 1850, the world's population more than doubled to over 1 billion people. It doubled again in only 80 years, passing 2 billion by 1930. And it is now increasing at a rate which should see the present number of some 3.2 billion people double yet again in 35 years.

For many experts such an ominous trend gives cause for alarm. The world population's current growth rate of 2 percent a year, they say, cannot be maintained for more than the briefest period of geologic time before humans are literally packed shoulder to shoulder all over the earth's surface. In the course of one century, such a rate of increase would multiply the number of humans sixfold—bringing it to more than 19.2 billion by 2065.

Yet UN experts, whose past estimates have fallen on the conservative side, predict that the rate of increase will move still higher—above 2 percent annually—during the next four decades. The prospects, in other words, are for an *increasing rate of increase* rather than a diminishing one, so that by the end of this century, within most of our lifetimes, population may be growing by more than 130 million in a single year.

DEATH CONTROL

Why this recent speedup in population growth? Basically, the answer is this: man's death rate has been dropping sharply while his birth rate has remained essentially unchanged—at those high levels which in earlier times insured the survival of the race. As one demographer puts it, "It is the combination of a medieval birth rate with a 20th century death rate that is responsible for the current high rate of population increase."[1]

Average life expectancy at birth in most advanced industrial nations now approaches 70 years, and, thanks to Western science, underdeveloped nations are in the swift process of catching up. For example, it took the U.S. some 80 years to increase the life expectancy of its white population from 43 to 63 years. This result has recently been attained by the people of Taiwan in two decades.

Statistics for 18 underdeveloped countries show that the crude death rate (the percentage of the population that dies each year expressed in deaths per thousand) fell by 6 percent in the 1930's and by almost 20 percent in the 1950's. Recent figures indicate that the rapid decrease in mortality rates continues to accelerate in these countries while there is no appreciable indication of change in the birth rate.

DOOMSDAY OR NONSENSE?

Eventually, the rate of increase might be expected to level off as life expectancy everywhere came up to the Western average of about 70 years. Thus the current phenomenon of rapidly falling death rates could prove

[1] Harold F. Dorn, "World Population Growth," in Philip M. Hauser (ed.), *The Population Dilemma*, Prentice-Hall, 1963, p. 18.

only a temporary booster to population growth. That is, once those whose life expectancy is now being stretched by advances in science begin to die off naturally from old age, the acceleration of population growth would come to a halt.

Nonetheless, concern over immediate trends has provoked some scientists into issuing "doomsday" warnings of what lies in store if growth rates climb unchecked. For example, a group of scientists at the University of Illinois has calculated that if growth rates rise as fast in the future as they have in the past, doomsday will fall on Friday the 13th of November, 2026. On that unlucky day, they say, the number of people on earth would approach infinity.

Such calculations have sharply irritated other demographers who believe that population problems are being sensationalized out of all proportion by phony "numbers games." They take exception to phrases like "population explosion," which they consider emotional and unscientific. In what field of growth, they ask, can 2 percent a year be considered "explosive"?

Others point out that doomsday predictions have been a part of the population controversy since the Rev. Thomas Malthus, almost 200 years ago, proclaimed his famous "law" concerning geometrical increase in human numbers and arithmetical increase in the food supply. Yet thus far history has shown such dire predictions to be false alarms. Some experts see no reason why, modern science and technology being what they are, mankind could not go on growing in both numbers and greater comfort for many years to come. A steady rise in the world's living standards, they believe, is not beyond the limits of the world's potential resources. Moreover, there are some indications that a rising living standard itself acts as an automatic brake on the birth rate.

Finally, demographers themselves are the first to admit that population trends are affected by almost as many variables—or "ifs"—as there are people on earth. One leading expert, Frank W. Notestein, puts it this way: "Population growth itself is a dependent variable, to be affected in large degree by the technological, social, economic and political developments of the future. The difficulty is not that of making predictions in terms of the present or of a reasonably anticipated setting. Rather, it is that of taking the predictions too seriously once they are made."

WHERE THE PROBLEM LIES

Whatever their differences, demographers are in agreement on this point: for the underdeveloped world, current population growth presents a critical, unparalleled and unsolved challenge. People are multiplying almost twice as fast in underdeveloped areas as in the industrially mature countries. Already about 70 percent of the world's adults and 80 percent of the world's children are concentrated in these so-called emerging nations.

No worldwide analysis of population trends can do justice to the critical nature of this problem. But an analysis by region—a comparison of Europe's demographic history with what has been happening in underdeveloped areas, for example—makes its dimensions apparent to the most complacent observer.[2]

The modern population boom got its start in the countries of northwestern Europe, where the death rate first began its dramatic decline. Germany provides a statistically reliable and typical example of what happened. In 1520, the average length of life was 20 years. By 1750 it had reached 30; by 1870, 40; by 1910, 50; by 1920, 60; and today it nears 70. Over most of this period birth rates held firm, the result being a steadily rising rate of population increase—the same number per thousand were being born, but fewer per thousand were dying. However, toward the end of the 19th century, after this process had been under way many decades in Europe, a series of reactions set in which not only resulted in a declining rate of population growth but in France during the interwar period threatened a *depopulation*.

These reactions took various forms. For example, between 1846 and 1932 some 27 million people left Europe's 10 most advanced countries to settle overseas, mostly in the U.S., Australia and South Africa. Other developments brought a sharp decline in the birth rate. People married at a later age. Birth control ideas and techniques spread rapidly despite opposition by church and state. The number of childless marriages rose, and the practice of induced abortions became widespread. By the 1930's, birth rates in most countries of northwest Europe were falling faster than death rates.

We may note that in all of this region, where population remains relatively stable, government policy had very little if anything to do with the reduction in population growth that took place. That reduction was brought about by the population itself, and in some cases birth control measures met with government opposition.

THE DIFFERENCE

Now let us turn to the underdeveloped nations, where the process of rapid growth got under way more recently. Here we are confronted from the start with a different set of circumstances, in that (1) the rate of population growth is far higher than Europe's was; (2) economic development is less advanced than it was in Europe at the peak of its population boom; and (3) the opportunity for emigration is virtually nil.

In other words, the underdeveloped nations are facing accelerated population growth with fewer economic resources or "escape hatches" than were available to other developing nations in the past. Moreover, because of an

[2] Cf. Kingsley Davis, "Population," *Scientific American*, September, 1963.

even swifter decline in death rates, the demographic history of the under-developed areas, by comparison with Europe's, is being telescoped into a few decades instead of taking several centuries. Thus the time for "reaction" is presumably much shorter than that enjoyed in the West.

What, then, are the prospects? Can resources be mustered to meet the needs of these expanding multitudes and provide a measure of advancement as well? Can the population growth rate be ignored or must active measures be taken to control it? If so, what form should these measures take? These are the questions at the heart of the great debate on population today.

WHAT CAN BE DONE?

*The world's resources, says one expert, could feed
95 billion people. Yet many of the 3.2 billion
people now alive are hungry tonight.*

Like all Gaul, the debate on population problems appears to be divided into three parts: Is there a need for action? What can be done? And what *should* be done? On the first of these questions there is probably the most general agreement. Most observers believe that immediate trends, particularly in underdeveloped areas, do call for some sort of action, whether it be simply to feed the growing number who are hungry or to stop the number who are hungry from growing.

In the last question lie the great moral issues—above all the matter of birth control—which have come to dominate the population debate in the public mind today. These issues will be taken up in later sections of this Fact Sheet. In this section the question to be explored is the second: What *can* be done?

THE FOUR POSSIBILITIES

Broadly speaking, there are just four ways in which current population problems might be resolved:
• Return to an increased death rate.
• Halt overcrowding through massive emigration.
• Raise production to satisfy growing needs.
• Reduce the birth rate.

Probably no one seriously advocates a return to higher death rates, although some economists have speculated that developing countries might hold off on public health investments until other sectors of the economy have a firmer footing. In this way, death rates would fall slowly, if at all, and the resources required for development would not have to be used to meet the consumption needs of a growing population. On the other hand, of course, (and aside from the morally questionable aspects of such an approach) a population wracked by malnutrition and disease hardly provides a firm base on which to build development plans.

The second alternative—massive emigration—has many drawbacks. The costs involved in moving great masses of people about the earth would be staggering—money better spent, perhaps, on resource development. Moreover, prosperous nations have been tightening their immigration laws in recent years, and under current circumstances it seems unlikely that Russia would willingly throw open the vast spaces of Siberia to an invasion by the Chinese, or that Australia would accept large numbers of nonwhites.

WHAT REMAINS?

This leaves two possibilities—resource development and/or birth control—around which the most interest centers. As with population growth itself, red warning signals flash when experts undertake analyses of world production, its trends and potentials. Figures on food production alone are both incomplete and uncertain.

Several estimates have been made, however, of the maximum population the earth's resources could support, given full utilization of existing technology. These estimates vary widely, one of the lowest of 2.8 billion, made in 1945, having already been surpassed. Others range from 7 billion (likely to be approached in this century) to 50 billion.

Perhaps the highest estimate has been made by Colin Clark, director of the Agricultural Economics Research Institute, Oxford, England. Clark calculates that the equivalent of 19 billion acres of the earth's surface would qualify as good agricultural land. If Dutch farming techniques were employed throughout, he concludes that 28 billion people could survive comfortably on one of the best diets known. If Japanese methods and nutritional standards were used, 95 billion people could inhabit the earth!

NEW TECHNIQUES

The UN estimates that as of mid-1963 world food production had increased by close to 50 percent since the outbreak of World War II in 1939. During the same period, population rose about 35 percent, so that an average improvement of more than 10 percent per person had taken place. But when regional breakdowns are analysed, much of the gain proves illusory. Soaring output has been concentrated in the advanced countries, many of them burdened by surpluses, while some developing areas have barely kept pace with growing populations.

The U.S. has shipped more than $12 billion in surplus food to underdeveloped areas in the last decade. But experts believe that shipping food from rich nations to poor will never meet the real problem. The needed export is agricultural techniques and skills. Rice yields per acre, for example, are more than three times as high in Japan as in India, and better utilization of fertilizers alone could double production in many parts of the world.

Agronomists generally agree that increasing food production is largely a matter of better techniques rather than more space. The UN estimates that about 10 percent of the world's land area is now under cultivation and that two or three times that much is suitable for farming. But recent history indicates that efforts to bring virgin areas into production, as in the U.S.S.R. "virgin lands" scheme, prove disappointing. In fact, as former Soviet Premier Khrushchev learned belatedly, successful farming is generally marked by intensive cultivation of a limited area, as in the U.S.

LET THEM EAT CAKE?

Meat is the most important foodstuff in short supply in the underdeveloped areas today. Low intake of animal protein is a major factor contributing to malnutrition, and raising that intake is a costly proposition. To increase consumption of animal protein by 16 percent, for instance, would mean a 67 percent increase in the cost of the diet.

Scientists have been experimenting with low-cost methods of enriching vegetarian diets in protein, however, and have made substantial progress toward an inexpensive solution of the problem. A properly processed oil-seed meal mixed with grain in the right ratio gives a cake that contains about 25 percent protein of meat-like quality. Some of these mixtures are now being manufactured and sold in various Latin American countries.

The UN estimates that giving everyone a nutritionally sound diet by A.D. 2000 will require a fourfold increase in food supplies in Asia, between three- and fourfold in Latin America, threefold in the Middle East and between two- and threefold in Africa. In all these areas such increases are entirely within resource potentials, with the possible exception of Asia, where the problem will be touch and go. As for the developed nations, at their present rate of progress they will be producing twice as much food as their populations will need by A.D. 2000.

But, as some experts have pointed out, there is little realism in speculating about the maximum number of people that the world could support at minimum levels of living. The crucial problem is to put subsistence economies on the road to economic development. If this can be done—and, these experts believe, it will require family planning—then the underdeveloped nations will ultimately be able to make self-sustaining progress. Thus viewed, population control is not an alternative to development—they go together.

"THE QUALITY OF LIFE"

In a 1963 speech, John D. Rockefeller 3d pointed to a related consideration: "Even if science by some magic could show the way to feed new billions of people, we still would not have solved the population problem. 'The quality of life' cannot be omitted from the solution. Indeed, there can be no true solution until society can assure every individual a chance to attain life's higher objectives; in short, an opportunity—in the fullest sense—to live as well as to survive."

That the development task is complicated by population growth seems clear enough. Just as one example, take the problem of housing.

On the generous assumption that a house lasts one century, it can be seen that the housing requirements of a stationary population would be satisfied by replacing houses at the rate of 1 percent a year. But if the population is *growing* by 1 percent a year, the number of new houses required each year must be automatically *doubled*.

In underdeveloped areas where population is growing by 2, 3 or more percent a year, housing construction would have to be tripled or quadrupled just to maintain existing standards. And, of course, the resources needed for housing compete with those needed for highways, factories and other types of output vital to industrialization.

BIRTH CONTROL?

Is birth control, then, the answer? It is not only religious groups that divide on this question. Scientists are divided, too. By no means are all of them convinced that birth control measures *could* accomplish a reduction in the birth rate, even if everyone were agreed they should be tried. The reason is simple: birth control touches on one of the most intimate and personal aspects of human life, one which even the most absolute dictatorship finds it difficult to control.

Past history indicates that governments such as those in Sweden, Poland and Japan moved to legalize abortion or provide family planning help and advice only *after* the people themselves had sharply reduced birth rates on their own initiative. And many experts believe it is neither hunger, nor the obvious discomforts of overcrowding, nor even necessarily the availability of contraceptive means that rouses a people to bring its rate of increase under control. "Poverty and deprivation alone are not likely to generate a slowdown of the birth rate," says demographer Kingsley Davis, "but personal aspirations are."

Such aspirations are usually related to the prospects and progress of economic development. Where poverty prevails it often seems in the interests of parents to have as many children as possible—all of them insurance for a secure old age. But when aspirations reach beyond acceptance of perpetual poverty, when the development process has gotten under way and its results are being felt, then more people in the underdeveloped countries will have personal incentives for family planning.

CHICKEN OR EGG?

For this reason, some observers believe the essential task is to push on with plans for economic development, letting the birth rate react in time by itself. But others are just as firmly convinced that economic development will prove a near hopeless task unless something is done quickly to bring birth rates under control.

In recent years science has made great strides in developing artificial means of controlling fertility. Birth control pills are now widely available in Western nations; a cheap, effective intrauterine coil has been developed. Mass distribution of such devices, development of attitudes favorable toward their use, and training of the personnel required to administer them could have a significant impact on birth rates in the underdeveloped countries over the next decade.

There has always existed one effective means of birth control advocated by the Catholic Church: total abstinence. In addition, the Church approves of the so-called rhythm method, which is based on abstinence during the period of the woman's ovulation cycle when conception is possible. A major difficulty with the rhythm method is the possibility of error, since it requires exact knowledge of the individual fertility cycle. As for total abstinence, many doubt that, given human nature, it is a feasible solution.

In the following two sections—case studies on population growth in Japan and Latin America—you will have an opportunity to examine the problems of birth control more closely.

JAPAN FINDS A SOLUTION . . .

Japan makes a good case study in population problems for several reasons. First, it is the only country of non-European stock to pull itself forward into the ranks of the world's advanced industrial powers. Second, it accomplished this feat despite one of the most serious problems of overcrowding ever to confront an aspiring nation. And finally, it has astonished demographers everywhere by its swift and decisive response to the population challenge, slashing its birth rate almost in half within a single decade.

For the century and a half prior to Commodore Perry's arrival in Japan in 1852, its population is believed to have remained stable at around 30 million. Within a few short years after Perry forced open the door, Japan abandoned its feudal isolation and launched upon a rapid ascent toward modernization and "great-power" status.

THE BOOM BEGINS

In the century that followed, population tripled to more than 90 million. Causal factors were the usual ones: birth rates ran high (36 per thousand by 1920) while death rates declined steadily. On the average between 1900 and 1940 Japan's population grew by about 1.2 percent a year—not an "explosive" increase compared to that occurring in many underdeveloped countries today, but rapid enough for a nation smaller than California.

Yet Japan's conservative rulers remained unperturbed in the face of this relentless growth. Their imperial designs on East Asia, fed by successive wars against Russia and China, provided (or so they thought) adequate scope for a population outlet. Hence official policy discouraged any efforts at birth control. But the Japanese people viewed matters differently. As early as 1925 there were signs of a falling birth rate. Japanese girls began marrying at a later age. As in Western Europe, the people were acting when their government would not.

By 1939 the birth rate had eased down to 27 per thousand. On the eve of World War II, Japan's population growth rate had declined to 1 percent a year, and efforts by the government to spur that rate during the war had little effect.

With defeat in 1945, Japan's population problems assumed a new note of urgency. The imperial solution for these problems had been scuttled by unconditional surrender. Millions of soldiers and civilians were, moreover, returning home from their overseas posts. The normal threat of a postwar "baby boom" lay in store. And under the American occupation the death rate was proceeding to decline to one of the lowest in the world.

What happened? As expected, the birth rate soared upward again in the immediate postwar years, hitting 34.3 per thousand in 1947. By 1956, however, it had plunged to 18.5, the swiftest reduction known in modern history.

The key factor in this spectacular drop was the Eugenic Protection Law of 1948, which relaxed legal restrictions against contraception, abortion and sterilization, and established what, in effect, amounted to birth control clinics throughout the country. Though originally enacted as a measure to protect women's health (even after the war the Japanese government continued to oppose any officially sponsored family planning program), the law has been gradually amended and broadly interpreted to include such grounds as economic hardship within its purview. Whatever its legislative intent, its real effect was to throw government support behind the type of wide-ranging birth control program for which private Japanese groups had been fighting.

The Japanese people themselves were quick to take advantage of the law's provisions. For example, the number of legal abortions recorded rose from 246,000 in 1949 to a peak of 1,170,000 in 1955. In 1952 the government's Institute of Public Health undertook a broad campaign to educate the public on contraception as a means of reducing this soaring figure. As a result, the number of abortion cases has been falling slowly but steadily since 1955. The number of voluntary sterilizations is said to be rising, in part because of the inconvenience or risks of failure involved in contraception, in part because of the risks to health sometimes posed by abortion and because more and more women undergo sterilization once their families have reached the "right" size.

WHAT LESSONS?

The law is still under attack in some Japanese quarters for contributing to moral delinquency. But a survey conducted in 1963 showed that 43 percent of the mothers questioned about contraception claimed their main motive was "to provide better education by limiting the number of children." Only 9 percent listed greater enjoyment of life, which might loosely be interpreted as self-indulgence, as their reason.

That official action can go far toward relieving population pressures is demonstrated by a study carried out in three rural Japanese villages after 1950. The study found that nine-tenths of the women concerned wanted to limit the size of their families. Courses in contraception were then provided by a government institute, and within three years the crude birth rate in each village fell by more than half.

Today Japan's population of some 97 million continues to grow because those born in the postwar baby boom are now establishing their own families (the birth rate stands at 17.3; the death rate at 7.4). But demographers believe that by 1980 the population will have stabilized or perhaps even begun a slight decline.

Yet Japan's solution for its population problems offers a doubtful example for the rest of Asia and the underdeveloped world. The Japanese are the most literate and economically advanced of all Asian peoples. They have, moreover, a long tradition of family planning at the grass-roots level that stretches back into feudal times, when abortion and infanticide were common. The current success with birth control, demographers agree, has been made possible because of the high level of intelligence, discipline and social responsibility of the Japanese people themselves.

. . . AND LATIN AMERICA SEEKS ONE

Latin America's population problem is not merely due to its present numbers nor to the lack of local resources to match swelling human needs.

control programs a condition to our foreign aid," he wrote in a magazine article, "but we should tell receiving nations how population growth threatens them and what can be done about it."

Late in 1963 the U.S. Congress moved to back the Administration's position by adopting the "Fulbright Amendment" on foreign aid. It authorized the Agency for International Development "to conduct research into the problems of population growth," and provided funds for that purpose.

CATHOLIC REACTION

Spokesmen for the Catholic Church who denounced the Draper report in 1959 have raised little if any objection to these subsequent developments. Their reaction has been variously attributed to such factors as a reluctance to clash with Mr. Kennedy, the first Catholic President, and to a "liberalizing ferment" within the Church itself on the birth control issue. However, it seems clear that the Church has no objection to taxpayer-supported research into the reproductive cycle *per se*.

As Senator Joseph S. Clark (D-Pa.) told his colleagues: "I suspect, particularly in the light of the position taken by so many eminent Catholic laymen and theologians, that one need not have any political timidity in advocating research into the problem of population control. . . . I received no adverse criticism of any consequence because I was advocating positive research and discussion in this area."

A WORLDWIDE SHIFT?

Indeed, to veteran advocates of population control, one of the most encouraging developments of recent years is the serious discussion and reexamination of the problem of "responsible parenthood" in which Catholics in many parts of the world are currently engaged. In 1963 the Ford Foundation and Georgetown University (a Catholic institution) set up a $225,-000 fund for a three-year study to develop a simple ovulation-detection method designed to perfect the rhythm method. In the same year, Dr. John Rock, a Catholic, and for many years professor of gynecology at Harvard University Medical School, published his much discussed book, *The Time Has Come*. In it he argued that an oral pill which he had co-developed and which prevented ovulation by chemical means was not in the category of mechanical birth control devices condemned by the Church and could be considered morally and theologically acceptable. Though Rock's argument is not officially accepted by the Church, a number of European Catholic theologians have recently expressed similar views. Pope Paul VI has said that the Church is giving "wide and profound study" to birth control problems, and last October three of the Church's most in-

It is, above all, a matter of growth rates that threaten to undo every plan for economic progress before it gets off the ground.

Taken as a whole, Latin America is growing at a rate of about 2.8 percent a year, a rate that would double the population in 25 years time. There were 91 million people in all of Latin America in 1920, compared to 117 million in the U.S. and Canada. By 1956, Latin Americans had surpassed their two northern neighbors in numbers, 187 million to 184 million. If current rates hold steady throughout the hemisphere, there will be 623 million people in Latin America by A.D. 2000, compared to 406 million in the U.S. and Canada. But current rates are expected to drop somewhat in the U.S. and to rise *still higher* among our neighbors to the south.

A GRIM OUTLOOK

The closer we look at this region, the bleaker the picture becomes. Those Latin American countries which are in the temperate zone—Argentina, Chile, Uruguay—are not only the most economically advanced but the ones where population is growing at the slowest rates. In the tropical zone, where poverty is greatest, the population advance is swiftest: 3.6 percent a year in Central America (Costa Rica, El Salvador, Guatemala, Honduras, Nicaragua), 3.1 percent in Mexico, 3.3 percent in Venezuela and 3.6 percent in Brazil. At such a rate Brazil's 80 million population will double in 19 years.

The age distribution of the existing population offers further cause for concern. Because of very high birth rates, more than 50 percent of the population in tropical South America is under 20 years of age, while 43–45 percent is under 15. This means that for each 1,000 adults aged 15 to 64 there are 850–900 dependents. By 1975 this "dependency load" of the adult population is expected to reach 890–940 per 1,000.

The strain that such a load places on economic development is enormous. Not only is almost half the population consuming resources without contributing toward their replenishment, but the educational investment called for under development plans will have to expand to all-devouring proportions.

To help Latin America cope with these problems, the U.S. has committed itself to a multibillion dollar aid program for economic development under the Alliance for Progress. And to insure its effectiveness, Washington has laid down certain conditions that must be met before funds are made available. In short, there are strings attached, and some experts are wondering why a program for birth control is not among them.

Until recently, at least, the answer has been that the Catholic Church has strongly opposed such programs. While recognizing that Latin America, with a third of the world's Catholics, is beset by serious population problems, conservative Catholic leaders have long opposed the use of "artificial" or mechanical birth control devices.

These Catholics have held that, quite apart from constituting a "moral evil," artificial birth prevention undermines those very qualities in man upon which successful development programs depend; namely, discipline, self-control, and the disposition to postpone present satisfactions for future gains. They are convinced that Latin America, with its abundant natural resources, could feed, shelter and clothe millions more if a proper emphasis were placed on resource development. Birth control, they say, is too often viewed as a cure-all, when the real needs are for land reform, better government, economic justice and education for the masses.

Within the past few years, however, a noticeable change has been taking place in the attitudes of some Latin American churchmen. In fact, as the next section of this Fact Sheet indicates, Catholics in many parts of the world are today engaged in a critical reexamination of their Church's stand on birth control. In addition, a number of recent studies in the area have cast the whole problem of responsible parenthood in a new perspective.

For example, one study of Catholic families in Puerto Rico, Peru, Chile and Mexico found that lower-class groups overwhelmingly favored smaller families and expressed a willingness to limit the size of their own when they know how to do it. Another study found that the number of illegal abortions has risen to shocking proportions. A survey of 1,890 women in Santiago, Chile revealed that 26 percent had had criminal abortions, the majority of these more than once. Of the 17 countries of this region for which statistics are available, in nine more than half the births are illegitimate.

WINDS OF CHANGE

Such statistics, and the widespread poverty that underlies them, have prompted some liberal Catholics to take a more tolerant view of birth control efforts. As a result, Latin American nations have been opening the door to experiments that only a few years ago would have been unthinkable.

Since 1961, for example, six countries have quietly permitted the establishment of contraceptive services in public hospitals. Throughout the area, family planning agencies have launched their activities in the open, in contrast to the cautious, discrete and word-of-mouth nature of such activities only five years ago. Even the U.S.-sponsored Alliance for Progress has been moving gingerly into the area.

FOR THE U.S.: WHAT POLICIES?

For more than a decade the U.S. has undertaken a program of economic assistance to underdeveloped countries—a multipurpose program aimed at

promoting peace, economic growth and the containment of communism. In recent years this program has been increasingly subjected to criticism. Even many who favor foreign aid wonder whether it can be effective unless the population boom in the underdeveloped countries is brought to a halt.

Because the subject of population control is both sensitive and controversial, U.S. policy-makers have, until relatively recently, been hesitant to take any official position on the issue. It was left to the nation's voluntary organizations and private foundations to deal with the problem in a variety of ways, depending on their interests and resources. For example, since 1952 the Ford Foundation has committed $24.2 million to programs in the broad field of population research and control in the U.S. and abroad.

U.S. POLICY RECORD

Given the growing urgency of the population problem, however, official U.S. concern has made itself manifest in recent years. In 1959 the so-called Draper report, drawn up by a panel of government-appointed experts, recommended, among other things, that the U.S. assist aid-receiving countries, upon request, in the formulation of their plans to deal with rapid population growth, and that it support studies on the problem and make the results available. But when asked about this recommendation at a press conference, President Eisenhower responded: "I cannot imagine anything more emphatically a subject that is not a proper political or governmental activity or function or responsibility. . . . This government has no, and will not . . . as long as I am here, have a positive political doctrine in its program that has to do with this problem of birth control."

For the time being the issue was dropped. But it was soon revived again under the Kennedy Administration. President Kennedy and his aids began by placing new emphasis on the population difficulties facing many foreign aid recipients. Gradually U.S. government-sponsored research into fertility control problems expanded. By December 1962 at the UN, the U.S. was offering, when requested, to help other countries "find potential sources of information and assistance on ways and means of dealing with population problems." It also supported a UN resolution calling for more information and research on the population problem. And shortly thereafter, the National Institutes of Health, a government agency, published a research inventory on birth control and the reproductive cycle, which the Administration made clear was available to any government.

At a press conference, Mr. Kennedy supported the idea that "this information be made more available to the world so that everyone can make their own judgment," and he called for continuing research into "the whole reproductive cycle."

Interestingly, by 1963 former President Eisenhower announced a change of view. "I still believe that as a national policy we should not make birth

fluential prelates called for an urgent reexamination of the official Catholic position.

Some Communist countries have recently been revising their views on population problems. According to classic Marxist dogma, population problems stem from failures in the capitalist system and can only be solved through "socialist production"—not population control. But in 1963, Soviet representatives to the UN Economic and Social Council announced their government's recognition that population growth had become an urgent world problem and offered technical assistance to help solve it.

In a number of Muslim nations—Turkey, Pakistan and the United Arab Republic, for example—government-sponsored birth control programs are now in operation.

THE BIG STEP

Advocates of birth control have been elated by these recent developments, yet they are fully aware that the longest and most difficult step of all for their cause is the one between approval and effective action. And on this score there is probably less ground for elation. India has had an extensive birth control program under way since 1950. Some 8,500 clinics have been established throughout the country, and 25,000 medical and social workers have been trained in family planning. Yet the president of India's Family Planning Association noted in 1963 that "despite all this useful activity and extensive coverage, the program has not yet succeeded in touching the core of the problem, which is to initiate a downward trend in the birth rate." Most other underdeveloped countries, it should be noted, lag far behind India in their treatment, and even their awareness, of population problems.

Thus, despite the encouraging developments of recent years, the urgency of the problem, as most population experts see it, remains undiminished. To its solution, the U.S., with its public health facilities and technical knowledge, could make a major contribution. But what official role, if any, should the U.S. play? What population policies would best serve our national interest?

LAISSEZ-FAIRE APPROACH

As might be expected, there is no consensus over how to deal with a problem that is so intimately related to the sources of life itself. On one side in the debate over population policy are those who advocate that the government take a laissez-faire position, i.e., simply do nothing. Some urge this on religious and moral grounds. They argue that in a matter which touches so deeply on religious convictions, the government should not use tax revenues to support policies morally repugnant to a large group of citizens. Others contend that for the U.S. to try to promote birth control programs abroad—urging population control on underdeveloped countries—would only arouse hostile reactions. Telling others to control their numbers is a delicate matter, to say the least, particularly when those who are doing the telling have no policy of their own to limit births at home. Finally, there are those observers who believe that fears about the population boom are unduly exaggerated. Left alone, they think, the situation will tend to take care of itself. Whatever problem exists, they say, can be adequately dealt with by private organizations and foundations, as in the past. At any rate, government should stay out of the field.

THE CASE FOR CONTROL

Advocates of population control are quick to reject these laissez-faire positions. While respecting the moral and religious convictions of birth control opponents, they believe that such convictions should not be allowed to stand in the way of needed action, especially in areas where the majority recognize the necessity for a population control program. Consequently, they offer a variety of alternatives, each calling for some degree of U.S. government action.

At one end of the spectrum are those convinced of the urgent need for drastic measures. They would suggest, for example, that the U.S. halt foreign aid to countries that fail to take steps designed to bring their population growth rates under control. Without such steps, they argue, aid for economic development mocks its own purpose by subsidizing precisely what underdeveloped countries don't need: more children.

Or take the matter of "death control." Here, too, those who view the "population explosion" as the major crisis of our time are ready to propose stern measures. They would have the U.S., in its medical and health programs for underdeveloped areas, shift primary emphasis to the curing of adult diseases and disabilities, allowing the infant mortality rate to remain high until a more vigorous adult population can achieve its development goals.

Other advocates of government action doubt the feasibility of such drastic measures. Moreover, they question whether birth control can be made a condition for foreign aid without arousing considerable resentment. They would say this: Offer to help countries with population problems. Show them how critical these problems can be in blocking development goals. Then, if they are willing, send in the supplies and the experts necessary to help solve the problem. Establish the needed health centers at the local level. Train workers in family planning. Supply the contraceptive means if the country cannot do it itself—though this last is generally the least expensive and difficult task involved in any birth control program. Then, while family planning takes hold (and as much as a decade may have to pass before significant results become apparent), keep the economic aid flowing.

In line with such recommendations, advocates of more vigorous U.S. action believe that the federal government should sharply increase its research program on reproduction. (Presently, the U.S. is spending a little more than $5 million annually.) They also urge that the U.S. step up its efforts both in and out of the UN to convince underdeveloped nations of the need for effective action.

Finally, there are those middle-of-the-roaders who are content with current U.S. policy. That policy, you will recall, consists in conducting research in the field of population control and delicately making the results of such research and related information available to countries that request assistance.

At the present stage of the world's population boom, is such a program doing too much? too little? or not enough?

FINAL REPORT OF THE
TWENTY-THIRD AMERICAN ASSEMBLY

———————————

At the close of their discussions the participants in the Twenty-third American Assembly at Arden House, Harriman, New York, May 2–5, 1963, on The Population Dilemma, reviewed as a group the following statement. Although there was general agreement on the final report, it is not the practice of The American Assembly for participants to affix their signatures, and it should not be assumed that every participant necessarily subscribes to every recommendation.

Never before in history have the security and welfare of mankind been so indivisible. Never before has man acquired the capability of achieving his own extinction. These circumstances require him to marshal his intelligence, control his emotions, and rise above his traditional thought and action in an unprecedented way. Failure to do so may threaten not only his prosperity, security and peace, but also his survival.

Among the serious threats to welfare and security, and therefore to peace, is the accelerating rate of world population growth. The less tangible but very real injury to personal development and the maintenance of family life must also be of concern. Rapid population increase and its accompaniments are obstructing economic development, and thereby contributing to frustration, social unrest and political instability in many areas of the globe. Rapid population growth also contributes to complex problems in the United States.

The Twenty-third American Assembly believes that:

A. *Present and prospective world rates of population growth cannot be maintained indefinitely. Such growth contributes substantially to the perpetuation of low levels of living for two-thirds of mankind, and creates difficult problems of adjustment in the economically advanced nations.*

Philip M. Hauser (ed.), *The Population Dilemma*, © 1963 by The American Assembly, Columbia University, New York, N.Y., pp. 178–183. Reprinted by permission of Prentice-Hall, Inc., Englewood Cliffs, N.J.

B. World birth rates must be reduced in view of the reductions in death rates already achieved.

C. Reduction of family size would produce important gains for many families as well as for entire nations. Unrestricted fertility tends to damage the health of the mother, impairs family life and restricts opportunity for adequately rearing and educating children.

The time has come for vigorous and coordinated action to alert mankind to the need for a reduced rate of population growth and to develop multilateral and bilateral programs to assist nations which desire to reduce their fertility.

I. WORLD PROBLEMS

A high birth rate obstructs the economic development of low income countries in a number of ways. It diverts resources and hampers economic growth in the less developed economies and makes it necessary to provide for a larger population rather than for a higher level of living. It contributes to imbalance in rural-urban and regional population distribution. It generates an age structure with large numbers of young dependents in relation to workers. It impairs efforts to improve the quality of a population by restricting per capita expenditures for improving health, raising educational levels, and teaching new occupational skills. It reduces natural resources per capita.

Reducing the birth rate and thereby lowering the rate of population increase is of course not the complete solution to the improvement of economic conditions in the less developed areas. It is a major element; but other factors—social and economic—are also involved. These include capital investment, technology, diversification of the economy, distribution of income, occupational skills, entrepreneurship, and attitudes and institutions favorable to innovation and social reform. The expansion of international trade and investment would also contribute to economic advance. More effective utilization of natural resources is required; in the short run world resources are sufficient to permit rising levels of living.

International migration can help many persons and temporarily ease some population pressures. It cannot, however, solve the world's major population problems.

RECOMMENDATIONS

The United Nations and the Specialized Agencies should:

1. *Expand activities in the field of population.*

They have significantly improved population data and research. They should now undertake more comprehensive and intensive population research, particularly on the interrelationships of population, economics and social change, and develop more effective programs for the dissemination of its findings.

2. Expand and strengthen the population staff and the regional population training and research centers.

This would enable the agencies better to assist nations to comprehend their own problems and formulate appropriate solutions.

3. Provide direct aid to countries wishing assistance in family planning programs.

The World Health Organization and other international agencies should recognize the consequences of their great achievements in reducing death rates; they should assist nations in dealing with the resultant population growth.

4. Encourage and support, especially through the WHO, biological and medical research in human reproduction.

5. Strive to contribute to the growing world consciousness of the implications of population growth through appropriate revisions of and additions to youth and adult educational materials prepared for world distribution by UNESCO.

II. THE POSITION OF THE UNITED STATES ON WORLD POPULATION PROBLEMS

The "Statement of the United States Policy" to the 17th General Assembly of the United Nations represents an important step forward. It offers the assistance of the United States to nations, upon request, "to find potential sources of information and assistance on ways and means of dealing with population problems." This policy should explicitly recognize that:

(1) Population growth in all countries affects the destinies of the world's people. It is an international problem of concern to all. (2) Parents everywhere should be free to decide how many children they should have. (3) Sustained progress in economic well-being requires the reduction of population increase.

RECOMMENDATIONS

In view of the relation of population to economic and social development, and the need for bilateral as well as multilateral programs of technical assistance, it is recommended that:

1. Since the ultimate objective of foreign aid is to improve living conditions, the United States give consideration to the way in which developmental plans are affected by population trends.

2. The United States extend assistance to developing nations, at their request, for the investigation of population problems and in support of programs to promote the voluntary regulation of fertility.

3. Administrative means be established by the federal government for disseminating knowledge about population problems and methods of regulating family size.

Such action is needed to implement the statement by President Kennedy of April 24, 1963, that the government could support increased research in fertility and human reproduction, and make the results more available to the world so that everyone could make his own judgment.

III. DOMESTIC POPULATION POLICY

There must be a greater concern by our national, state and local governments with our own population problems.

The postwar resurgence in population growth coupled with the growth of metropolitan areas has created complex problems not only at the state and local levels but also on a regional and national basis.

Rapid population growth has undoubtedly contributed to additional effective demand and thus to increased economic growth. Although there are no insuperable economic difficulties in the short run, we see increasing dangers in the continuation of the present rate of growth that would double the population every forty years with the prospect of constricted social opportunities and progressive crowding.

Accelerated population growth has already intensified problems of urban congestion, education and transportation, and contributed to pollution of air and water and crowding of outdoor recreational facilities. It has required federal, state and local governments to provide new and expanded public facilities and services, with consequent increased taxation. Furthermore, the wave of young workers now entering the labor force constitutes a serious challenge to our economy, which is already confronted by readjustment to the advent of automation. These challenges will require special attention.

RECOMMENDATIONS

This American Assembly therefore recommends:

1. Intensified investigation of our population trends and problems —including their long-range as well as their short-term implications.

2. Accelerated research through the United States Public Health Service and private agencies, on the biological and medical aspects of human reproduction so that a variety of improved methods of fertility control are developed.

3. *Assumption of responsibility by the federal, state and local governments for making available information concerning the regulation of fertility and providing services to needy mothers compatible with the religious and ethical beliefs of the individual recipient.*

Freedom of decision regarding family size is a basic human right which in practice is now effectively withheld from a portion of the American people. This discrimination would be eliminated by making fully available to all adults through public and private agencies information and service regarding the various methods of family planning which accord with the ethical and religious convictions of those involved.

4. *The cultivation with the assistance of schools, religious organizations and other cultural media, of a sense of responsibility concerning marriage and parenthood, including the responsibility of bringing into the world only those children whom parents are prepared adequately to care for and educate.*

5. *Recognition that the United States is an economic and social unit, to the end that all of our citizens, no matter what their area of origin or race, are adequately prepared for full participation in the life of any part of the nation.*

Since the end of the war, millions of persons have moved to urban parts of the United States. Many are ill-prepared for life in the areas to which they moved. In consequence, problems of accommodation are severe for the migrants and for the communities to which they come.

6. *Our immigration policy should be in accord with the following principles:*
   a. selection among applicants without discrimination by race or country or origin
   b. total immigration not to exceed the present level except in emergencies
   c. exclusion of persons who do not meet established personal standards such as those relating to literacy and health, save under extraordinary circumstances
   d. consideration of (1) special skills, abilities and employment opportunities, and (2) kinship to persons already present in this country

7. *The acceleration of economic growth and increased employment opportunities in view of the current levels of unemployment and the impending increase in the labor force.*

8. *More research on the resources of the United States and other parts of the world with attention to the lessening of waste and protection of the claims of oncoming generations.*

9. *Appointment by the President of the United States of a Commission to inform, after investigation, the government and the American people of the nature of population problems at home and abroad*

with respect to: implications for all aspects of American life, and relevance to our efforts, in cooperation with international agencies, to promote economic and social progress throughout the world.

.   .   .

The vast majority of the people of the world, including a large proportion of the people of the United States, do not yet recognize the full implications of present population trends. The Twenty-third American Assembly cannot emphasize too strongly that time is running out for the formulation and implementation of world and national population policy.

To continue to ignore world and United States population problems is to ignore the welfare and security of all peoples. We must not remain complacent in the face of a major threat to world peace and survival.

SUPREME COURT
OF THE UNITED STATES

No. 496.—October Term, 1964.

| Estelle T. Griswold et al., Appellants, *v.* State of Connecticut. | On Appeal From the Supreme Court of Errors of Connecticut. |

[June 7, 1965.]

Mr. Justice Douglas delivered the opinion of the Court.

Appellant Griswold is Executive Director of the Planned Parenthood League of Connecticut. Appellant Buxton is a licensed physician and a professor at the Yale Medical School who served as Medical Director for the League at its Center in New Haven—a center open and operating from November 1 to November 10, 1961, when appellants were arrested.

They gave information, instruction, and medical advice to *married persons* as to the means of preventing conception. They examined the wife and prescribed the best contraceptive device or material for her use. Fees were usually charged, although some couples were serviced free.

The statutes whose constitutionality is involved in this appeal are §§ 53–32 and 54–196 of the General Statutes of Connecticut (1938). The former provides:

> Any person who uses any drug, medicinal article or instrument for the purpose of preventing conception shall be fined not less than fifty dollars or imprisoned not less than sixty days nor more than one year or be both fined and imprisoned.

Section 54–196 provides:

> Any person who assists, abets, counsels, causes, hires, or commands another to commit any offense may be prosecuted and punished as if he were the principal offender.

The appellants were found guilty as accessories and fined $100 each, against the claim that the accessory statute as so applied violated the Fourteenth Amendment. The Appellate Division of the Circuit Court affirmed. The Court of Errors affirmed that judgment. 151 Conn. 544, 200 A. 2d 479. We noted probable jurisdiction. 379 U.S. 926.

We think that appellants have standing to raise the constitutional rights of the married people with whom they had a professional relationship. *Tileston v. Ullman*, 318 U.S. 44, is different, for there the plaintiff seeking to represent others asked for a declaratory judgment. In that situation we thought that the requirements of standing should be strict, lest the standards of "case or controversy" in Article III of the Constitution become blurred. Here those doubts are removed by reason of a criminal conviction for serving married couples in violation of an aiding-and-abetting statute. Certainly the accessory should have standing to assert that the offense which he is charged with assisting is not, or cannot constitutionally be, a crime.

This case is more akin to *Truax v. Raich*, 239 U.S. 33, where an employee was permitted to assert the rights of his employer; to *Pierce v. Society of Sisters*, 268 U.S. 510, where the owners of private schools were entitled to assert the rights of potential pupils and their parents; and to *Barrows v. Jackson*, 346 U.S. 249, where a white defendant, party to a racially restrictive covenant, who was being sued for damages by the covenantors because she had conveyed her property to Negroes, was allowed to raise the issue that enforcement of the covenant violated the rights of prospective Negro purchasers to equal protection, although no Negro was a party to the suit. And see *Meyer v. Nebraska*, 262 U.S. 390; *Adler v. Board of Education*, 342 U.S. 485; *NAACP v. Alabama*, 357 U.S. 449; *NAACP v. Button*, 371 U.S. 415. The rights of husband and wife, pressed here, are likely to be diluted or adversely affected unless those rights are considered in a suit involving those who have this kind of confidential relation to them.

Coming to the merits, we are met with a wide range of questions that implicate the Due Process Clause of the Fourteenth Amendment. Overtones of some arguments suggest that *Lochner v. New York*, 198 U.S. 45, should be our guide. But we decline that invitation as we did in *West Coast Hotel Co. v. Parrish*, 300 U.S. 379; *Olsen v. Nebraska*, 313 U.S. 236; *Lincoln Union v. Northwestern Co.*, 335 U.S. 525; *Williamson v. Lee Optical Co.*, 348 U.S. 483; *Giboney v. Empire Storage Co.*, 336 U.S. 490. We do not sit as a super-legislature to determine the wisdom, need, and propriety of laws that touch economic problems, business affairs, or social conditions. This law, however, operates directly on an intimate relation of husband and wife and their physician's role in one aspect of that relation.

The association of people is not mentioned in the Constitution nor in the Bill of Rights. The right to educate a child in a school of the parents' choice—whether public or private or parochial—is also not mentioned. Nor is the right to study any particular subject or any foreign language. Yet the First Amendment has been construed to include certain of those rights.

By *Pierce v. Society of Sisters, supra*, the right to educate one's children as one chooses is made applicable to the States by the force of the First and Fourteenth Amendments. By *Meyer v. Nebraska, supra,* the same dignity is given the right to study the German language in a private school. In other words, the State may not, consistently with the spirit of the First Amendment, contract the spectrum of available knowledge. The right of freedom of speech and press includes not only the right to utter or to print, but the right to distribute, the right to receive, the right to read (*Martin v. Struthers,* 319 U.S. 141, 143) and freedom of inquiry, freedom of thought, and freedom to teach (see *Wieman v. Updegraff,* 344 U.S. 183, 195)—indeed the freedom of the entire university community. *Sweezy v. New Hampshire,* 354 U.S. 234, 249–250, 261–263; *Barenblatt v. United States,* 360 U.S. 109, 112; *Baggett v. Bullitt,* 377 U.S. 360, 369. Without those peripheral rights the specific rights would be less secure. And so we reaffirm the principle of the *Pierce* and the *Meyer* cases.

In *NAACP v. Alabama,* 357 U.S. 449, 462, we protected the "freedom to associate and privacy in one's association," noting that freedom of association was a peripheral First Amendment right. Disclosure of membership lists of a constitutionally valid association, we held, was invalid "as entailing the likelihood of a substantial restraint upon the exercise by petitioner's members of their right to freedom of association." *Ibid.* In other words, the First Amendment has a penumbra where privacy is protected from governmental intrusion. In like context, we have protected forms of "association" that are not political in the customary sense but pertain to the social, legal, and economic benefit of the members. *NAACP v. Button,* 371 U.S. 415, 430–431. In *Schware v. Board of Bar Examiners,* 353 U.S. 232, we held it not permissible to bar a lawyer from practice, because he had once been a member of the Communist Party. The man's "association with that Party" was not shown to be "anything more than a political faith in a political party" (*id.,* at 244) and not action of a kind proving bad moral character. *Id.,* at 245–246.

Those cases involved more than the "right of assembly"—a right that extends to all irrespective of their race or ideology. *DeJonge v. Oregon,* 299 U.S. 353. The right of "association," like the right of belief (*Board of Education v. Barnette,* 319 U.S. 624), is more than the right to attend a meeting; it includes the right to express one's attitudes or philosophies by membership in a group or by affiliation with it or by other lawful means. Association in that context is a form of expression of opinion; and while it is not expressly included in the First Amendment its existence is necessary in making the express guarantees fully meaningful.

The foregoing cases suggest that specific guarantees in the Bill of Rights have penumbras, formed by emanations from those guarantees that help give them life and substance. See *Poe v. Ullman,* 367 U.S. 497, 516–522 (dissenting opinion). Various guarantees create zones of privacy. The right of association contained in the penumbra of the First Amendment is one, as we have seen. The Third Amendment in its prohibition against the quartering of soldiers "in any house" in time of peace without the consent of the owner is another facet of that privacy. The Fourth Amendment explicitly affirms the "right of the people to be secure in their persons, houses, papers, and effects against unreasonable searches and seizures." The Fifth Amendment in its Self-Incrimination Clause enables the citizen to create a zone of privacy which government may not force him to surrender to his detriment. The Ninth Amendment provides: "The enumeration in the Constitution, of certain rights, shall not be construed to deny or disparage others retained by the people."

The Fourth and Fifth Amendments were described in *Boyd v. United States*, 116 U.S. 616, 630, as protection against all governmental invasions "of the sanctity of a man's home and the privacies of life."[1] We recently referred in *Mapp v. Ohio*, 367 U.S. 643, 656, to the Fourth Amendment as creating a "right of privacy, no less important than any other right carefully and particularly reserved to the people." See Beaney, The Constitutional Right to Privacy, 1962 Sup. Ct. Rev. 212; Griswold, The Right to be Let Alone, 55 N.W.U.L. Rev. 216 (1960).

We have had many controversies over these penumbral rights of "privacy and repose." See, e.g., *Breard v. Alexandria*, 341 U.S. 622, 626, 644; *Public Utilities Comm'n v. Pollak*, 343 U.S. 451; *Monroe v. Pape*, 365 U.S. 167; *Lanza v. New York*, 370 U.S. 139; *Frank v. Maryland*, 359 U.S. 360; *Skinner v. Oklahoma*, 316 U.S. 535, 541. These cases bear witness that the right of privacy which presses for recognition here is a legitimate one.

The present case, then, concerns a relationship lying within the zone of privacy created by several fundamental constitutional guarantees. And it concerns a law which, in forbidding the use of contraceptives rather than regulating their manufacture or sale, seeks to achieve its goals by means having a maximum destructive impact upon that relationship. Such a law cannot stand in light of the familiar principle, so often applied by this Court, that a "governmental purpose to control or prevent activities constitutionally subject to state regulation may not be achieved by means

---

[1] The Court said in full about this right of privacy:

"The principles laid down in this opinion [by Lord Camden in *Entick v. Carrington*, 19 Howell's State Trials 1029] affect the very essence of constitutional liberty and security. They reach farther than the concrete form of the case then before the court, with its adventitious circumstances; they apply to all invasions on the part of the government and its employes of the sanctity of a man's home and the privacies of life. It is not the breaking of his doors, and the rummaging of his drawers, that constitutes the essence of the offence; but it is the invasion of his indefeasible right of personal security, personal liberty and private property, where that right has never been forfeited by his conviction of some public offence,—it is the invasion of this sacred right which underlies and constitutes the essence of Lord Camden's judgment. Breaking into a house and opening boxes and drawers are circumstances of aggravation; but any forcible and compulsory extortion of a man's own testimony or of his private papers to be used as evidence to convict him of crime or to forfeit his goods, is within the condemnation of that judgment. In this regard the Fourth and Fifth Amendments run almost into each other." 116 U.S., at 630.

which sweep unnecessarily broadly and thereby invade the area of protected freedom." *NAACP* v. *Alabama*, 377 U.S. 288, 307. Would we allow the police to search the sacred precincts of marital bedrooms for telltale signs of the use of contraceptives? The very idea is repulsive to the notions of privacy surrounding the marriage relationship.

We deal with a right of privacy older than the Bill of Rights—older than our political parties, older than our school system. Marriage is a coming together for better or for worse, hopefully enduring, and intimate to the degree of being sacred. It is an association that promotes a way of life, not causes; a harmony in living, not political faiths; a bilateral loyalty, not commercial or social projects. Yet it is an association for as noble a purpose as any involved in our prior decisions.

Reversed

Family Planning Association

KARACHI BRANCH

IS AIMING

AT

BETTER FAMILY LIFE

FOR YOU

Through Services in :

★ FAMILY LIMITATION
★ STERILITY SERVICE
★ PREMARITAL GUIDANCE
★ POSTMARITAL PROBLEMS

No 1
(2nd Print)

Hafeez Art Press, Karachi-1

FAMILY PLANNING ASSOCIATION is a voluntary and non-profiting organisation which functions with financial help and cooperation of the public who desire to provide or/and avail the services of the Association. Considering the growing and urgent need of family planning, it is hoped that we will be able to avail generous assistance from Karachi Municipal Corporation and other organisations. We are also grateful to the Govt. of Pakistan for their financial aid.

WHAT IS FAMILY PLANNING ?

(a) CONCEPTION CONTROL ADVICE to families who have more children than they can look after satisfactorily by :-

    i.   Advising and teaching the use of contraceptives to the WOMEN.

    ii. Advising and teaching MEN the ways and means of family limitation.

    iii. Advise to space children on health and other grounds.

    iv. SURGICAL STERILIZATION of suitable men without unsexing.

(b) INVESTIGATE ADVISE AND TREAT sterile couples.

(c) PREMARITAL examination and advise.

(d) POSTMARITAL PROBLEMS. Helping the married coupley in their numerous post-marital problems.

WHY FAMILY PLANNING ?

In the present social set-up northing is likely to work well unless it is pre-planned. Whether it be the limitation of the number of children, spacing the children or to have children when a family has none; it is desirable to plan with a view to achive one's objective and personal and family happiness.

Family Planning has become a necessity. It is equally urgent both at the personal and national levels. The main factors motivating family planning are :-

i. HEALTH FACTOR : To attain and maintain better standard of health of children, and the parents, particularly the mother.

ii. ECONOMIC FACTOR : To partially solve the problems of the limited economic resources of a given family.

iii. SOCIAL FACTER : To meet the ever increasing social demands with limited resources—, an acute problem majority of our families are facing to-day.

HOW FAMILY PLANNING ?

The Association is conducting a Model Clinic, where advise and help is given to those who ask for it, regarding the best procedure that a given family may adopt under their circumstances to limit the size of their families. Arrangement has also being made for :-

1. Advise and help to the families who are not bleassed with children.

2. Pre-marital guidance.   } Marriage
                                       Counselling

3. Advise on post-marital problems. }

Hours of Work
9 a.m. to 12-30 p.m.
All week days.

SURGICAL STERILISATION

OF

MALE

WITHOUT UNSEXING
IS THE
SAFEST
CHEAPEST
EASIEST
&
100 % SURE METHOD
KNOWN TODAY

We recommend this method of Family Limitation to

Couples :-

1. Who are round about 35 years.
2. Who have atleast 3 children.
3. Atleast one of the three should be a boy or a girl.

Treaty Series No. 10 of 1958

BASIC AGREEMENT

Between the Government of Ceylon and The Royal Swedish Government for Technical Co-operation in the Field of Family Planning

Signed at Colombo on 22nd May, 1958

Presented to Parliament
by
The Minister of External Affairs

PRINTED AT THE GOVERNMENT PRESS, CEYLON

TO be purchased at the GOVERNMENT PUBLICATIONS BUREAU, COLOMBO

OCTOBER 1958   Price : 15 cents   Postage : 10 cents

BASIC AGREEMENT BETWEEN THE GOVERNMENT OF CEYLON AND THE ROYAL SWEDISH GOVERNMENT FOR TECHNICAL CO-OPERATION IN THE FIELD OF FAMILY PLANNING

ARTICLE 1

The Government of Ceylon and the Royal Government of Sweden agree to co-operate in order to promote and facilitate a pilot project in Community Family Planning to take place in two or more rural areas in Ceylon with the aim of extending such activities on the basis of the experience found on a nation wide scale.

ARTICLE 2

The purpose of the project shall be:—

(a) to make a scientific assessment of the attitudes towards family planning in the areas concerned.
(b) to investigate the possibilities of family planning in the areas concerned.
(c) to give instruction in the methods of family planning to the people in the areas, and
(d) to assist in training Ceylonese health personnel in work of this kind.

ARTICLE 3

This project shall be implemented in accordance with a plan agreed upon between the Central Committee for Swedish Technical Assistance and the Family Planning Association of Ceylon, who shall be entrusted by their respective Governments with full power to carry out the project.

ARTICLE 4

For the purpose stated in Article 2, the Central Committee for Swedish Technical Assistance shall particularly provide for a total period of three years, the services of a Chief Technical Adviser and the necessary equipment and supplies.

ARTICLE 5

The Government of Ceylon shall provide, or cause to be provided for a total period of three years one clerk experienced in statistical work and two midwives and also office accommodation for the Chief Technical Adviser.

ARTICLE 6

All funds, material and equipment of any kind which are brought to Ceylon for the specific purpose of implementing any program or project developed under this Agreement shall be admitted into Ceylon free of customs and import duties and all other taxes and service charges, and shall be free of currency and foreign exchange controls.

ARTICLE 7

Swedish personnel provided under this Agreement, shall be exempt in Ceylon from all Ceylonese income tax, social security tax or other personal tax or property tax on personal property intended for their own use, including customs and import duties on personal effects and equipment imported into Ceylon for their own exclusive use on their arrival in Ceylon.

ARTICLE 8

This Agreement shall enter into effect as from the date of signature and shall remain in effect for three years from that date, unless terminated in accordance with the provisions of Article 9. It may be prolonged beyond the period of three years by agreement between the two Governments. It may also at any time be amended by such agreement.

ARTICLE 9

This Agreement may at any time be terminated by either Government by the giving of no less than six months' notice in writing to that effect.

ARTICLE 10

On the termination of this agreement, or at such time as is provided in the agreement concluded in accordance with Article 3 above, all property, supplies and equipments acquired or employed in Ceylon for the development of projects under this Agreement shall become and remain the property of the Ceylonese Government.

ARTICLE 11

Any difference of opinion which may arise between the two organisations mentioned in Article 3 or otherwise concerning this Agreement shall be settled by an exchange of views between the two Governments.

In witness of this Agreement the Government of Ceylon and the Royal Government of Sweden have signed this document, at Colombo this Twenty-second day of May, One Thousand Nine Hundred and Fifty-eight in Two Copies in English.

(Sgd.) P. B. G. KALUGALLE,	(Sgd.) ALVA MYRDAL,
On behalf of	On behalf of
the Government of Ceylon	the Royal Government of Sweden

ANNOTATED BIBLIOGRAPHY

BOOKS

Bibliographical Data	*Annotation*
American Assembly, Columbia University, *The Population Dilemma*, P. M. Hauser (ed.), Prentice-Hall, 1963. 187 pp.	Chapters on Population and Economic Development; Resources in the United States and the World. Excellent for overall coverage.
Appleman, Philip, *The Silent Explosion*, Beacon Press, 1965. 139 pp.	Told from personal experience. Seven chapters, all vital, including A Million More Mouths Each Week. Discusses ideology of Communists, conservative Catholics, and liberals toward population.
Balestra, Pietro, and N. K. Rao, *Basic Economic Projections, United States Population 1965–1980*, Stanford Research Institute, Menlo Park, Calif., 1964. 70 pp.	An invaluable set of tables and figures showing such items as Projected Birth and Death Rates by State, Male Births per 1,000 Female Births, and Actual and Projected Birth Rates for the United States.
Bates, Marston, *The Prevalence of People*, Scribner, 1955. 261 pp.*	Written by a biologist. Excellent chapters on Human Reproduction, The Control of Reproduction, and The Idea of Eugenics.
Bogue, D. J., *The Population of the United States*, Macmillan, 1959. 859 pp.	Excellent tables. Wide statistical coverage.
Brown, Harrison, James Bonner, and John Weir, *The Next Hundred Years*, Viking, 1957. 175 pp.*	Short, pithy chapters. Prepared for leaders of American industry. Chapters on World Food Production, New Knowledge and New Food, Production of Scientists and Engineers.
Chen, Kuan-I, *World Population Growth and Living Standards*, College and University Press, 1960. 86 pp.*	Eighteen pages of statistical tables on a wide variety of subjects. Excellent short review of the problem.
Cipolla, Carlo, *The Economic History of World Population*, Penguin, 1962. 126 pp.*	Excellent short summary of the population dilemma.
Drogat, Noel, *The Challenge of Hunger*, J. R. Kirwan (tr.), Newman Press, 1962. 156 pp.	Chapters on The Geography of Hunger Malnutrition and The F.A.O. (Food and Agriculture Organization of the U.N.) Fights Hunger. Very interesting reading.

* Indicates bibliography.

BOOKS (continued)

Bibliographical Data	Annotation
Fabre-Luce, Alfred, *Men or Insects?* Robert Baldick (tr.), Hutchinson, 1964. 155 pp.*	Published in Paris in 1962. Includes discusion of euthanasia, abortion, Sweden vs. France. Interesting reading. Not as sensational as the title sounds.
Fagley, Richard M., *The Population Explosion and Christian Responsibility*, Oxford, 1960. 234 pp.	Chapters on Eastern Orthodoxy and Parenthood, the New Testament and Parenthood, Roman Catholicism and Parenthood, Protestantism and Parenthood.
Freedman, Ronald, et al., *Family Planning, Sterility and Population Growth*, McGraw-Hill, 1959. 495 pp.	Includes results of interviews on fertility trends. Chapters on The Use of Methods to Regulate Conception; Family Size in Different Social and Economic Groups; and Population Growth, 1955–2000.
Freedman, Ronald (ed.), *Population: The Vital Revolution*, Anchor, 1964. 267 pp.	Sections on newly developing countries, Latin America, India, Japan, Communist China, Soviet Union, and Europe. Nineteen essays by different authors.
Garst, Jonathan, *No Need for Hunger*, Random House, 1963. 173 pp.	Entertainingly written in the first person. Good descriptions of food problems in El Salvador and Brazil, and of the Alliance for Progress.
Glass, David V. (ed.), *Demography*, U.N.E.S.C.O., 1957. 200 pp.	An exposition of the methods by which demography is taught in various countries.
Greep, Roy O., *Human Fertility and Population Problems*, Schenkman Publishing Co., 1963. 278 pp.	Proceedings of a seminar sponsored by the American Academy of Arts and Sciences with the support of the Ford Foundation. Chapters on Taiwan and Legal Abortion.
Hauser, Philip M., *Population Perspectives*, Rutgers, 1960. 171 pp.	Chapters on The World Population Explosion, The United States Population Explosion, The Metropolitan Area Explosion. Graphs, maps.
Hauser, Philip M., and Otis D. Duncan, *The Study of Population*, University of Chicago, 1959. 851 pp.	Reports on demographic research in France, Germany, Italy, Brazil, the Pacific. Chapters on Genetics and

* Indicates bibliography.

BOOKS (*continued*)

Bibliographical Data	Annotation
	Demography and Economics and Demography.
Huxley, Julian, *The Human Crisis*, University of Washington, 1963. 88 pp.	Lectures by Huxley delivered under the John Danz Fund.
Kiser, Clyde V. (ed.), *Research in Family Planning*, Princeton, 1962. 662 pp.	Papers presented at a 1960 conference. Wide geographic coverage—India, Asia and the Middle East, Japan, U.S., Latin America. Articles on communication problems and fertility control.
Malthus, Thomas F., Julian Huxley, and Frederick Osborn, *On Population: Three Essays*, Mentor, 1960. 138 pp.	Excellent for gaining an historical and philosophical background of the problem.
McCormack, Arthur, *People, Space, Food*, Sheed and Ward, 1960. 279 pp.*	Interesting chapters on Food from New Sources, Food and Science, and More Food from Existing Sources.
McCormack, Arthur, *World Poverty and the Christian*, Hawthorn, 1963. 158 pp.*	Sections on The Extent of World Poverty, The Population Explosion and World Poverty, Hunger and Poverty Can Be Wiped Out, The Church's Teaching on International Social Justice, and Economics and Christian Humanism.
Mudd, Stuart (ed.), *The Population Crisis and the Use of World Resources*. Indiana University, 1964. 535 pp.	Compiled by the World Academy of Art and Science. Chapters on The Unwanted Child, Better Genes for Tomorrow, The Problem of Abortion, The Place of Sterilization, and a series of chapters on population problems in given parts of the world, including India, China, Latin America, U.A.R., Pakistan.
Organski, Katherine, and A. F. K. Organski, *Population and World Power*, Knopf, 1961. 263 pp.*	Treats population problems from the viewpoint of power politics.
Osborn, Fairfield (ed.), *Our Crowded Planet: Essays on the Pressures of Population*, Doubleday, 1962. 233 pp.*	Sponsored by the Conservation Foundation. Sections on India, Japan, Latin America. Part IV is entitled The Population Problem and Religion.
Peterson, William, *The Politics of Population*, Doubleday, 1964. 338 pp.	Treatment of demography in The Netherlands and U.S. Chapters on

BOOKS (continued)

Bibliographical Data   *Annotation*

urban planning, religious statistics, and planned migration.

Rock, John, *The Time Has Come: A Catholic Doctor's Proposals to End the Battle over Birth Control*, Knopf, 1963. 204 pp.*

A gynecologist discusses legal battles over birth control in Massachusetts and Connecticut. Includes a summary of how contraceptive pills were developed.

Sagi, Westoff P., et al., *The Third Child*, Princeton, 1963. 206 pp.

Excellent chapters on Religion and Religiousness and on Predicting Fertility.

Sax, Karl, "The Population Explosion," in *Headline Series, Foreign Policy Association*, No. 120 (Nov.–Dec., 1956), Foreign Policy Association, 1956. 61 pp.

Good graphs. Famine may become severe unless population control is undertaken. Excellent introductory study.

Sax, Karl, *Standing Room Only*, Beacon Press, 1955. 192 pp.*

Good for overall viewpoint.

Smith, T. Lynn, *Fundamentals of Population Study*, Lippincott, 1960. 520 pp.*

Figures, maps, graphs. Excellent chapters on Internal Migration; Race, Color, Ethnic Stock, and Nativity; and Mortality Trends.

Stycos, J. Mayone, *Family and Fertility in Puerto Rico*, Columbia, 1955. 314 pp.*

Chapters on Attitudes toward Fertility, Attitudes toward Birth Control, and the Dynamics of Birth Control Use.

Stycos, J. Mayone, and Kurt W. Back, *The Control of Human Fertility in Jamaica*, Cornell, 1964. 369 pp.*

A thorough study of Jamaica, including the results of an experimental program offered to control births.

Vogt, William, *People! Challenge to Survival*, Sloane, 1960. 257 pp.

Written for popular consumption. Recommended for pleasant reading.

Wrong, Dennis H., *Population and Society*, Random House, 2nd rev. ed., 1964. 134 pp.*

Excellent summation of the problem.

Zimmerman, Anthony, *Catholic Viewpoint on Overpopulation*, Hanover House, 1961. 214 pp.

Ten chapters, including Japan, The Morality of Rearing Large Families in Overpopulated Areas.

ANNOTATED BIBLIOGRAPHY

PERIODICALS

Periodical	Author	Title, Date	Annotation
America	F. C. Madigan	Asian population conference. 110: 188–189; Feb. 8, 64. Population program; worldwide American population control policy. 112: 216; Feb. 13, 65. Reply, 112:408; Mar. 27, 65.	Discussion and statistics. Some negative arguments. Discusses President Johnson's statement of intent to help work with world population.
American Academy of Political and Social Science Annals	T. Sellin (ed.)	A crowding hemisphere: population change in the Americas. All of 316:1–136; Mar., 58.	Excellent on U.S., Canada, Caribbean, Latin America; 15 articles.
American Association of University Women Journal	J. D. Rockefeller	Population: decision by default. 57:4–6; Oct., 63.	Philosophies presented are challenging.
American Economic Review	R. A. Easterlin	U.S. baby boom in historical perspective. 51:869–911; Dec., 61.	Seventy-three-item bibliography at conclusion.
American Historical Review	W. L. Langer	Europe's initial population explosion. 69:1–17; Oct., 63.	Good historical background. Does not discuss present.
American Sociological Review	E. G. Stockwell	Relationship between population growth and economic development. 27:250–252; Apr., 62.	Reply given in Aug., 62. Has coverage of both points of view.
Barron's National Business and Financial Weekly		Advertisement 42:8; May 14, 62.	

PERIODICALS (*continued*)

Periodical	Author	Title, Date	Annotation
Catholic World	T. K. Burch	Facts and fallacies about world population growth. 190:345–351; Mar., 60.	Considers fallacies concerning why population will decrease. Both sides of issue.
Christian Century	P. K. Jewett	Case for birth control. 78:651–652; May 24, 61.	Theological point of view for birth control.
	R. M. Fagley	Population problems and the church. 79:744–777; June 13, 62.	Theological foundation for birth control. Protestant.
	J. A. O'Brien	Population explosion demands worldwide action. 81:43–46; Jan. 8, 64.	Need for integrated plan of aid, immigration, birth control.
Commonweal	T. K. Burch	Population and Parenthood. 80: 328–331; June 5, 64.	This entire issue is concerned with birth control.
	J. O'Gara	Race against hunger. 81:62; Oct. 9, 64.	Advocates some form of birth control and aid to have-not countries.
Contemporary Review	R. Malik	Population explosion and India. 199:25–27; Jan., 61.	Good background on India.
Demographic Yearbook		Sales Section, United Nations, N.Y.	All issues applicable. $8, one per year. Vital statistics.
Demography		Community and Family Study Center, 1126 E. 59th St., Chicago, Ill.	All issues applicable. $7, one per year.
Economist		Seventy million	Good for present

PERIODICALS (continued)

Periodical	Author	Title, Date	Annotation
		Britons? 207:413–414; May 4, 63.	and future of Britain.
Foreign Affairs	J. Zlotnick	Population pressure and political indecision. 39: 683–694; July, 61.	Compares U.S. with Russia and China. Material on both sides of the question.
Foreign Service Journal	T. Dohrman	Critical dimensions in overpopulation; will mankind be able to restore the balance between population and food resources? 40:21–24; Dec., 63.	Excellent for survey of present situation.
Fortune	C. Clark	Do population and freedom grow together? 62:136–194; Dec., 60.	Author says yes. Biographical sketch of author. Gain freedom and economic wealth together.
Intercom	Foreign Policy Association	Focus on world population. 6, no. 1:13–72; Jan.–Feb., 64.	Presents a detailed breakdown of organizations interested in population.
International Labour Review		Projections of population and labour force. 83: 378–399; Apr., 61.	Tables showing the labor situation in various countries.
International Planned Parenthood News		International Planned Parenthood Federation, 64 Sloane St., London, S.W.1, England.	All issues applicable. A 4-page leaflet giving mostly news. Monthly except July and August. $2 per year.
Journal of Educational Sociology	H. H. Punke	Population, foreign aid and ethical values. 34: 328–332; Mar., 61.	Defends ethics of not helping the very poor.

PERIODICALS (*continued*)

Periodical	Author	Title, Date	Annotation
Journal of Geography	R. C. Klove	Growing population of the United States. 60:203–213; May, 61.	Maps showing population changes. Descriptive.
	P. C. Morrison	Middle America, land of too many and too little. 60:112–120; Mar., 61.	Bibliography. Points out why underdeveloped countries cannot follow U.S. growth.
	C. L. White	Whither South America: population and natural resources. 60:103–112; Mar., 61.	Good description of raw materials of South America, difficulties and possibilities for development.
Journal of International Affairs	J. C. Hurewitz	Politics of rapid population growth in the Middle East. 19:26–38; 65.	A detailed discussion of the population problem in the nations of the Middle East. Relates this problem to the role of the U.S. in this area. Suggests that population explosion in the Middle East is hindering social and economic development.
Law and Contemporary Problems		Population control. 25:379–629; Summer, 60.	Series of articles on variety of subjects, including population control in Japan, India, and Puerto Rico.

PERIODICALS (continued)

Periodical	Author	Title, Date	Annotation
National Education Association Journal	Research Division	How much the United States population will grow from 1960 to 1970; summary of population projections. 51:22; Jan., 62.	Good chart.
National Review		Population explosion: symposium. 17:633–648; July 27, 65. Discussion, 17:706; Aug. 24, 65.	Four separate articles entitled The Avalanche, What Exit for Asia, How Births Can Be Controlled, and Catholics and Population. All excellent.
New Republic		Fighting world famine. 153:7–8; Aug. 7, 65.	Discusses agricultural production around the world.
New York Times Magazine	E. Fremont-Smith	Malthus—again. Sep. 23, 62; p. 68.	Good background on Malthus and his views.
North Central Association Quarterly	R. B. Thompson	Population explosion: its effects on education. 35: 297–299; Apr., 61.	Doesn't suggest control in itself. Suggests alternatives for education if control doesn't occur.
Population and Vital Statistics Report		Department of Economic and Social Affairs, Statistical Office, United Nations, N.Y.	All issues applicable. Quarterly. $1 per year. Excellent for current statistics on such items as births and deaths.

PERIODICALS (continued)

Periodical	Author	Title, Date	Annotation
Population Bulletin of the United Nations		Department of Economic and Social Affairs, United Nations, N.Y.	All issues applicable. Issued irregularly. No. 6 (1962) gives annotated bibliography of demographic publications of U.N.
Population Bulletin		Population Reference Bureau, 1755 Massachusetts Ave., N.W., Washington, D.C. 20036.	All issues applicable. 6 issues per year. $3 per year.
Population Index		Office of Population Research, Princeton University, Princeton, N.J.	All issues applicable. Quarterly. $10 per year.
Population Studies		Population Investigation Committee, London School of Economics and Political Science, London, England.	All issues applicable. 3 issues per year. $8.50.
Saturday Review	H. Brown and E. K. Fedorov	Too many people in the world? 45: 16–20; Feb. 17, 62, and 45:15–16; Sep., 62.	Debate between a Russian and America's Harrison Brown.
	G. Clark	Solving the inhuman equation; can arms control end the population crisis? 46:15–16, 18–19; Feb. 16, 63.	Yes, and nothing can until the arms crisis is solved.
	R. N. Gardner	Politics of population; concerning U.N. resolution on population growth and	Illustrated. Charts on population now and in the year 2000.

PERIODICALS (continued)

Periodical	Author	Title, Date	Annotation
		economic development. 46:10–12, 37–38; Sep. 7, 63.	
Science		Greater role for U.N. specialized agencies seen in meeting problem of population outrunning resources. 129:882–884; Apr. 3, 59.	Gives reasons why U.N. has been ineffective so far in doing more.
	H. von Foerster et al.	Doomsday: Friday, 13 November, A.D. 2026. 132:1291–1295; Nov. 4, 60.	Bibliography. Mathematical formulas for population prediction.
	D. S. Greenberg	Population: new U.S. interest in offering assistance reveals lags in underdeveloped nations. 143:1016–1017; Mar. 6, 64.	Apathy on the part of underdeveloped countries.
Science News Letter		Priority for population. 84:381; Dec. 14, 63.	Discusses resolution of Senators Clark and Gruening requesting presidential commission on population.
Scientific American		Fertility and economic growth; India. 210:56; June, 64.	Plots fertility curve for India.
		Technological and economic development. 209 (312 pp.); Sep., 63.	Thirteen articles on various phases of how nations can attain self-sustaining growth, in-

PERIODICALS (continued)

Periodical	Author	Title, Date	Annotation
			cluding articles on food, water, energy, minerals, and the development of Nigeria, India, and Brazil. Article by K. Davis pointing to evidence that personal aspirations will slow population growth.
Senior Scholastic		Tomorrow's world population; too many? 83:18–20; Sep. 27, 63.	Some break in the problem in Europe, but outlook not hopeful unless action taken.
Social Progress		Religion, population, and the law. 53, no. 2; Nov., 62.	Issued by Presbyterian Distribution Service, 225 Varick St., New York, N.Y.
Social Studies	H. M. Boodish	Expanding population problem. 51:267–270; Dec., 60.	What life would be like for 50 billions.
Teachers College Record		Education and birth control. 65: 149–151; Nov., 63.	Literacy before birth control.
		Human numbers racket. 66:232– 234; Dec., 64.	Concerned with Connecticut Supreme Court decision and Demographic Yearbook report on population increase.
Thought: Fordham University	C. G. Wilbar	To feed the hungry: unless the	Single nos. $1.75. Fordham

PERIODICALS (continued)

Periodical	Author	Title, Date	Annotation
Quarterly		basic biological situation of the unity of mankind is seriously acknowledged, we cannot solve worldwide problems like hunger and the population problem. 38: 487–498; Winter, 63.	University Press, 441 Fordham Road, New York, N.Y. 10058.
United States Department of State Bulletin	R. N. Gardner	Politics of population: a blueprint for international cooperation. 48: 906–914; June 10, 63.	An address. Good on both sides of population control.
	R. N. Gardner	Population growth, economic development, and the U.N. statements, Dec. 10 and 13; with text of resolution, Dec. 18, 62. 48:14–20; Jan. 7, 63.	The position taken by the U.S. before the U.N. Council. Good on both sides of population control.
	F. O. Wilcox	World population and economic development. 42: 860–867; May 30, 60.	Address of Apr. 29, 1960. Good on both sides of issue. What can be done other than birth control?
United States News and World Report		Population problem. 47:122–123; Dec. 7, 59.	Statement by Catholic bishops of the United States.
	R. M. Scammon	What's ahead in the population boom. 54:68–71; May 6, 63.	An interview. Good for information as to predicted patterns in U.S. suburbs,

PERIODICALS *(continued)*

Periodical	Author	Title, Date	Annotation
			specialized city areas, racial balance.
		Way the United States is growing, what it means. 56: 82–85; Jan. 13, 64.	Charts and statistics for U. S. growth.
	P. M. Hauser	How population explosion is changing the United States. 57:58–63; Aug. 31, 64.	An interview. Explains fine points of what demographers have predicted and why.
Virginia Quarterly Review	E. R. Black	Population growth and economic development. 37:321–331; Summer, 61.	Rich must help poor. Population must be curbed.
World Politics	S. N. Afriat	People and population. 17:431–439; Apr., 65.	Supports restraint on parenthood.

ANNOTATED BIBLIOGRAPHY

D O C U M E N T S[1]

Source	Annotation
Plenary Meetings, The United Nations, 17th session, Vol. III, Dec. 18, 1962, pp. 1171–1179.	By 69–0 with 27 abstentions, U.N. passed resolution encouraging U.N. agencies to speed up their study of population. See also discussions that led up to Dec. 18.
Hearings before the Committee on the Judiciary, U.S. House of Representatives, "Study of Population and Immigration Problems," Special Series, Aug. 16, 1962–June 17, 1963.	87th Congress, 2nd session No. 1: Population of the United States, Aug. 16, 1962. 130 pp. No. 2: Population of the World, Aug. 29, 1962. 32 pp. No. 3: Manpower in the U.S. with Projection to 1970, Aug. 30, 1962. 31 pp. No. 4: Asian Populations: The Critical Decades, Sept. 13, 1962. 31 pp. 88th Congress, 1st session No. 5: Trends in Canadian Population; Population Trends in Mexico, Mar. 11, 1962. 79 pp. No. 6: The Demographic Position of the Caribbean; The Growth of Population in Central and South America, Mar. 27, 1963. 186 pp. No. 7: The Population of Western Europe, June 13, 1963. 27 pp. No. 8: Recent Demographic Changes in Eastern Europe, June 17, 1963. 71 pp.
"The Time Has Come to Speak Out on the Problem of Population Control," *Congressional Record*, 88th Congress, 1st session, Vol. 109, Part 11, Aug. 15, 1963, pp. 15237–15251.	A speech by Senator Joseph S. Clark of Pennsylvania.
"Population Control Is Receiving Serious Attention," *Congressional Record*, 88th Congress, 1st session, Vol. 109, Part 14, Oct. 10, 1963, pp. 19196–19215.	A speech by Senator Ernest Gruening of Alaska.

[1] Chronologically arranged.

MATERIALS AVAILABLE FOR PURCHASE[1]

American Eugenics Society, Inc., 230 Park Ave., New York, N.Y. 10017
Mayone Stycos, *Female Sterilization in Puerto Rico.* 25¢
Nan Aheard, *Regulation of Offspring and the Roman Catholic Church.*
25¢

Association for Voluntary Sterilization, 515 Madison Ave., New York, N.Y.
10022
Alan F. Guttmacher, *Sterilization: Facts and Arguments.* 10¢
Herman M. Moser, *Sterilization of Incompetent.* 15¢

The Community and Family Study Center, The University of Chicago, 1126
East 59th St., Chicago, Ill.
Richard Frank and C. Tietze, *Birth Control Made Easy and Inexpensive.*
40¢
Men: The Truth about Birth Control. 20¢
The Birth Control Pill and Aerosol Foam. 5¢

Family Life Bureau, National Catholic Welfare Conference, 1312 Massachu-
setts Ave., N.W., Washington, D.C. 20005
John C. Ford, *Morality and the Pill.* 5¢
John R. Maguire, *About "Those" Catholic Marriage Laws.* 10¢
Norman St. John-Stevas, *Sterilization and Public Policy.* 50¢

Hugh Moore Fund, 60 East 42nd St., New York, N.Y. 10017
News Items. A four-page release, published irregularly by the Population
Policy Panel of the Hugh Moore Fund. Single copies free. Ask to be put
on mailing list.
The Population Bomb: Is Voluntary Human Sterilization the Answer?
Single copies free
Marriner S. Eccles, *The Population Explosion and Your Taxes.* Single
copies free
Adolph W. Schmidt, *Business Profits and the Population Explosion.* Sin-
gle copies free

Paulist Press, National Catholic Reading Distributors, Harristown Road, Glen
Rock, N.J.
George A. Kelly, *Overpopulation, A Catholic View.* 75¢
William J. Gibbons (ed.), *Population, Resources and the Future.* 25¢

Planned Parenthood Federation of America, World Population Emergency
Campaign, 515 Madison Ave., New York, N.Y. 10022
M. A. Calderone, *Illegal Abortion as a Public Health Problem.* 10¢
A. C. Tietze et al., *Family Planning Service in Rural Puerto Rico.* 5¢
Spirals, Loops and Rings Tested as Contraceptives. 15¢
J. M. Jones, *Does Overpopulation Mean Poverty.* 75¢
L. Day, *Our Irresponsible Birthrate.* 5¢

The Population Council, 230 Park Ave., New York, N.Y. 10017
This organization issues its material free only to university libraries and

---

[1] Only representative items are listed, to demonstrate what materials are available
(materials of this nature go out of print quickly). Students are urged to write for lists
of releases.

research institutions in Africa, Asia, and Latin America. It also releases valuable bibliographies, which list such items as the following:

Mary S. Calderone (ed.), *Manual of Contraceptive Practice*, Williams and Wilkins, 1964.

C. Tietze and H. Lehfeldt, "Legal Abortion in Eastern Europe," *Journal of the American Medical Association*, 175; Apr. 1, 61.

The Population Reference Bureau, Inc., 1755 Massachusetts Ave., N.W., Washington, D.C. 20036

Interstellar Migration and the Population Problem. 10¢

110,000,000 Babies. 10¢

Marriage and the Co-ed. 10¢

Mexico: Problem of People. 50¢

The World's Great Cities. 50¢

The Population Research Project, George Washington University, Washington, D.C.

Samuel Baum, *Population, Manpower, and Economic Development in Eastern Europe.* $1.25

Harold L. Geisert, *The Caribbean: Population and Resources.* $1.25

Harold L. Geisert, *Population Problems in Mexico and Central America.* $1.25

Carr B. Lavell, *Population Growth and the Development of South America.* $1

Kathryn T. Louka, *The Role of Population in the Development of Southeast Asia.* $1.25

Richard W. Stephens, *Population Factors in the Development of North Africa.* $1.25

Population Research and Training Center, The University of Chicago, 1413 East 60th St., Chicago, Ill. 60637

Patricia Hodge, *Population Projections for the City of Chicago and the Chicago Metropolitan Area, 1970 and 1980.* $1

D. M. Pappenfort, *Journey to Labor: A Study of Births in Hospitals and Technology.* $1.50

Sales Section, The United Nations, New York, N.Y.

Bibliography available from the Bureau of Social Affairs, Department of Economic and Social Affairs, The United Nations. Nonsales items are requested from the issuing organization.

The Future Growth of World Population. Sales No.: 58.XIII.2. ST/SOA/Ser.A/28. $1

Population Growth and Manpower in the Philippines. Sales No.: 61.XIII.2. ST/SOA/Ser. A/32. $1

Population and Food Supply. Freedom from Hunger Campaign Basic Study No. 7. Sales No.: 62.I.22. 50¢

Asia and the Far East Seminar on Population. Bandung, 21 No. to 3 Dec. 1955. Sales No.: 57.II.H.1. 60¢

Future Population Estimates by Sex and Age. Report I: The Population of Central America (including Mexico), 1950–1980. Sales No.: 54.XIII.3. 70¢

SUGGESTED SPEECH SUBJECTS

Informative Speeches: Round One

1. Food Problems in Brazil
2. Population Problems in Taiwan
3. Population Problems in India
4. Population Problems in Japan
5. Population Problems in Jamaica
6. Population Problems in the U.S.S.R.
7. Population Problems in The People's Republic of China
8. Population Problems in Puerto Rico
9. Population Problems in Ceylon
10. Population Problems in Pakistan
11. Population Problems in Latin America
12. World Food Production
13. The Sea as a Source of Food Supply
14. The Population Explosion in Large Cities in the United States
15. The Population Explosion in California
16. Recent Population Growth Has Greatly Increased the Percentage of the Population under Twenty-Five Years of Age
17. The Alliance for Progress and Population Control
18. Mortality Rates in Developed and Underdeveloped Countries
19. The Development of the Contraceptive Pill
20. Population Growth Expected in the Twenty-first Century
21. Mathematical Formulae for Predicting Population Increases
22. Life on Earth with a Population of Fifty Billion
23. The Relationship between Literacy and Birth Control
24. Underdeveloped Countries Do Not Use the Birth-Control Facilities Available to Them
25. New Sources of Food through Chemistry

Informative Speeches: Round Two

26. Abortion Practices in Japan
27. The Prevalence of Abortion in the United States
28. The Current World Population Growth
29. Papal Encyclicals on Birth Control
30. The Status of Voluntary Sterilization
31. Research and Programs in Population Control Are Being Generously Supported
32. The Position of the United States Supreme Court on Birth Control
33. The Policy of the Catholic Church in the United States on Birth Control
34. The Food and Agriculture Organization of the United Nations
35. The Problems Involved in Communicating Information on Birth Control
36. Increasing the Food Supply by Better Use of Fertilizers
37. The Role of Power Politics in the Population Explosion
38. Famine in the World Today

39. The Differential Birth Rate
40. The Growth of Population in the United States
41. The Science of Eugenics
42. Demography
43. Methods of Regulating Conception
44. The Attitude of the Protestant Episcopal Church on Population Control
45. The Attitude of the Presbyterian Church on Population Control
46. Protestantism and Parenthood
47. Dr. John Rock
48. T. R. Malthus
49. Population Growth in the City of London
50. Euthanasia

Persuasive Speeches: Round One

1. The psychological effects of overcrowding will be so disastrous that population control is imperative.
2. Communist countries are interested in using population growth as a means of bringing new recruits to communism.
3. Properly planned housing in the future can provide a means of living with the population explosion.
4. The population explosion is not as severe as many persons believe.
5. The Roman Catholic Church opposes only the method, not the aims, of birth control.
6. The widespread use of contraceptives will result in a decided decrease in population growth.
7. An increase in population results in increased job opportunities.
8. The population explosion should cause the United States to stop immigration.
9. The United States government should begin immediately on extensive research on population control.
10. The elimination of former population controls, such as famine, war, and disease, has caused the population explosion.
11. Population growth will annihilate the world by 2026.
12. Russia can increase her population materially, whereas the United States cannot.
13. Population control cannot be achieved until the arms race is controlled.
14. As Senators Joseph Clark and Ernest Gruening have suggested, the President should create a presidential commission on population.
15. An increase in population will drastically change life in the United States.
16. Population growth is not a serious problem because it will level off for natural reasons.
17. Population growth is more dangerous than the atom bomb.

Persuasive Speeches: Round Two

18. Population growth will produce a famine in Asia by 1980.
19. Population growth is exceeding agricultural growth.

20. The uneven distribution of the world's population justifies a redistribution of territory.
21. The United States cannot justify foreign aid when population growth in recipient nations continues to outstrip economic growth.
22. Public and private organizations should be permitted to distribute information on birth control to married and unmarried persons.
23. Euthanasia should be encouraged as one means of controlling population.
24. Children unwanted by lower-income-bracket families provide a major problem that can be eliminated by birth control.
25. Birth control can produce better genes for the peoples of tomorrow.
26. Sterilization should be expanded as a means of birth control.
27. Planned migration can serve as a major way to control overpopulation.
28. The only way to prevent overpopulation is by governmental regulation of the size of families.
29. Only through population control can the Caucasian retain his leadership in world society.
30. It is immoral to continue to produce large families in overpopulated areas.
31. The United States hesitates to help others with overpopulation because it has no problem of its own.
32. The use of contraceptives is contrary to religious law.
33. Abortion should be legalized to reduce population growth.
34. Persons in high socioeconomic brackets have no more right to large families than do persons in lower socioeconomic brackets.

Debate Propositions

1. *Resolved:* that abortion should be legalized in the United States.
2. *Resolved:* that overpopulation is the greatest problem facing the world today.
3. *Resolved:* that the United States should accompany foreign aid programs to overpopulated countries with programs of population control.
4. *Resolved:* that information on birth control should be disseminated by public agencies to unmarried persons.
5. *Resolved:* that the state has the right to regulate population growth.
6. *Resolved:* that research in population control will develop methods of birth control which will regulate population growth without state intervention.
7. *Resolved:* that artificial methods of birth control are immoral.
8. *Resolved:* that overpopulation will destroy the world.
9. *Resolved:* that birth control can produce a super-race.
10. *Resolved:* that new sources of food supply will be developed which will exceed the needs of population growth.

Discussion Subjects

1. Should the United States sponsor programs in foreign countries aimed at population control?

2. Should governments enact legislation which would limit the size of families?
3. Should abortion be legalized to limit population growth?
4. Should the United States government expand immediately its system of federal parks to prepare for future population growth?
5. What should be the attitude of the church toward sterilization and euthanasia?
6. Can India achieve economic progress without effective birth control?
7. What specific steps should the United States take to prepare for population growth?
8. What effects will shifts in population have upon white supremacy?
9. The curriculum of the secondary school should include a program designed to encourage birth control.
10. What are the obligations of the richer countries toward the poorer, over-populated countries?

II

BUSINESS ETHICS

SELECTED READINGS

THE WORD "BUSINESS" in this unit has been given a broad enough definition to include the professions, such as law, medicine, and the church. Not much material relevant to the teacher has been included, because of the separate unit on teacher education. The federal and state governments are definitely "big business," and are pertinent to this unit.

As with teacher education, the more sensational articles are by those who are depreciating the ethics of American business. A vigorous search was made for materials complimentary to business ethics, and, although many were found, their style and verve do not compare well with those of the derogatory critics. Any resulting bias, the editors hope, results from the materials available, and not from their manner of presentation.

The student of business ethics will find himself confronted with many more opinions and assertions than he will documented evidence. Research in this unit will be considerably different from that on population control, where much of the material is quite specific. Evidently we know considerably less about just how business ethics function than we would like to know. This should be considered a strength, and not a weakness. The intangibility of the material should present a challenge to the student's curiosity.

Speakers should avoid taking the attitude of "getting the businessman." Before offering blanket condemnations—or making sweeping commendations—the student should be certain that he has considered both sides of the problem. The sensational speeches in this unit should be sacrificed for what should be a serious consideration of the businessman's dilemma.

Students should interview businessmen, professors of business administration, the local office of the Better Business Bureau, and consumers to supplement their library research. An hour spent in a local advertising agency or with an important businessman in the community will do much to make the reading matter in this unit come to life. State and federal representatives can offer pertinent material. Students should inquire about local grievance committees in the professions, such as law, medicine, and dentistry.

Speeches on the general philosophy of ethics are probably not pertinent to this unit. Students interested in such philosophical discussions should make an effort to apply their theories to the practical business world of today.

HOW ETHICAL ARE BUSINESSMEN?

RAYMOND C. BAUMHART, S.J.

WHAT WOULD YOU DO IF—

. . . as a director of a large corporation, you learned at a board meeting of an impending merger with a smaller company? Suppose this company has had an unprofitable year, and its stock is selling at a price so low that you are certain it will rise when news of the merger becomes public knowledge. Would you buy some stock? Or tell a friend? Or tell your broker?

. . . as president of a company in a highly competitive industry, you learned that a competitor had made an important scientific discovery which would give him a substantial advantage over you? If you had an opportunity to hire one of his employees who knew the details of the discovery, would you do it?

WHAT DO YOU THINK ABOUT—

. . . an executive earning $10,000 a year who has been padding his expense account by about $500 a year?

. . . an executive owning stock in a company with which his own company regularly does business?

. . . the idea that management should act in the interest of shareholders alone?

These problems were posed as part of a lengthy questionnaire on business ethics completed by some 1,700 *HBR* executive readers—34% of the 5,000 cross section polled. This high rate of return, and the hundreds of thoughtful essays written by these anonymous administrators on the margins of their questionnaires and on separate letterheads paint a picture of executives' deep concern over business behavior. (For a profile of these respondents, see Exhibit I.)

Harvard Business Review, 39:7–19, 156–176; July–August, 1961. Reprinted by permission.

71

During the past decade, much has been written about ethics in business. Most of the books and articles are based on the experiences of one man, or on a priori reasoning. Few authors have approached business ethics empirically, surveying the ideas, problems, and attitudes of a large number of businessmen. This study employs such an empirical approach.

We hoped that in the process of securing and reporting the data, we would prompt top management to re-examine fruitfully its thinking and practices. In addition, we wished to give scholars the businessman's point of view, that is, what he regards as ethical problems and unethical behavior—though, of course, this is not meant to imply that ethics is a matter of statistics, or that a majority response constitutes an ethical answer.

Here are some of the highlights of our study:

℃ *Executives are alert to the social responsibilities of business as these are expressed in general terms. They see the corporation as a human society, a microcosm of the larger society in which it functions.* (See the section on "Business Responsibility?")

℃ *As for specific business practices, executives often disagree about what is the ethical thing to do.* (See "I'M Ethical, But Is HE?")

℃ *Though our respondents profess a lofty level of ethical aspiration for themselves, they reveal a lower opinion of the practices of the "average" businessman.* (See "Cynicism.")

℃ *Executives say that the man most likely to act ethically is one with a well-defined personal code. If he also has a boss who is highly ethical, his behavior will be consistently upright. But watch out, say executives, for there are many pressures for unethical conduct.* (See "Ethical Influences.")

℃ *Executives admit and point out the presence of numerous generally accepted practices in their industry which they consider unethical. Our respondents cite many daily problems in which the "economic" solution conflicts with the "ethical" solution.* (See "Chapter & Verse.")

℃ *If unethical practices are to be reduced, executives say that top management must lead the way. The men at the top must be individuals of principle, who unmistakably reveal their ethical attitude, not only verbally, but also by forceful actions.* (See "Pressure.")

℃ *As a help in correcting unethical practices, most executives would welcome a written code of ethics for their industry. But this code must have "teeth," be capable of enforcement, and embody specific guides for conduct if it is to do the job.* (See "Code of Ethics.")

℃ *Most executives believe that organized religion and clergymen have been lax in providing guidance for the ethical problems of business. At the same time, the welcome which businessmen give to clerical advice is di-*

rectly proportional to the amount of knowledge that the individual clergy-man has about business. (See "Role of Religion.")

Now, for the details, let us turn to the specifics of our findings, so that you can compare your thinking and your views with those of the executives surveyed and interviewed in our study.

BUSINESS RESPONSIBILITY?

Polybius, the Greek historian, summarized a nation's decline in a single

EXHIBIT I. *Profile of the Executives Responding*

Management position

Top management	= chairman of the board; board member; owner; partner; president; division or executive vice president; vice president; treasurer, secretary-treasurer; controller; secretary (to the corporation); general manager; general superintendent; editor; administrative director; dean; and assistants thereto.	45%
Upper middle management	= functional department head (e.g., advertising, sales, promotion, production, purchasing, personnel, engineering, public relations, brand manager, and the like).	27
Lower middle management	= assistant to functional department head; district manager; branch manager; section manager; and the like.	12
Nonmanagement personnel	= all others employed in business.	9
Professional	= doctor; practicing lawyer; practicing CPA; professor; consultant; military officer; government official; union official; clergyman; and the like.	7

Formal education		Income group	
High school or less	5%	Under $10,000	12%
Some college	19	$10,000–19,999	45
Bachelor's degree	36	$20,000–29,999	23
Graduate school	40	$30,000–39,999	8
		$40,000–49,999	4
		$50,000–74,999	4
		$75,000–99,999	2
		$100,000 and over	2

Age		Company size by number of employees	
Under 30 years	6%	1–49	15%
30–34	12	50–99	7
35–39	16	100–249	10
40–44	18	250–499	9
45–49	17	500–999	10
50–54	13	1,000–9,999	26
55–59	10	10,000–19,999	7
60–65	5	20,000 or more	16
Over 65	3		

Industry

Manufacturing consumer goods	16%	Construction	2%
Manufacturing industrial goods	25	Mining or extraction; oil	2
		Retail or wholesale trade	7
Engineering, research and development	6	Transportation, public utilities	5
Management consulting and business services	6	Advertising, media, publishing	4
Banking, investment, insurance	10	Consumer services	3
		Other	14

NOTE: Of the 1,700 total returns, 1,531 were received in time for machine tabulation, and the balance inspected and found to have no significant demographic or opinion differences.

sentence: "At Carthage, nothing which results in profit is regarded as disgraceful."[1] Modern critics have leveled this same charge at U.S. business, and we wondered if executives still adhere to this Carthaginian creed. To find out, we asked respondents to comment on a recent statement by a student of business:

❡ ". . . the businessman exists for only one purpose, to create and deliver value satisfactions at a profit to himself. . . . If what is offered can be sold at a profit (not even necessarily a long-term profit), then it is legitimate. . . . The cultural, spiritual, social, and moral consequences of his actions are none of his occupational concern."[2]

From top to bottom of the corporate ladder, a convincing 94% say: "We disagree!" As one personnel director sees it: "This man lives in a vacuum, ignoring the society that gave him his opportunity, his responsibility to make it better rather than worse as a result of his existence." In twentieth

[1] *The Histories of Polybius* (New York, G. P. Putnam's Sons, 1923), III, p. 393.
[2] Theodore Levitt, "Are Advertising and Marketing Corrupting Society? It's Not Your Worry, Levitt Tells Business," *Advertising Age*, October 6, 1958, p. 89.

century America, it seems, some things which result in profit are regarded as disgraceful—even by professional profit-makers.

In fact, our respondents indicate that they regard untempered profit maximization as immoral—agreeing with the thesis advanced in *HBR* recently by Professor Robert N. Anthony.[3] Five out of every six executives in our survey reacted affirmatively to this paraphrase of his view:

❏ "For corporation executives to act in the interest of shareholders alone, and not also in the interest of employees and consumers, is unethical."

Further, the answers of our executive panel reveal attitudes far different from those of the legendary rugged individualist. For example, only one executive in five agrees with the traditional dictum, "Let the buyer beware." But don't conclude that the "ethical" attitude revealed by these answers stems solely from a desire to do what is right *because* it is right. This conclusion would ignore the belief of our respondents that "sound ethics is good business in the long run." Only one respondent in a hundred disagrees with this statement!

Apparently management does believe that shady or ruthless operations might make money for a time, but that a corporation cannot mistreat the public for long and still survive. Once stung, the public has a long memory. For the long run, say executives, sound ethics not only is good public relations but also is conducive to making money.

Are executives as socially responsible as these findings suggest? We wonder, especially in light of the fact that 15% of our panel agree with the statement that "whatever is good business is good ethics." This response prompts us to exercise caution in praising our panel's posture of social awareness. To say that "whatever is good business is good ethics" makes economic efficiency the norm of ethical behavior; in other words, the economic consequences of a business transaction determine whether it is right or wrong. This is the same as saying that if a thing makes money, it is good —and sounds pretty much like that Carthaginian creed that nothing resulting in profit is disgraceful. The small size of this group doesn't alter the fact of its existence.

However, looking at the sum of our information about the social consciousness of the executives responding, we gain the over-all impression that most businessmen have a definite awareness of their social responsibilities. They view the corporation as being more than a money-making producer of goods and services. Their level of ethical ideals appears to be high. There is even substantial agreement among them that a few specific practices are absolutely wrong. Thus:

- 88% regard providing a "call girl" as always unethical.[4]
- 86% say they regard padding expense accounts as always unethical.

[3] "The Trouble with Profit Maximization," *HBR*, November–December 1960, p. 126.
[4] That some of these practices are especially controversial is attested to by the fact

Clearly, these executives see a business enterprise as a society of human beings—a society with obligations not only to the people who provide capital, but also to employees, customers, suppliers, government, and even, at times, competitors.

I'M ETHICAL, BUT IS *HE?*

Although our respondents profess a lofty level of ethical aspiration for themselves, they reveal a lower opinion of the practices of the "average" businessman. It is commonly observed that there is sometimes a discrepancy between what a man says he thinks or does, and what he *actually* thinks or does. Such a discrepancy is very likely to be present in answers to questions which require ethical choices, as in this study. Replies to such queries often correspond more closely to the image which the respondent would like others to have of him than to a realistic picture of himself. It is human to try to picture oneself in the most favorable way.

We wanted to take this tendency into account in our study, and so we asked some of our case situation questions in two different ways. One half of our panel was asked: "What would you do?" The other half: "What would the *average* executive do?" These questions and their replies are shown in Exhibit II. The differences in the answers of the two groups are striking.

Such differences certainly need closer scrutiny. Could they have been due to a flaw in our sampling? Apparently not. Our panel was split on a random basis. On checking, the two halves of our sample match demographically; in fact, the two halves of our sample are so very much alike in their opinions that the replies to the 25 questions which all executives were asked are, statistically, virtually identical. Hence, the differences in the replies of the two groups must clearly signal that our respondents did recognize the ethical content in the questions, and reacted accordingly.

Actual business practice, then, is probably closer to what respondents say "the average executive would do" in Exhibit II than it is to what they say "I would do." On this basis, the number of executives who apparently condone expense account padding and would use privy knowledge for personal financial gain is hardly reassuring.

---

that we received a number of letters from purchasing agents protesting our connecting purchasing agents with "call girls" in the questionnaire and requesting that we refrain from publishing our findings. The question was included for methodological reasons, with no evidence in the questionnaire itself that we believed this to be a prevalent practice by purchasing agents or that we were singling them out for attention. As was originally intended, the findings are reported above by Father Baumhart without explicit reference to purchasing agents; but, in the light of public editorializing about our asking the question, we feel that we must take some notice of it, if only to avoid the appearance of yielding to pressure tactics on the part of an important segment of American business.

—*The Editors*

EXHIBIT II. *I'm More Ethical Than He*

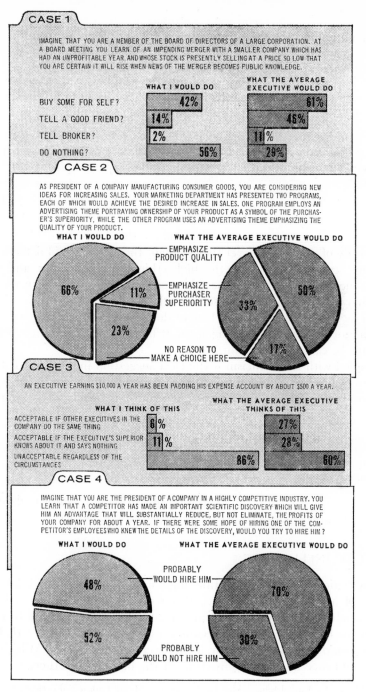

CASE 1

IMAGINE THAT YOU ARE A MEMBER OF THE BOARD OF DIRECTORS OF A LARGE CORPORATION. AT A BOARD MEETING YOU LEARN OF AN IMPENDING MERGER WITH A SMALLER COMPANY WHICH HAS HAD AN UNPROFITABLE YEAR, AND WHOSE STOCK IS PRESENTLY SELLING AT A PRICE SO LOW THAT YOU ARE CERTAIN IT WILL RISE WHEN NEWS OF THE MERGER BECOMES PUBLIC KNOWLEDGE.

	WHAT I WOULD DO	WHAT THE AVERAGE EXECUTIVE WOULD DO
BUY SOME FOR SELF?	42%	61%
TELL A GOOD FRIEND?	14%	46%
TELL BROKER?	2%	11%
DO NOTHING?	56%	29%

CASE 2

AS PRESIDENT OF A COMPANY MANUFACTURING CONSUMER GOODS, YOU ARE CONSIDERING NEW IDEAS FOR INCREASING SALES. YOUR MARKETING DEPARTMENT HAS PRESENTED TWO PROGRAMS, EACH OF WHICH WOULD ACHIEVE THE DESIRED INCREASE IN SALES. ONE PROGRAM EMPLOYS AN ADVERTISING THEME PORTRAYING OWNERSHIP OF YOUR PRODUCT AS A SYMBOL OF THE PURCHASER'S SUPERIORITY, WHILE THE OTHER PROGRAM USES AN ADVERTISING THEME EMPHASIZING THE QUALITY OF YOUR PRODUCT.

WHAT I WOULD DO — 66%, 11%, 23%

WHAT THE AVERAGE EXECUTIVE WOULD DO — 50%, 33%, 17%

EMPHASIZE PRODUCT QUALITY / EMPHASIZE PURCHASER SUPERIORITY / NO REASON TO MAKE A CHOICE HERE

CASE 3

AN EXECUTIVE EARNING $10,000 A YEAR HAS BEEN PADDING HIS EXPENSE ACCOUNT BY ABOUT $500 A YEAR.

	WHAT I THINK OF THIS	WHAT THE AVERAGE EXECUTIVE THINKS OF THIS
ACCEPTABLE IF OTHER EXECUTIVES IN THE COMPANY DO THE SAME THING	6%	27%
ACCEPTABLE IF THE EXECUTIVE'S SUPERIOR KNOWS ABOUT IT AND SAYS NOTHING	11%	28%
UNACCEPTABLE REGARDLESS OF THE CIRCUMSTANCES	86%	60%

CASE 4

IMAGINE THAT YOU ARE THE PRESIDENT OF A COMPANY IN A HIGHLY COMPETITIVE INDUSTRY. YOU LEARN THAT A COMPETITOR HAS MADE AN IMPORTANT SCIENTIFIC DISCOVERY WHICH WILL GIVE HIM AN ADVANTAGE THAT WILL SUBSTANTIALLY REDUCE, BUT NOT ELIMINATE, THE PROFITS OF YOUR COMPANY FOR ABOUT A YEAR. IF THERE WERE SOME HOPE OF HIRING ONE OF THE COMPETITOR'S EMPLOYEES WHO KNEW THE DETAILS OF THE DISCOVERY, WOULD YOU TRY TO HIRE HIM?

WHAT I WOULD DO — 48%, 52%

WHAT THE AVERAGE EXECUTIVE WOULD DO — 70%, 30%

PROBABLY WOULD HIRE HIM / PROBABLY WOULD NOT HIRE HIM

NOTE: The figures for Cases 1 and 3 in this table do not add to 100% since some respondents gave more than one answer to the case problem.

CYNICISM

The possibility that general business behavior is quite different from the personal ethical attitudes reported by our respondents is increased by their cynicism about typical executive behavior. This cynicism is illustrated by our panel's reaction to this observation by a friendly critic of business, who said:

  ❡ "The American business executive tends to ignore the great ethical laws as they apply immediately to his work. He is preoccupied chiefly with gain."[5]

Almost half of our panel agree. This same cynicism is underscored in replies to a later question about adoption of industry-wide ethical practices codes. Four of every seven executives believe that businessmen "would violate a code of ethics whenever they thought they could avoid detection."

If our respondents possess the high ethic described earlier, and at the same time are cynical about the ethics of other executives, then undoubtedly they do not identify themselves with the "average" executive. Would such a lack of identification be true of doctors, lawyers, or professors? And does it not suggest that management still has a distance to go before it can truly be called a profession?

Coupled with this cynicism is the clear suggestion in our data that some executives have a "double ethic." This double ethic consists of applying one standard to friends and another standard to strangers. Some examples:

  • Many executives who would tell a friend secret news of a forthcoming merger would not tell their broker.
  • Essay answers about practices of pricing, hiring, and rebidding on contracts reveal the existence of an ethic which has a special niche for friends.

Favoring friends can be an expression of gratitude, which is praiseworthy —unless the gratitude is displayed at the expense of justice.

ETHICAL INFLUENCES

This cynicism, this double ethic, undermines—as we shall see later—the ability of an executive to believe that written codes of ethics will really work. Such cynicism must certainly be considered when trying to predict a man's behavior in a touchy situation, especially *if he believes that most others would behave unethically if they were in his position.* Which is going to influence him more—his ethic, or the behavior of others?

[5] Rabbi Louis Finkelstein, "The Businessman's Moral Failure," *Fortune*, September 1958, p. 116.

We asked a random one half of our respondents to rank five factors according to the influence they exert on an executive to make *ethical* decisions. The five factors are: company policy, industry climate, behavior of superiors, behavior of equals, and personal code of behavior. We asked the other random one half of our respondents to rank five similar factors according to the influence they exert for *unethical* decisions. The rather remarkable results can be found in EXHIBIT III.

EXHIBIT III.   *Influences on Executive Behavior*

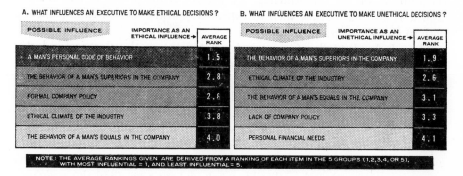

What can we learn from the rankings? Here is one line of interpretation:

▼ If an executive acts *ethically* (Part A), this is attributable to his own set of values and his ability to resist pressure and temptation, with some credit due to his superiors and company policy.

▲ If an executive acts *unethically* (Part B), it is largely because of his superiors and the climate of industry ethics.

A wag might say that this sounds like the legendary playwright who blamed all his failures on inept casts and stupid audiences, and accepted the praise for his successful shows as his rightful due. On the other hand, a friend of business might say that it is a hopeful sign that many executives indicate they follow their own consciences in making decisions.

NOT HIS KEEPER?

It is obvious that those around a man influence his behavior. But to what extent does this influence operate? Are executives "other-directed" rather than "inner-directed," as David Riesman suggested in *The Lonely Crowd?* Do executives look mainly to the company for their standards; are they the "organization men" described by William H. Whyte, Jr.? Or, more simply, what do our data say about the following item from the *Wall Street*

Journal, commenting on the recent antitrust decisions in the electrical industry: "The simplest, if not the complete, answer [to why high-ranking executives had knowingly done wrong] goes back to the organization man"?[6]

Close examination of our data reveals a tendency in every age group, company milieu, and management level for a man to accept the values of his superiors. This tendency, stemming from a respect for the talents of the superior as well as for his authoritative position, should be acknowledged by every administrator as a part of his power for good or evil. The larger the number of his subordinates, the greater is his power in this matter. And it is also natural for men to expect responsible action from someone with so much power.

Thus, Judge J. Cullen Ganey, in his statement on the electrical industry antitrust cases, despite the absence of probative evidence, felt compelled to say that "the real blame is to be laid at the doorstep of the corporate defendants and those who guide and direct their policy."[7] And the public has been reluctant to accept the idea that the electrical equipment companies' top managements are blameless, for the public holds these men in a position analogous to the parents of a 21-year-old who has done serious wrong. Though the parents be liked and respected, they must endure the common opinion that they should somehow have prevented the son's mistake. Our data would indicate that this belief is based on the facts of executive behavior: men do look to their superiors for guidance.

Have the troubles of the electrical industry introduced bias into the answers given to our questions? Undoubtedly. A pilot study preparatory to the present survey was completed before Judge Ganey's January decision, and we can compare results from the two studies.[8] There is a noteworthy difference in the ranks assigned in the question discussed above.

In the pilot study, formal company policy was ranked as the second most important factor influencing ethical behavior; superiors were ranked as the third. In the present study, these two factors have changed places, presumably because of the ineffectuality of policy directives used by the defendant companies. Also, from the time of the pilot study to the present one, there has been a slight increase in the percentage of men who say that unfair pricing or price collusion is the source of a personal role conflict.

Also of interest is our finding that financial need is ranked as *least* important of the five factors influencing unethical behavior. We doubt that money is unimportant to our respondents. A partial answer undoubtedly

[6] John Bridge, "Antitrust and Organization Man," *Wall Street Journal*, January 10, 1961, p. 10.

[7] *New York Times*, February 7, 1961, p. 26.

[8] In conducting the pilot study, the author was ably assisted by the Reverend Alexander D. Stewart, William J. Gies, Roger L. Hall, Robert J. Russell, and Robert C. Valtz.

lies in the fact that some 86% of the executives responding have five-figure incomes. At least the pressures of starvation are not at the door. What is important is to note that bad example, pressure from superiors or equals, and industry environment are seen by our respondents as more closely related to dishonest behavior than is the need for money.

We asked John J. Brennan, Jr., Vice President and Treasurer of Electronics Corporation of America, how he interpreted our findings. Here are the remarks he made in reply:

> "The pattern and level of corporate ethical standards are determined predominantly by the code of behavior formulated and promulgated by top management. The rest of the organization, almost perforce, will follow these ethical operating precepts and examples; but in the absence of such norms, the same organization will be motivated by individual, and possibly inconsistent, codes of behavior.
>
> "The crucial matter, therefore, is whether or not each individual comprising top management has a well-defined, high-standard personal code of behavior. If each has this clear, objective, consistent concept of ethics— however acquired—he has the yardsticks, the guiding principles, against which to measure the ethical import of his decisions.
>
> "The executive whose concepts of ethics are vague, and whose principles of ethics are ill-defined—and possibly even vacillating and inconsistent—is in constant danger of yielding to expediency and even pursuing unethical practices; or, worse, providing an undesirable environment wherein his subordinates can make such decisions based solely on their own personal ethical principles, with no frame of ethical reference from the top.
>
> "Of course, a well-defined personal code, however high in standards, does not of itself ensure ethical conduct; courage is always necessary in order to assert what one knows to be right."

A Nestor of the business world once said that the best advice he could give to a young man embarking on a business career was: find a good boss. Our data suggest a corollary: *if you want to act ethically, find an ethical boss.*

Hearty approval of this notion came from James J. Valtz, Export Manager of the Allied Kid Company, who said:

> "My advice to the young is: find an ethical boss. I was profoundly impressed as a young man by the example of our company's founder, Solomon Agoos. His behavior in the financial crisis of 1920, when the market for leather goods broke, was exemplary.
>
> "All of his employees appreciated the level at which he wanted the business conducted. For example, no one would think of yielding to pressure from even the largest foreign customer for false invoices, which would enable the customer to evade customs duties."

The importance of this is underlined by looking at the differences in rankings that one's fellow executives have in influencing a man's behavior.

These peers are said to have little influence for *ethical* behavior, but are relatively important in influencing *unethical* conduct. In other words, an executive's fellows are more likely to drag him down than to lift him up. Why?

OPPORTUNITY FOR GOOD

Clearly, then, the opportunity for any one administrator to influence ethical behavior effectively is immense, if only by refraining from encouraging unethical behavior. The importance of this influence increases if the belief of ethical businessmen—that they are not like the average executive —makes them reluctant to take responsibility for improving the behavior of others.

Such reluctance is characterized by statements like "if he wants to lie and cheat, that's his business." But such apparent indifference is meretricious. Lewis B. Ward, Professor of Business Research at the Harvard Business School, compares this reluctance to the "I won't squeal" attitude that students take about cheating by others—an attitude which has led to the downfall of academic "honor systems" in some colleges. Without the exercise of individual responsibility, how can group morality do other than deteriorate? If one's fellow executives encourage dishonesty—explicitly or by silence—how long will it be before men believe they "are suckers for being honest"?

Edmund Burke said, "All that is necessary for the forces of evil to win in the world is for enough good men to do nothing." This is a universal problem. It confronts us as bus passengers when we see a couple of toughs strong-arm another passenger. It confronts all of mankind when a strong nation tries to force its will on a small one. It confronts a business executive when he sees wrong being done in his industry. The responsibility is clear: *I am my brother's keeper.*

CHAPTER & VERSE

Every industry develops its own way of doing things, its generally accepted practices. Since industry climate is an important influence on unethical behavior, how does this influence manifest itself in specific practices that are generally accepted in the industry?

To find out, we asked:

❡ "In every industry, there are some generally accepted business practices. In your industry, are there any such practices which you regard as unethical?"

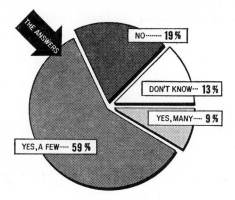

Taking away those who "don't know," we have the startling finding that four out of five executives giving an opinion affirm the presence in their industry of *practices which are generally accepted and are also unethical!*

Surely a candid admission! And, just as surely, a clarion call for corrective action! Generally accepted practices are the sun and rain of an industry climate. When a goodly number of these practices are unethical, how can the climate be otherwise? And, as our respondents have said, an unethical climate is an important influence on decision makers.

If our respondents, and their fellow leaders in American industry, are in earnest in professing lofty ethics, industry practices are a logical starting place for putting their ideals into operation.

More than half of our respondents were willing to tell us the "one practice in their industry they would most like to see eliminated." We have analyzed and grouped the replies, and Exhibit IV contains chapter and verse of the unethical practices that our executives want erased in their own industries.

Perhaps seeing some of their answers will give a sense of their sincerity and good will in reporting these practices. Thus:

- INSURANCE EXECUTIVE: "Seeking preferential treatment through lavish entertainment."
- MANAGER, CONSUMER SERVICES COMPANY: "Kickback to purchasing department employees."
- PERSONNEL DIRECTOR, WESTERN MANUFACTURING FIRM: "The idea that industry should have a few women employees on the payroll for entertainment of prospective customers."
- FINANCIAL COUNSEL: "Payoffs to government officials."
- SECRETARY, CONSTRUCTION FIRM: "Price rigging between supplier and contractor."
- PRESIDENT OF SMALL COMPANY: "Accounts of similar size, purchasing ability, and credit rating are charged prices varying as much as 25%

EXHIBIT IV.   *The Unethical Practices Executives Want to Eliminate*

(Per cent of total executives specifying this practice)

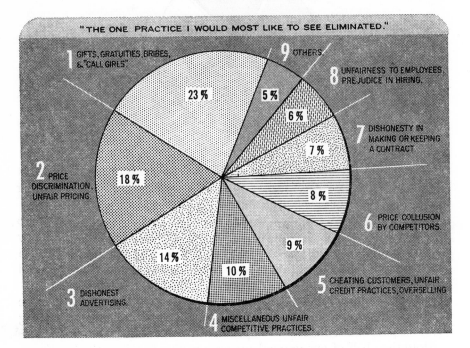

"THE ONE PRACTICE I WOULD MOST LIKE TO SEE ELIMINATED."

1 GIFTS, GRATUITIES, BRIBES, & "CALL GIRLS" — 23%

2 PRICE DISCRIMINATION, UNFAIR PRICING — 18%

3 DISHONEST ADVERTISING — 14%

4 MISCELLANEOUS UNFAIR COMPETITIVE PRACTICES — 10%

5 CHEATING CUSTOMERS, UNFAIR CREDIT PRACTICES, OVERSELLING — 9%

6 PRICE COLLUSION BY COMPETITORS — 8%

7 DISHONESTY IN MAKING OR KEEPING A CONTRACT — 7%

8 UNFAIRNESS TO EMPLOYEES, PREJUDICE IN HIRING — 6%

9 OTHERS — 5%

(by our competitors). So far, we have not deviated from our policy of charging the same price to everybody."

• PRESIDENT, CONSUMER SERVICES COMPANY: "Occasional exchanges of price information prior to contract bidding."

• VICE PRESIDENT, COMPANY MAKING INDUSTRIAL PRODUCTS: "The payment or large gifts to employees of other companies, customers, or competitors for 'favors' or information."

• SALES MANAGER, PHARMACEUTICALS: "Misleading ad claims."

• TOP EXECUTIVE, MASS COMMUNICATIONS FIRM: "Deliberate distortion of facts."

• RESEARCH AND DESIGN EXPERT: "Ambiguous advertising intended to mislead consumers."

• YOUNG FINANCIER: "Mutual fixing of rates of interest to be charged a borrower at two or more banks."

• VICE PRESIDENT, MANUFACTURING COMPANY: "Underbidding with the intention of substituting inferior workmanship or materials."

• PRESIDENT, CONSULTING FIRM: "Selling a 'tremendous bill of goods' of which the buyer knows too little."

• MANAGER, MIDWESTERN BANK: "Loaning customer more than he needs or more than is prudent for him to borrow."

The place for correction to begin is with such "accepted" industry practices. They need not be tolerated and certainly provide a convenient place to begin the difficult job of self-regulation. And these activities are a practical place to begin, for each executive knows about them, and is able to do something about them directly.

DRAWING THE LINE

Of course, to decide exactly where to draw the line on many of these issues is not easy. For example, the majority of executives regard gift giving as an "unwise practice." Similarly, the majority think that "a company should have a written policy about gifts." But only 27% of these same executives are willing to stipulate a $100 maximum value for gifts. Presumably, the other 73% are of the opinion that there are situations where gifts of greater value are appropriate and acceptable.

With respect to gift giving, as well as to owning stock in a company which does business with one's own company, most *HBR* readers (and rightly, in this reporter's opinion) refuse to say that the practice is *always* unethical. The broad principle is clear: an executive must be loyal to his company. But not every gift promotes disloyalty or results in the recipient's favoring one supplier over another. Nor does every executive who owns stock in a company which does business with his own face a conflict of interest.

These are complex problems; often they involve, simultaneously, several ethical principles. The details of each particular case determine the application of the various principles and, consequently, make the difference between an ethical and an unethical practice. At the same time, this inability or unwillingness to draw immediate and fast lines raises two serious questions: (1) How do executives react to having to make decisions with strong ethical content? (2) Do executives need better guidelines to help them make the correct decision in such situations?

ROLE CONFLICT

The first of these questions relates to what a social scientist calls "role conflict." A role conflict confronts an executive when he is required to fill simultaneously two roles (patterns of behavior) which present inconsistent or contradictory expectations. For example, the behavior expected of an executive as an "economic man" often differs from what is expected of him as an "ethical man." To investigate such situations, we posed the following question:

℃ "Probably there have been times when you have experienced a conflict between what was expected of you as an efficient, profit-conscious businessman and what was expected of you as an ethical person. Please describe the situation which has been for you the source of deepest concern because of such a conflict."

Nearly half of our respondents generously spent the time necessary to supply us with an essay answer. Surprisingly, one out of every four executives reporting says that he has *experienced no such conflict!*

It is difficult to believe that these men never experienced a situation in business where cheating, lying just a little, or using a minor shady practice could have brought them some advantage. All such situations contain role conflicts. In fact, even in the most reputable company, whose top management makes it relatively easy for executives to act ethically, it seems unlikely that all such temptations are absent. Perhaps some respondents believed they were being asked to reveal a conflict in which they had acted unethically, and replied "no such conflict" because, in the situation, they had acted ethically.

But it is hard to escape the conclusion that many executives who answered "no such conflict" have a deficient notion of ethics, or lack an awareness of the social implications of business decisions. One professor of business administration, commenting on these answers, said that they reminded him of some executives who identify as ethical problems only those situations involving large sums of money. He has now overcome his surprise at such statements as, "Our company has no ethical problems. The last one we had was five years ago when the treasurer absconded with $50,-000."

SPECIFIC SITUATIONS

What kinds of conflicts were mentioned by the remaining 75%? They cover a wide range and make fascinating reading. Firing and layoffs were reported by 102 executives as being the problems over which they had experienced the deepest concern. Thus:

- In the words of one training supervisor: "When it is necessary to reduce the work force, the decision of separating the older, less efficient employees, or the younger employees with greater technical skills and vigor, is a real tough problem."
- An eastern plant manager sees a similar problem in a broader context: "No provision in our society for providing useful work for well-meaning, moral, hard-working individuals who just can't make the grade in the occupation they have chosen, and must be dismissed for efficiency reasons. This is a most serious problem for me, and I have fired many persons for this reason."
- The president of a small company has the same problem, but a different solution: "Discharge of ethical but incompetent employees. I can't do it."
- A well-paid vice president is anxious about "employees with long, good records, and whose work becomes inefficient. How long can I carry them on the payroll? What is the measure of my loyalty to a man who helped build my business?"
- The product supervisor in a large manufacturing company is especially aware of one facet of the layoff problem: "Treatment of clerical-

level, salaried employees during periods of economic recession. This group seems always to take the brunt of any work-force reductions."

• Finally, a southern personnel director thoughtfully observes: "It has always concerned me that the industry's regular [periodic] reductions in work force should always bear so heavily on the 'little people'—particularly when adversity has not always been equally shared by stockholders and top management."

That final quotation deserves some reflection on our part. No doubt most discharges and layoffs are ethical, and probably the conflicts cited by some of the 102 are waged between their head and their heart, rather than between economic efficiency and ethical behavior. But justice can, at times, demand that the brunt of a recession be borne by stockholders and executives, rather than by the little people. Perhaps we should recall here that 73% of our respondents agree that "for corporation executives to act in the interest of shareholders alone, and not also in the interest of employees and consumers, is unethical." But it will take a secure and courageous administrator, indeed, to stand up and suggest reducing prices and dividends instead of reducing the number of wage earners.

COMMUNICATIONS

One in ten of our respondents has experienced deepest concern over a problem in honest communication—of telling the whole truth. Some examples:

• A vice president, industrial manufacturing, is disturbed by "requests by customers for false billings to avoid taxes or help in their depreciation schedules."

• A controller reports he had to decide how to handle "a good friend caught cheating on his expenses."

• A securities salesman finds that "my customers often approach me with an idea that would be profitable to me, but which I feel is unwise for them. At times, my best advice will cost me a sale and perhaps a customer."

COLLUSION & GIFTS

Opportunities for collusion and other sharp practices in pricing are the next most frequently mentioned conflict—by 79 executives. For instance:

• The president of a small southern company mentions "the use of extreme pressure by competition to force me to collude with them to fix prices."

• A sales manager is annoyed by "price differentials extended to 'price buyers,' but not to loyal customers—a rotten practice."

• And the treasurer of a small retailing firm puts a perennial problem in the form of a question: "What is a *fair* profit at retail level for installment purchases?"

Gifts, entertainment, and kickbacks compose the fourth most prevalent conflict category for 56 men. Specifically:

• A top executive in one of our giant corporations deplores "attending industry 'junkets' in the name of promoting the welfare of the industry, which are actually only 'binges' at the expense of neglected stockholders for whom we are trustees and managers."

• A western sales manager is bothered by "the excessive entertainment which some buyers seem to feel it is our duty to supply. I feel a buyer who can be bought for entertainment is not a moral person fundamentally, and I don't trust him."

• The head of a consulting firm notes a conflict with a happy ending: "As manager of a business, I was asked for a kickback by the buyer of an important customer; I refused the request and lost the customer. For months after, I was not sure I was right from a business angle. Now, years later, I know I was right, for the concern came to me for management counsel."

PRESSURE

A number of executives, 40 to be exact, though they cite different kinds of conflicts, stress an important theme in their essays: pressure from superiors played a part in the situation in which they had experienced the deepest concern. For example:

• A controller resents "repeatedly having to act contrary to my sense of justice in order to 'please.' In upper middle management, apparently, one's own ethical will must be subordinated to that of interests 'at the top'—not only to advance, but even to be retained."

• A young supervisor is concerned with "pressure to get too much work out of too few people in too short a time."

• A division manager is unhappy over "strong pressures for superior results which lead to compromise of personal integrity in operations."

• The sales manager of a very large corporation phrases his views most bluntly: "The constant everyday pressure from top management to obtain profitable business; unwritten, but well understood, is the phrase 'at any cost.' To do this requires every conceivable dirty trick."

But many men voice more than these generalized anxieties, and cite specific practices toward which they are being pushed—and which they do not like. Thus:

• A high-salaried assistant manager is worried because "my management has, in effect, required that I go along with certain antitrust violations involving restraint of trade."

• Another executive says: "As controller, I prepared a P & L statement which showed a loss. An executive vice president tried to force me to falsify the statement to show a profit in order to present it to a bank for a line of credit. I refused, and was fired on the spot."

• A young engineer testifies that he was "asked to present 'edited' results of a reliability study; I refused, and nearly got fired. I refused to defraud the customer, so they had others do it."

• Still another engineer deplores "cheating in the makeup of reports caused by demanding improvement in index numbers."

Of course, the task of top management is to get results. And to do so every executive must apply some sort of pressure or sanction to subordinates in order to obtain excellent work. A good boss ought to have the ability to "stretch" his men. But it is important that he not "overstretch" them, physically, psychologically, or ethically.

How can a top executive guard against pushing his men too far? By knowing them. By taking the time to understand them. By reflecting on the kinds and amount of pressure he is applying to them. To gain such knowledge requires excellent two-way communication between the boss and his subordinates. Such clear communication is especially important in large, decentralized corporations.

Without careful observation of what is going on, a superior can unwittingly hand down impossible demands—even in a memo that, for example, insists on a certain share of market, or sets too large a sales or profit goal for the period. Perhaps the possible injustice of such demands can be seen by comparing this situation to the father who insists that his son, whose I.Q. is 100, get a straight-A report card.

Impossible demands, say our respondents, especially if accompanied by an implied "produce or get out" attitude, can quickly result in unethical behavior. One certainly wonders if the lonely subordinate, faced with demands like these, does not occasionally dream about a union for middle management, complete with seniority and grievance procedures.

A common retort—and defense—of top management on this issue maintains that "it is only fair that pressure be kept on subordinates. After all, stockholders and competitors keep the pressure on top management all the time."

Yet few *top* executives in our survey specifically mention such pressures. Perhaps "pressure" is part of a self-induced image of how a president or vice president *should* act. This reporter doubts that widely disparate and anonymous stockholders exercise specific pressure on top management comparable to the pressure that top executives bring to bear on their subordinates. As for the pressure of competition, few industries operate under conditions of absolutely free competition. Perhaps, the very fact that executives blame competitive pressure for widespread unethical behavior is a good sign that cutthroat competition exists in an industry and ought to be modified.

Though most of the 40 men say that pressure from superiors was for *unethical* behavior, several volunteered the information that their particular bosses had helped them to act ethically:

- According to one vice president, "I am fortunate in that my top management has never countenanced any deviation from ethical procedures. In our company we are expected to base decisions on what is right, without regard for possible loss."
- This influence is echoed by a California sales manager: "The company I work for, the largest of its kind, was founded by a Christian gentle-

man. Policies are ethical in the strictest sense. For twenty years I have needed only to follow policy."

CODE OF ETHICS?

This brings us to the second question posed earlier in the article: Do executives need better guidelines to help them make the best decision in situations with an ethical dimension? Will they welcome such guidelines? To put it another way, granting the presence of many unethical practices in American industry (and we have presented ample evidence that executives believe this is so), what can be done to improve matters? Here is one possible step: *draw up a code of ethics.*

It is true that a number of industries already have ethical codes. In fact, in 1958 the National Association of Manufacturers issued a Code of Moral and Ethical Standards. The NAM code was designed in part to answer criticism of big business for not having a norm for measuring corporate morality that was comparable to the 1957 AFL-CIO Ethical Practices Code. But the NAM code, like so many industry codes, has been ineffectual. Perhaps this is because such codes have no enforcement provisions and are filled with generalities and platitudes that signify little but good will.

To find out what executives think of ethical codes, and what kind of a code they might want, we posed a number of questions. The first was:

 ❡ "How do you feel about an effort to develop a code of ethical practices for your industry? How would you react if a group of experienced executives in your industry tried to draw up such a code?"

The answer is a resounding *"good idea!"* Only one man in ten opposes such an effort. Indeed, the pattern is overwhelming:

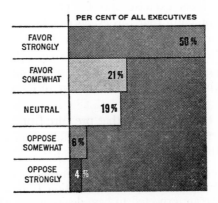

	PER CENT OF ALL EXECUTIVES
FAVOR STRONGLY	50%
FAVOR SOMEWHAT	21%
NEUTRAL	19%
OPPOSE SOMEWHAT	6%
OPPOSE STRONGLY	4%

To get a deeper understanding of their reply, let us look at some of the spontaneous comments written in the questionnaire margins:

- A management consultant feels he "would regret the necessity of a code, but would favor one strongly."
- A Kansas engineer favors the code, which he sees as "written to control the minority."
- A public utilities executive not only favors a code, but thinks it would be "easy to enforce if management wants it enforced."
- A California Rotarian adds that "after 26 years in business, I think a code would be a triumph of optimism over experience."
- A labor relations director adopts a similar tone: "I have seen the AFL-CIO code operate—codes don't solve any problems."
- Opposition to codes comes from a Pennsylvania marketer who "thinks the stimulus to act ethically should come from outside business, social, or trade organizations."

WHAT A CODE CAN DO

We wanted to probe the reasons why executives favor or oppose an ethical code, and thereby find out not only how a code could operate, but also whether it could be made to work at all. To find out, we posed the following hypothetical situation:

❧ "Assume, for the moment, that an ethical practices code has been drawn up for your industry by experienced executives. What do you think such a code and its reasonable enforcement would accomplish?" We asked for comments on seven ideas. These themes with the opinions of executives are summarized in Exhibit v. Looking for a pattern, we see the following:

- 71% believe a code would raise the ethical level of their industry.
- 87% believe that a code would not be easy to enforce.
- Executives split pretty evenly over the problem of whether a code would reduce sharp practices in tough, competitive situations.
- 88% would welcome a code as a useful aid when they wanted to refuse an unethical request impersonally.
- 81% disagree with the idea that codes protect inefficient firms.
- 81% agree that a code would help executives by defining clearly the limits of acceptable conduct.
- Finally, executives split again (this time 57% agree) over the thorny problem of whether people would violate the code whenever they thought they could avoid detection.

Summing up, their replies indicate a moderate optimism about the potentialities of a code, coupled with a strong belief that enforcement and adherence would be difficult jobs.

The near-unanimous agreement on the idea that a code would help executives in making decisions deserves additional discussion. Why would a code help? After all, a code is a form of restriction on business behavior. Perhaps the following illustration best portrays why men are sometimes willing to impose restrictions on themselves:

Suppose that you and your family live on a high hill, with a lovely, large back yard. The yard's only drawback is that it ends in a long, sheer drop on three sides. You have two obvious choices: (1) You can caution

EXHIBIT V. *What Consequences Do Executives Expect from Industry Codes?*

PER CENT OF ALL EXECUTIVES GIVING THIS RATING TO EACH CONSEQUENCE

POSSIBLE CONSEQUENCES OF A CODE	AGREE	PARTIALLY AGREE	NEUTRAL	PARTIALLY DISAGREE	DISAGREE
THE CODE WOULD RAISE THE ETHICAL LEVEL OF THE INDUSTRY.	36 %	35 %	12 %	7 %	10 %
THE CODE WOULD BE EASY TO ENFORCE.	2	7	4	23	64
IN SITUATIONS OF SEVERE COMPETITION, THE CODE WOULD REDUCE SHARP PRACTICES.	13	38	9	19	21
EXECUTIVES WOULD WELCOME THE CODE AS A USEFUL AID WHEN THEY WANTED TO REFUSE AN UNETHICAL REQUEST IMPERSONALLY.	59	28	5	4	4
THE CODE WOULD PROTECT INEFFICIENT FIRMS AND RETARD THE DYNAMIC GROWTH OF INDUSTRY.	3	8	8	11	70
THE CODE WOULD HELP EXECUTIVES BY DEFINING CLEARLY THE LIMITS OF ACCEPTABLE CONDUCT.	48	33	7	5	7
PEOPLE WOULD VIOLATE THE CODE WHENEVER THEY THOUGHT THEY COULD AVOID DETECTION.	13	44	8	20	15

all who enter the yard about the danger of falling over the edge; consequently, no one will go closer than six or eight feet, and you yourself will often be anxious about how close you are to it. Or (2) you can build a fence six inches from the edge, and eliminate anxiety at the same time that you gain more space for playing and gardening.

There are many businessmen who are willing to "fence themselves in" with an ethical practices code, provided that experienced executives in their industry have a hand in formulating it, because the fence will increase the area in which they can securely and ethically do business.

A code of ethics can help in other ways, say executives. For example, take situations in which it is difficult to refuse an unethical request—such as when it comes from a friend or associate. A direct refusal gives a holier-than-thou impression—and seriously jeopardizes what otherwise may be very pleasant interpersonal relationships. Faced with such a request, one looks for a way to refuse without offending. A specific code of ethics, say seven out of eight of our respondents, would provide an impersonal and welcome way of refusing such a request.

What about opposition to industry codes? Some of it is undoubtedly rooted in the belief that "you can't legislate virtue." In the words of a young manager of personnel relations for a large corporation, "I feel that this cannot be legislated, and that an attempt to draw up a code would be a sham."

Such an objection appears to confuse what is internal to a person with what is external. Presumably, most men acknowledge that a written rule can't change a man's heart. However, our respondents favor a written code not because it can change men internally, but because it can make it easier for good men to conform their external behavior to their internal ideals. At the same time, a code can discourage wrongdoers by making it easier to detect and punish unethical behavior.

WILL A CODE WORK?

All these things are what a code can do. But will a code actually work? As noted, our executives have mixed feelings on this subject. They agree that a code would be difficult to enforce; they don't know whether it would help reduce sharp practices in really competitive situations. Also, they are cynical (as mentioned earlier) about the behavior of other businessmen, with four out of every seven agreeing that "people would violate the code whenever they thought they could avoid detection."

Realistically, our panel sees enforcement as a major problem, and backs this up with marginal comments of "I would not think an enforcement agency is feasible," or "A code is impossible to police."

In order to discover the most acceptable form of enforcement, we posed the following question:

❡ "Assume that an ethical practices code has been drawn up for your industry. Which of the following groups would you choose to enforce the code?"

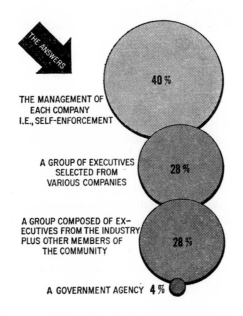

THE ANSWERS

THE MANAGEMENT OF EACH COMPANY I.E., SELF-ENFORCEMENT — 40%

A GROUP OF EXECUTIVES SELECTED FROM VARIOUS COMPANIES — 28%

A GROUP COMPOSED OF EX-ECUTIVES FROM THE INDUSTRY PLUS OTHER MEMBERS OF THE COMMUNITY — 28%

A GOVERNMENT AGENCY 4%

SELF-ENFORCEMENT?

How realistic is this seeming preference for self-enforcement? Note that 60% of the executives prefer some form of outside regulation. One element is clear: executives want to keep for themselves the greater share of responsibility for enforcement. Only 4% would use a government agency.

Much of our other evidence questions the current effectiveness of self-enforcement. We have seen, for example, that internal company pressures (by superiors and fellow executives) are important influences on ethical behavior. We have also seen that executives believe that such internal enforcement has failed to reach its potential for creating ethical behavior and has been effective in those firms where top management has taken a strongly ethical stand. It is not, then, that self-enforcement cannot work, but rather that it has not been made to work. Perhaps this is the very reason why so many (60%, to be exact) would prefer a form of business regulation which is largely external to the company.

But even such external forms of enforcement have many difficulties. To illustrate, let us consider the "Standards of Practice" of the American Association of Advertising Agencies. It is clear from our data that a good number of *HBR* executives identify dishonest advertising as the one unethical practice they would most like to see eliminated from their industry. Yet no one can deny that the broad standards put forth by the AAAA are carefully worded. From such evidence, one can hardly escape the assumption that the Committee for Improvement of Advertising Content is not enforcing the Standards of Practice as rigorously as executives (and probably the public) would like.

Perhaps one flaw in the AAAA code is a reluctance to believe that an ounce of prevention is worth a pound of cure. The fact that all regulation takes place *after* an advertisement has done its work, in effect, means that one can get around the code. If, as the executives responding in this survey indicate, most executives would violate a code when given the chance, then it is logical to conclude that specific norms, spelling out in advance what the committee regards as wrong, would be more effective as preventive regulation than such general statements as "misleading exaggerations" and "misleading price claims."

After seven years of operation and some 300 decisions, the AAAA committee ought to be able to formulate more detailed directives than the two quoted above, directives which will make it more difficult for corner-cutters to plead that they didn't intend to mislead consumers. The AAAA problem is presented here not because it is unique or egregious, but simply because it aptly exemplifies the flaw in many industries and in many existing codes: the absence of specific, detailed statements of what industry members regard as unethical, and the teeth to put these statements into action.

Which industry would care to lead the way?

More specifically, *how* can an industry begin to lead the way? How can the detailed norms needed for an effective code be formulated? Here the achievement of the American Psychological Association in formulating its *Ethical Standards of Psychologists* is a good model. The APA used an empirical approach, gathering data about the ethical problems confronting psychologists. Members of the APA were asked to "describe a situation they knew of firsthand, in which a psychologist made a decision having ethical implications, and to indicate what the correspondents perceived as being the ethical issues involved."[9]

These reports were examined to discover patterns in the problems and thereby to provide a plan for organizing the information supplied. After the reports were categorized into six ethical areas, they were analyzed to obtain a number of specific problems in each area. Following this analysis, six committees were appointed, each concentrating on the specific ethical problems of a single area. After much discussion and thoughtful study, these committees hammered out the *Ethical Standards of Psychologists*. With adaptation to its own circumstances, any industry could produce its own code in the same way. The issue is not whether it can be done, but whether top management wants it done.

TOP MANAGEMENT

With this in mind, there remains one fundamental question: Should the difficulties of enforcement or the likelihood of limited success deter efforts to construct industry codes? This answer can only come from top management which, as Adolf A. Berle, Jr., wrote, "has substantially absolute power. Thus the only real control which guides or limits their economic and social action is the real, though undefined and tacit, philosophy of the men who compose them."[10] That this power operates, for good or evil, is attested to by our executives when they indicate that "if you want to be ethical, find an ethical boss." The time for each member of top management to make more explicit his philosophy, his ethic, is right now.

Henry Ford II, speaking in Minneapolis on April 20, 1961, concurred with this view:

> "It is up to us in our various companies and industries to see to the establishment of our own formal principles of ethical practice, plus the effective means of self-policing those principles."[11]

[9] *Ethical Standards of Psychologists* (Washington, D.C., The American Psychological Association, 1953), p. vi.

[10] *20th Century Capitalist Revolution* (New York, Harcourt, Brace and Company, 1954), p. 180.

[11] *New York Times*, April 21, 1961, p. 16.

Among the administrators most optimistic about a code of ethics for businessmen is John B. Shallenberger, President of the Connellsville Corporation. Mr. Shallenberger, in his capacity as Research Officer of the Comite International de l'Organisation Scientifique, recently had the unique opportunity of interviewing some 7,500 managers in 109 different countries. Here is his opinion, based on his globe-circling research:

"In about 40% of these confidential interviews, I detected a desire to talk about ethics in business. This was not the subject of the interview, and any mention of the subject was spontaneous on the part of the manager being interviewed. Thus, it became evident that there lies deep-seated in the minds of managers a desire to do good, a kind of noble aspiration which seeks expression. Many managers indicated a latent desire to do greater good than they felt they could in the role they were expected to play as managers.

"In my opinion, based on wide and intimate exposure to top managers, they are potentially a great force for good. All that is needed is a code, a delineation of parameters of performance, or a set of guidelines by which to steer one's course of management behavior, plus a general recognition by boards of directors and stockholders that managers desire to perform their duties on a high ethical plane and for the benefit of mankind.

"Managers are shy to speak openly of ethics, just as most people blush to mention God in daily conversation. But when the way is opened for free and socially accepted discussion of ethics and morals, managers will be the first to reveal deep-seated desires that, in their fulfilling, would bring powerful forces to bear on the improvement of the lot of multitudes of people.

"Two effective steps would go a long way toward unleashing this latent force, and I submit them as a proposal for action:

1. Codification of ethical standards of manager performance.
2. Establishment of a 'Hippocratic Oath' to be administered by a suitable body of authority to all persons admitted to top-management levels."

ROLE OF RELIGION

But what about the more traditional institutions for improving human behavior? We wondered what *HBR* subscribers thought of the efforts of organized religion to assist the businessman. Our interest stemmed from the discussion initiated last year by J. Howard Pew, a director of the Sun Oil Company. Mr. Pew, speaking as President of the United Presbyterian Foundation, charged the Church with meddling in secular affairs.[12] To look into this issue, we asked:

❡ "In your opinion, how much guidance did your church and clergymen provide for the ethical problems you and your business acquaintances faced in the last five years?"

---

[12] In a speech in Chicago on March 19, 1960, before the National Council of Presbyterian Men.

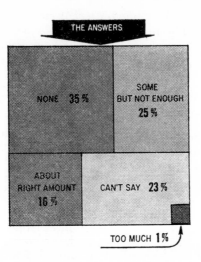

Why did 23% refuse an opinion? Some of the 23% were men in our sample who have no religious affiliation, and therefore felt that the question was not addressed to them. Perhaps others prefer not to criticize the clergy. But probably the principal reason is the lack of communication between businessmen and the clergy. The arresting conclusion is, in any case, that for those who gave an opinion, 4 out of every 5 were dissatisfied with what organized religion had or had not done.

It would be erroneous to conclude that all those who are dissatisfied would be willing and ready to accept help from the clergy for business problems. For nearly 20% of this group indicate both that their church has been of no help to them in the past five years and that they want no help. And for many different reasons:

> • A young New York stockbroker: "The average clergyman has such a scant understanding of the U.S. economy that his intervention in this area would be a mistake."
> • A Louisiana insurance broker: "I don't believe the clergy should be permitted to preach to businessmen."
> • The president of a small financial institution: "If the clergy would stick to their business of preaching the gospel, they and business would be better off. The clergy admits the weakness of their faith when they turn from the gospel and try to get into other fields of influence and preach a doctrine of social gospel."
> • Or, as another president writes: "The writer's religious convictions are not in need of assistance." But, curiously enough, he states elsewhere in his reply that "it is more difficult to know what is right than to do it."

Though the view that the Church should make no effort to help businessmen as businessmen is clearly present in our survey, and its presence will disturb many clergy, it is a minority view. In fact, a minority of comparable size thinks that the Church's recent efforts to assist business ethics have been adequate. The top executive of one of the country's giant corporations blames businessmen for not hearing the Church's message: "Too few men understand or listen."

Most executives who criticize organized religion's current lack of guidance in business ethics hope for religious help in the future. And they give some clear indications of their preference for Church practice:

    ❦ Executives strongly favor traditional forms of guidance (sermons, writing) over recent innovations (such as the presence of a clergyman at the office or factory).
    ❦ Executives prefer the explanation of ethical principles over (a) the application of these principles to typical business situations, and (b) the motivation to do good rather than evil.
    ❦ Executives like the idea of a clergyman meeting regularly with small groups of businessmen to discuss management problems.

The preference for "explanation of ethical principles" over "applications" deserves study. Here are some of the comments:

    — A personnel director: "I don't think the average clergyman knows enough about business to be specific."
    — A president: "The question of competency enters here. The personality and ability of the preacher or padre makes all the difference."

Such reservations about the level of business knowledge possessed by the average clergyman are common in our replies. Presumably, they were born during a sermon when an ill-informed cleric ventured into economic waters well over his head.

On the other hand, our data intimate that most businessmen welcome the assistance of clergymen who are well educated in business, economics, and the social sciences. Indeed, many of our respondents favor the idea of regular meetings, attended by a small group of businessmen and a clergyman, for the purpose of discussing problems in business ethics. The idea is receiving a thorough trial from a number of Catholic Employers and Managers Study Groups.

A Louisiana vice president likes the idea because it will help the clergy to understand the complexity and pressures of businessmen's problems, for "too many clergymen are 'ivory tower' fellows."

Similarly, as Vincent P. Stanton, Investment Analyst for Loomis-Sayles & Company, points out: "This is an encouraging sign, for it indicates an active, rather than merely a passive, interest in improving business ethics."

MEDIAL NORMS

Businessmen, trying to cope with the prickly problem of writing specific industry codes, could use the assistance of competent moral philosophers and theologians. One form which this aid might profitably take is the construction of *medial norms* to provide guidance for the solution of everyday problems in business.

Such medial norms are needed. In America, there is widespread acceptance among businessmen of the handful of general ethical principles which are the foundation of Judaeo-Christian civilization. But between these general principles (such as "Thou shalt not steal") and the concrete problems of the businessman (such as whether or not price-fixing is stealing from customers) a wide gap appears.

If scholars cooperate with businessmen, this gap can be filled with medial norms, refinements, and applications of the general principles. These norms would shed light not only on daily business decisions but also on the content of industry codes. Naturally, because specific business problems change, ample provision would have to be made for altering the medial norms when advisable.

PLANT PASTORS

Several companies, including LeTourneau Incorporated, Texas Aluminum, Reynolds Tobacco Co., and D-X Sunray Oil, have employed "plant pastors," i.e., clergymen available at the plant or office for individual consultation by employees. We asked our executives for their opinion on using chaplains in industry. Their response does not encourage this practice. Most men prefer such consultation to take place at the synagogue, parsonage, or rectory.

Why the lack of interest in plant pastors? Mr. Stanton suggested:

"Perhaps administrators are wary of the many practical problems which appear to be involved. For example, it may be difficult to find a clergyman with the understanding of complex business relationships necessary to apply ethical principles to specific problems successfully. Will the clergyman be forced into the role of a judge rather than a guide? Will he seem to represent either a management or labor viewpoint, and hence lose some of his effectiveness? What denomination should he come from, and will this be acceptable to all? Will he be heard by those who should hear him, if contact is purely voluntary, as it should be?"

WHAT OF THE FUTURE?

Anyone who is pessimistic about U.S. business ethics would qualify his views after reading a sample of our completed questionnaires. They contain many heartening examples of courageous decisions made for ethical reasons. Thus:

• A sales manager refused to give a "payoff required to secure distribution of a consumer product in a grocery chain. Have been tempted but have not gone along with this 'under-the-counter' dealing. Our sales are hurt as a result."

• The president of a company engaged in mass communication faced the choice of "giving up a valued client of long standing and great profitability, and having to resort to laying off hard-to-replace employees; or yielding to the client's demand to do something I didn't believe in. I chose the former course."

With men like these holding some of the reins of industry, surely there is reason for hope. Of course, the continuing good influence of organizations like Better Business Bureaus and the Federal Trade Commission affords additional reason for optimism.

Someone has defined a leader as a man who raises his own standards above the ordinary and is willing to let other people judge him by these raised standards. Here are several signs that ethical leadership is present in business today:

(1) The forthright speech delivered recently by Henry Ford II not only reproved the actions of some of his acquaintances, but also promised that the Ford Motor Company would maintain the highest standards of business integrity.

(2) The Gillette Company, in its 1960 Annual Report, introduced a section specifying company practice with respect to gift taking and conflicts of interest. Perhaps shareholders in other firms would like to see this idea adopted, and even extended.

(3) The Association of National Advertisers and the American Association of Advertising Agencies recently invited all advertising media to criticize advertisements considered offensive, and have developed a procedure for evaluating the criticisms.

This survey provides useful empirical knowledge about the problems and views of executives concerning business ethics. Some of the findings are not complimentary to businessmen. They are reported, not to chastise, but to reveal specific areas for improvement.

Only the candor of our respondents made this report possible. Presumably, they chose to reveal these business shortcomings in the hope of remedying them. Our recommendations for action are based on the confidential opinions generously supplied by *HBR* readers. It is their hope, and ours, that industry will act on these candid sentiments by rectifying behavior from within, rather than delaying until regulation comes from without.

It is noteworthy that, in our responses, there were no major differences of opinion among the various levels of management. The same is true of analysis by industry, business activity, and income levels. (We are, however, still examining our data for differences in opinion by age, education, and religious affiliation and hope to have some interesting information for you at a future date.)

Further, the desire for *change* permeates executive belief from the top to the bottom of the corporate structure. But this change will not come about, say executives, merely by hoping for it, instituting half-measures, or issuing platitudes. The time has come for courageous top-management leadership to implement executives' desires to raise the level of business ethics.

ETHICS AND THE RULE OF LAW

WAYNE A. R. LEYS

———————•▸◄•◄———————

Abstract: What is a businessman's moral duty when there is real uncertainty in the law? Uncertainty in the meaning of legal regulations must
be distinguished from uncertainty that the law will be enforced and uncertainty that the law will accomplish its intended purpose. Assuming a
moral obligation to obey laws that are reasonably clear in their applications, a businessman has no obligations to guess that an uncertain law requires the greatest conceivable sacrifice. There is no moral culpability in
trying to secure interpretations that are convenient and profitable. A manager does, however, have an obligation not to expose his enterprise to un-
bearable risks and not to sabotage the rule-making process, though there
may be hopeless disagreement as to the identity of those who are doing
these things. The common objections to bare compliance with law do not
identify a fault in the attitude toward law but rather a defect in extralegal
matters. As long as systems of social control are imperfect, there is good
reason for not lumping legal and extralegal duties together under the word
"responsibility."

What is a businessman's moral duty when there is real uncertainty
whether a contemplated action will be held to be legal or illegal? This is,
I believe, one of the most puzzling problems of business ethics. The problem is encountered in those gray areas that are subject to regulation but

*Wayne A. R. Leys, Ph.D., Wilmette, Illinois, has been Professor of Philos-
ophy and Dean of the Graduate Division, Roosevelt University, since 1955.
From 1945 to 1955 he was the first Dean of Faculties and Vice-President of
Roosevelt University. During the Second World War, he served as a public
panel member of the National War Labor Board. He has directed research
projects concerned with occupational ethics and the public interest. He is author of Ethics for Policy Decisions (1952), coauthor of Philosophy and the
Public Interest (1959), and a contributor to Nomos and other symposia. He is
currently serving as chairman of the American Philosophical Association's Committee to Advance Original Work.*

The Annals of the Americal Academy of Political and Social Science, 343:32–38;
September, 1962. Reprinted by permission of the publisher and the author.

where regulation does not follow clearly defined rules. The gray areas include business practices that may or may not be attacked as violating the antitrust laws depending upon who is in office in the coming years. The gray areas include tax declarations which may or may not be accepted depending upon the reasoning of a revenue agent or a judge as yet undesignated. They include matters subject to health and building codes of which interpretation will vary according to whether a spectacular fire or accident gives vote-catching value to the codes. And, then, there are employment practices during those times when regulatory bodies are just beginning to establish their standards or when a political upset at the polls foreshadows a change in standards.

Do businessmen deserve moral censure if they are convicted of violating law that was difficult to predict? Should the penalty of moral disgrace be added to the woes of Mr. Unlucky Guesser while Mr. Lucky Guesser enjoys a good reputation as well as his profits? Is bare compliance with the law sufficient? Is a manager morally obligated to make sacrifices that are beyond what he believes to be the minimum legal requirements? Does business ethics require fulfillment of the alleged purposes of a law even when the law, as officially interpreted, seems to be satisfied with something less than that?

The issue here is our duty when we act in the presence of uncertain law. The uncertainty, it must be emphasized, is in the meaning and application of law. Such uncertainty may be created by the loose wording of a statute or by the granting of broad discretionary powers to an administrative agency or by something else.[1]

THREE KINDS OF UNCERTAINTY

Uncertainty in the very meaning of the law needs to be distinguished from some other kinds of uncertainty. I am not here concerned with (1) uncertainty as to whether lawbreakers will be detected and punished; nor (2) the uncertainty that the law will accomplish its intended purpose. I am not trying to give aid and comfort to those who take chances by violating laws whose applications are reasonably predictable.

I am not talking about laws that are clear in meaning but are inefficiently enforced. If I take a cleverly disguised pleasure trip, I do wrong in claiming an income-tax deduction for "business trip expense," even though no revenue agent is likely to catch the violation. By contrast, what I am discussing

[1] The vague reference to "something else" merely recognizes that there are several kinds of uncertainty in law. For examples of kinds that will not be stressed in this paper see H. L. A. Hart and A. M. Honoré, *Causation in the Law* (Oxford: Oxford University Press, 1959). These authors are concerned with laws whose administration requires judgments of causation, of the foreseeability of cause-and-effect relationships, etc.

in this article is the expenditure which the revenue regulations do not clearly make deductible or nondeductible.[2]

I am not referring to laws that are uncertain in the sense that they may not accomplish their stated purpose in exceptional cases. If I find myself in unusual circumstances where a group of employees can be kept off relief only by my paying them less than the minimum wage, the payment of substandard wages is nevertheless a violation of law. To argue that such a violation is morally defensible is a mistake.[3] It is to raise an issue that is quite different from the case where no one can be very sure whether the Wages and Hours Division of the Department of Labor has jurisdiction.

BUSINESSMEN'S OBLIGATIONS

The ethical issues presented by these various kinds of uncertainty may not, in all cases, be so sharply distinguishable. For purposes of exposition, however, I shall assume that it is everyone's moral obligation to obey a law whose applications are reasonably clear, whether or not violators are likely to be caught, and regardless of the probability that the law will fail to have desired effects.

By contrast, I shall argue on the immediate ethical question: (1) that a businessman has no obligation to guess that an uncertain law requires him to make the greatest conceivable sacrifice; (2) that managers who take big risks in the gray areas have, nevertheless, an obligation to their enterprises to be prudent in the assumption of such risks; and (3) that there are some as yet poorly defined duties to avoid tactics that increase the uncertainty of law or prevent the regulatory processes from being as intelligent as possible.

These opinions might be tested by examining recent cases in which judgments of monopoly, deception, and negligence were hard to predict. But some of the recent judgments have aroused strong passions. In the hope, therefore, of avoiding the weak logic of strong passion, I propose the examination of a public policy that had the force of law twenty years ago, namely, the wartime wage stabilization.

The reader may think that wage stabilization is an odd set of regulations

[2] This is not the place to review the philosophical arguments for law observance. They usually raise the question, "What would happen if everyone did that?" The question is particularly apt for those who want to evade a law that they do not like while expecting other people to obey other laws (which the other people do not like). The so-called "generalization argument" was considerably tightened in a recent book by Marcus G. Singer, *Generalization in Ethics* (New York: A. A. Knopf, 1961).

[3] The mistake is a confusion of the general effects of a public policy (which justify the public policy) with the specific effects of an act that comes under the policy. See John Rawls, "Two Concepts of Rules," *The Philosophical Review*, Vol. 64 (1955), pp. 3–32, and Richard Brandt, *Ethical Theory* (Englewood Cliffs, N.J.: Prentice-Hall, 1959), Chap. 15.

to select for study of the businessman's problem of law observance. Generally speaking, it was the unions that tried to break through the wartime ceiling on wage rates. The reader may recall that businessmen objected to other wartime labor policies, such as union security and checkoff. Why not take them for study instead?

THE CASE OF WAGE REGULATION

No, the puzzles of compliance with an uncertain law are easier to understand when we examine a law that is strongly supported in the business community. Then, we can see the contrast between "what is good for the nation" and "what is good for the company," without the distraction of pro and anti business polemics. In the case of wage stabilization, the overwhelming majority of employers agreed with its immediate purpose: labor shortages must not be allowed to push wages to competitive levels. Twelve million men were being taken out of the labor force while government spending was pushing production to almost double its previous volume. Without controls, wage increases would set off an inflation that might interfere with the financing of the war and have many other bad consequences.

At the same time, employers were trying to keep their own operations going. They were tempted to offer illegal wages, at least for certain classes of scarce labor. The enforcement problems thus arising were greatest in the construction industries, but they were also acute in many trades not closely related to the war effort that were losing skilled workers to steel, aircraft, oil, and so on.

You may recall that, after some false starts, the federal government announced what sounded like a firm public policy in the autumn of 1942. Wage stabilization and price control were believed to be necessary for the effective prosecution of the war. The President, by Executive Order Number 9250, directed the National War Labor Board not to approve "any increase in the wage rates prevailing on September 15, 1942, unless such increase is necessary to correct maladjustments or inequities, to eliminate substandards of living, to correct gross inequities, or to aid in the effective prosecution of the war." The War Labor Board interpreted the executive order to mean, among other things, that, except for inequities and substandards, groups of employees could not receive increases amounting to more that 15 per cent of their average straight-time rates prevailing on January 1, 1941.[4]

The wage-stabilization policy had the force of law. It was administered by a regulatory agency of unprecedented size. Its sanctions included the

[4] See the policy statement of November 6, 1942, in *The Termination Report* of the National War Labor Board (Washington, D.C.: U.S. Government Printing Office, 1948), Vol. I, pp. 187–188.

threat of governmental seizure, the disallowance of expenses for tax purposes, and cancellation of employment privileges as well as fines and imprisonment.

In spite of the apparent simplicity of the policy and the heavy penalties for violations, wage stabilization had its gray areas. Some managers were tempted to contrive questionable wage contracts. The managers were, in numerous instances, under strong pressure from a union. They were experiencing great difficulty in recruiting and holding a work force. Many of them were competing for employees with companies and industries that, by historical accident or by clever evasion, were offering higher wages. The demand for ever greater production came from the usual sources plus the armed services and an aroused, patriotic public opinion.

GRAY AREAS

What were the gray areas? Prior to the fall of 1942, there was uncertainty about the extent of increases that would be permitted because of increases in the cost of living. During the early part of 1943, no one could say for sure what the prevailing wage rates were in various areas; inequities, therefore, were arguable from competing sets of data. In 1944 there continued to be uncertainty about fringe benefits—such as paid vacations and welfare funds—and new incentive wage plans. Throughout the war, there was difficulty in classifying some jobs. Reclassification of jobs and of workers in jobs remained a wordy art; it never became a science.

Was an employer morally culpable if he guessed that a convenient and employee-holding increase in one of these gray areas would be approved? Was he doing anything wrong when, in these same gray areas, he guessed that he would be upheld in resisting an increase that was inconvenient and unprofitable for him?

To have called such an employer unethical would have been to misunderstand the intertwined rule-making and adjudicating processes. Take as an illustration the classification of jobs and the determination of prevailing rates for those jobs. Several seasons were required to accumulate and analyze the information that was needed to determine prevailing area rates. During long months, the staff and members of the War Labor Board were securing this knowledge by hearing arguments about the comparability of various jobs. The process of establishing regulations depended upon the exchange of ideas and the persuasive efforts of interested parties. In some instances, it was only when an interested party tested the gray area that anything like a definable rule emerged from the process. The man who did not press his claim left the determination to parties that had other needs and, possibly, adverse interests. He might even be victimized by a statistical error, like the one in the Cleveland region, discovered too late to be rectified without a lot of trouble.

If it was not unethical per se to probe the gray areas by interpreting regulations in the manner most convenient for one's business, were there no
ethical limits to partisanship? Suppose that I had been desperate for machinists and that I had decided to classify ordinary machinists, with routine
maintenance duties, as tool makers? Or suppose that I had a plentiful supply of assemblers and that I introduced a piece-rate plan which would repay
normal effort with the equivalent of the straight-time rate of thirty-five
cents per hour? The uncertainty of War Labor Board rulings was common
knowledge. According to a joke that went the rounds, there were only eight
"common laborers" left in the airframe industry in California. So, why not
stretch the definitions?

LIMITS ON GAMBLING

There were two restraints on such gambling. The first was an obligation
to my company to be prudent in its management. If I took a very long
chance on the interpretation of an uncertain government policy, I accepted
not merely the chance of increased profits but also the chance of an adverse
order from the War Labor Board and, with that adverse order, the possibility of trouble from other war agencies. There was also the prospect of
hurting reputations, that of the company and my own. As with any risks,
I was duty bound to ask whether the company and I could afford to take
these risks.[5]

The second ethical restraint on partisanship in the wage-stabilization
process was a poorly defined obligation to be "co-operative"—to an extent.
The business community, the unions, the lawyers, and "the public" had
somewhat different expectations, but none of them condoned conspiracies
to keep the rule-making processes from clearing up gray areas. According to
many opinions, an interested party might exhaust all legal remedies while
fighting and delaying a rule or an order that he believed to be incorrect. He
might take heroic risks to secure what he believed to be the purpose of
wage stabilization. But whatever admiration there was for a man who went
down fighting usually disappeared if the man was found to have falsified
records or to have otherwise tried to corrupt the wage-stabilizing process.

A complicated set of regulations, such as the wartime wage stabilization,
could not be developed and applied in neatly separated activities called
"rule-making" and "adjudication."[6] When anyone saw how necessary was
the interplay of partisan contention and official judgment, he might wish

[5] There is always a danger that a gray-area tester will become a black-and-white area
violator. It is one thing to say, "I'll take a chance that the Board or the courts will not
punish people who do XYZ." It is quite another thing to say, "The government pun-
ishes people who are convicted of ABC. I'll do ABC, on the chance that I won't be
caught and convicted."

[6] This point is well developed with reference to a number of regulatory agencies in
Mark S. Massel, "The Regulatory Process," *Law and Contemporary Problems,* Vol. 26
(Spring 1961), pp. 181–202.

that the entire procedure should become a problem-solving process and each participant be judged by the extent to which he helped to solve the problems. The flaw in this broad-minded view that the participants could not agree on the precise nature of the problem which they were all helping to solve.[7]

SUMMARY

Summarizing these reflections upon wage stabilization, I should say that:

(1) Where there is real uncertainty in a public policy that has the force of law, a man does not violate his obligation to be law abiding if he guesses that a profitable or convenient activity will be upheld;

(2) He does, however, assume a risk for himself and his company, and he has an obligation to his company to assume no greater risks than his company can afford, both by way of possible legal penalties and possible moral censure from a not-too-discriminating public;

(3) He also has an obligation not to sabotage the rule-making process, but the judgment of his fidelity to this obligation is controversial. There will be agreement that he has such an obligation but not on what it is.

May the foregoing conclusions be accepted as stating the relation of law and ethics in business generally? I do not know. The reader may think of many situations in which very different opinions seem reasonable. I shall, in concluding, anticipate only one objection.

What about the objection that no man may ethically do that which, in his opinion, destroys or damages a common good, even though such an action is within the law? Consider two examples.

(1) A businessman helps to merge two enterprises. The merger will provide handsome tax advantages for himself and others who will be leaving the scene. But the businessman knows that it is a monstrous merger, for the operations that are combined require managerial skills so varied that no single management is likely to possess them all.

(2) A manufacturer discovers that he can greatly increase his profits by making and distributing a product that is probably well within the law but, in his opinion, it is dangerous to health and should be prohibited by law. In spite of these qualms, the manufacturer seizes his profit opportunity.

IMPERFECTION OF LAW

These two cases are examples of imperfection in our system of social control. There are discrepancies between the good, as someone sees it, and the

---

[7] See Gail Kennedy, "The Process of Evaluation in a Democratic Community," *The Journal of Philosophy*, Vol. 56 (March 12, 1959), pp. 253–263. Although Professor Kennedy held out hope of an eventual consensus concerning the nature of public problems, Charner Perry and I found such optimism to be rather rare. See Leys and Perry, *Philosophy and the Public Interest* (Chicago, 1959).

actual results achieved by law. Law, custom, and public opinion are formed by men who aim at good results. But legislators sometimes tolerate evils because the costs of enforcing an effective law would be too high or because they have not been able to resolve their differences regarding the good to be obtained or the means to be used.

Our society accepts and is grateful for the voluntary sacrifices of men who go beyond the call of duty. They partially mitigate the evils that arise from the imperfections of legally enforceable regulations. Most of us educate our children so that they will make some sacrifices of this character. If moral education is successful, the children have to do more than stay within the law in order to retain their own self-respect and the respect of the kind of persons they have been taught to seek out.

What about the citizen who does not have a conscience that makes him feel responsible for the common good? Should we not put moral pressure on him, so that he does not use the imperfections of the law to pursue antisocial purposes? Must we tolerate the chiseler, the loophole artist, and the questionable character who barely complies with the law?

My answer to this question is that, in a free country, anyone may voice his objections to anything. But the objections to minimal compliance with lawful regulation are misdirected if we say that the bare-compliance man has a faulty attitude toward the law. It is his attitude toward common goods other than the law that we find deficient. What irks us is his indifference to health and public safety and national security and future solvency.

I hope that these distinctions will not sound Pickwickian. They seem to me to be needed for the following reasons. First, not all common goods are likely to be secured and preserved by legislation and the regulatory processes: amoral education that lumps all legal and extralegal responsibilities together and calls them "responsibility" obscures the voluntary nature of a considerable part of morality. Second, the misplacement of charity and love in the development of judicial and administrative regulation overlooks the need in the regulatory processes for partisan attitudes and the mutual criticism that partisan attitudes make possible.

a statement on
BUSINESS ETHICS
and
A CALL FOR ACTION

WITH SOME QUESTIONS FOR BUSINESSMEN

BUSINESS ETHICS ADVISORY COUNCIL
organized by the
U.S. DEPARTMENT OF COMMERCE
Washington 25, D.C.

WHAT IS THE BUSINESS ETHICS
ADVISORY COUNCIL?

On May 17, 1961, a group of outstanding American businessmen, educators, clergymen, and journalists met at the Department of Commerce in Washington, D.C. They gathered at my invitation for the purpose of exploring as a Council some approaches to the development of ethical guidelines that might be useful to the business community.

On that occasion I said:

"There has been a great deal of discussion recently about the state of business ethics and the need for some very careful thought to help establish an approach to the problem. Here at the Department of Commerce we feel an obligation to assist business in this effort. It is not a critical approach that we seek—but rather a constructive one.

"The government looks to you as a Council to advise the business community. We have no preconceived notions regarding the development of a code of ethics or your method of approach. We seek your considered opinion as to what tools business and industry can best use to pursue its own search for the highest ethical performance. Public confidence in our business community is shaken. Both government and industry are anxious to do everything possible to achieve renewed public faith in the ethical ideal of management. I sincerely hope the Council will look into the problem, seek the tools and programs that answer needs, and finally educate and encourage businessmen to use them."

Out of that meeting and subsequent meetings of the Council and its subcommittee have come the inspiring Statement on Business Ethics and a Call for Action, and the Questions for Businessmen which are published here. The Council first presented its Statement and Questions to President Kennedy, during a White House meeting, on January 16, 1962.

At that meeting the Council explained that these documents should be regarded as its first report. The Council defined its further work as a long-range implementation program to help the business community to accelerate the improvement of ethical performance. As the Council stated to the President, "This program will involve working with key businessmen and association leaders in industry to encourage adoption, updating, and activation of company and industry codes. Schools of business administration and the major religious groups will be asked to increase awareness and study of problems of business ethics by businessmen, students, and the public at large. In addition, foundations and universities will be asked to sponsor studies in depth of various ethical problems of business. The aid of government agencies will also be sought in some of these efforts."

In publishing the Council's Statement and Questions at this time the

Department of Commerce is performing its proper role in this important undertaking. We are seeking to help the American business community to develop techniques and programs to help itself. We look upon the Council's Statement and Questions as starting points from which businessmen will be moved to initiate programs of ethical inquiry in their own companies. Each one must do this for himself—and in his own best way. This is, after all, the only method of real achievement in a democratic society.

Luther H. Hodges
Secretary of Commerce

A STATEMENT ON BUSINESS ETHICS
AND A CALL FOR ACTION

The ethical standards of American businessmen, like those of the American people, are founded upon our religious heritage and our traditions of social, political, and economic freedom. They impose upon each man high obligations in his dealings with his fellowmen, and make all men stewards of the common good. Immutable, well-understood guides to performance generally are effective, but new ethical problems are created constantly by the ever-increasing complexity of society. In business, as in every other activity, therefore, men must continually seek to identify new and appropriate standards.

Over the years, American businessmen in the main have continually endeavored to demonstrate their responsiveness to their ethical obligations in our free society. They have themselves initiated and welcomed from others calls for the improvement of their ethical performance, regarding each as a challenge to establish and meet ever higher ethical goals. In consequence, the ethical standards that should guide business enterprise in this country have steadily risen over the years, and this has had a profound influence on the performance of the business community.

As the ethical standards and conduct of American private enterprise have improved, so also has there developed a public demand for proper performance and a keen sensitivity to lapses from those standards. The full realization by the business community of its future opportunities and, indeed, the maintenance of public confidence requires a continuing pursuit of the highest standards of ethical conduct.

Attainment of this objective is not without difficulty. Business enterprises, large and small, have relationships in many directions—with stockholders and other owners, employees, customers, suppliers, government, and the public in general. The traditional emphasis on freedom, competition, and progress in our economic system often brings the varying interests of these groups into conflict, so that many difficult and complex ethical problems can arise in any enterprise. While all relationships of an enterprise to these groups are regulated in some degree by law, compliance with law can only provide a minimum standard of conduct. Beyond legal obligations, the policies and actions of businessmen must be based upon a regard for the proper claims of all affected groups.

Moreover, in many business situations the decision that must be made is not the simple choice between absolute right and absolute wrong. The decisions of business frequently must be made in highly complex and ever-changing circumstances, and at times involve either adhering to earlier standards or developing new ones. Such decisions affect profoundly not only the business enterprise, but our society as a whole. Indeed, the responsible position of American business—both large and small—obligates each participant to lead rather than follow.

A weighty responsibility therefore rests upon all those who manage business enterprises, as well as upon all others who influence the environment in which business operates. In the final analysis, however, the primary moral duty to establish high ethical standards and adequate procedures for their enforcement in each enterprise must rest with its policymaking body —its board of directors and its top management.

We, therefore, now propose that current efforts be expanded and intensified and that new efforts now be undertaken by the American business community to hasten its attainment of those high ethical standards that derive from our heritage and traditions. We urge all enterprises, business groups, and associations to accept responsibility—each for itself and in its own most appropriate way—to develop methods and programs for encouraging and sustaining these efforts on a continuous basis. We believe in this goal, we accept it, and we encourage all to pursue its attainment.

SOME QUESTIONS FOR BUSINESSMEN

The following questions are designed to facilitate the examination by American businessmen of their ethical standards and performance. They are intended to illustrate the kinds of questions that must be identified and considered by each business enterprise if it is to achieve compliance with those high ethical standards that derive from our heritage and traditions. Every reader will think of others. No single list can possibly encompass all of the demands for ethical judgments that must be met by men in business.

1. GENERAL UNDERSTANDING:

Do we have in our organization current, well-considered statements of the ethical principles that should guide our officers and employees in specific situations that arise in our business activities, both domestic and foreign? Do we revise these statements periodically to cover new situations and changing laws and social patterns?

Have those statements been the fruit of discussion in which all members of policy-determining management have had an opportunity to participate?

Have we given to our officers and employees at all levels sufficient motivation to search out ethical factors in business problems and apply high ethical standards in their solution? What have we done to eliminate opposing pressures?

Have we provided officers and employees with an easily accessible means of obtaining counsel on and resolution of ethical problems that may arise in their activities? Do they use it?

Do we know whether our officers and employees apply in their daily activities the ethical standards we have promulgated? Do we reward those who do so and penalize those who do not?

2. COMPLIANCE WITH LAW:

Having in mind the complexities and ever-changing patterns of modern law and government regulation:

What are we doing to make sure that our officers and employees are informed about and comply with laws and regulations affecting their activities?

Have we made clear that it is our policy to obey even those laws which we may think unwise and seek to have changed?

Do we have adequate internal checks on our compliance with law?

Have we established a simple and readily available procedure for our officers and employees to seek legal guidance in their activities? Do they use it?

3. CONFLICTS OF INTEREST:

Do we have a current, well-considered statement of policy regarding potential conflict of interest problems of our directors, officers and employees? If so, does it cover conflicts which may arise in connection with such activities as: transactions with or involving our company; acquiring interests in or performing services for our customers, distributors, suppliers and competitors; buying and selling our company's securities; or the personal undertaking of what might be called company opportunities?

What mechanism do we have for enabling our directors, officers and employees to make ethical judgments when conflicts of interest do arise?

Do we require regular reports, or do we leave it to our directors, officers and employees to disclose such activities voluntarily?

4. ENTERTAINMENT, GIFTS, AND EXPENSES:

Have we defined our company policy on accepting and making expenditures for gifts and entertainment? Are the criteria as to occasion and amount clearly stated or are they left merely to the judgment of the officer or employee?

Do we disseminate information about our company policy to the organizations with which we deal?

Do we require adequate reports of both the giving and receiving of gifts and entertainment; are they supported in sufficient detail; are they subject to review by appropriate authority; and could the payment or receipt be justified to our stockholders, the government, and the public?

5. CUSTOMERS AND SUPPLIERS:

Have we taken appropriate steps to keep our advertising and sales representations truthful and fair? Are these steps effective?

How often do we review our advertising, literature, labels, and packaging? Do they give our customers a fair understanding of the true quality, quantity, price and function of our products? Does our service as well as our product measure up to our basic obligations and our representations?

Do we fairly make good on flaws and defects? Is this a matter of stated policy? Do we know that our employees, distributors, dealers and agents follow it?

Do we avoid favoritism and discrimination and otherwise treat our customers and suppliers fairly and equitably in all of our dealings with them?

6. SOCIAL RESPONSIBILITIES:

Every business enterprise has manifold responsibilities to the society of which it is a part. The prime legal and social obligation of the managers of a business is to operate it for the long-term profit of its owners. Concurrent social responsibilities pertain to a company's treatment of its past, present and prospective employees and to its various relationships with customers, suppliers, government, the community and the public at large. These responsibilities may often be, or appear to be, in conflict, and at times a management's recognition of its broad responsibilities may affect the amount of an enterprise's immediate profits and the means of attaining them.

The problems that businessmen must solve in this area are often exceedingly perplexing. One may begin his reflections on this subject by asking—

Have we reviewed our company policies in the light of our responsibilities to society? Are our employees aware of the interaction between our business policies and our social responsibilities?

Do we have a clearly understood concept of our obligation to assess our responsibilities to stockholders, employees, customers, suppliers, our community and the public?

Do we recognize and impress upon all our officers and employees the fact that our free enterprise system and our individual business enterprises can thrive and grow only to the extent that they contribute to the welfare of our country and its people?

THE WHITE HOUSE

Statement of the President at Meeting of Business Ethics Advisory Council, January 16, 1962

I have reviewed with Secretary Hodges the report and progress you have made in the development of a program to stimulate and assist business leaders and trade association groups in attaining high ethical standards, and I am delighted.

But your statement of principles can only be a beginning. In the last analysis, high ethical standards can be achieved only through voluntary effort. The principles you have outlined will establish guideposts, give direction and help whole industries and companies to initiate codes and standards.

I am confident that American business will respond, but in addition to helping businessmen, your work should assist the general public to achieve a broader understanding of these problems—for ethics is a matter of concern to us all.

The free world watches us closely for leadership in this field, the uncommitted nations seek examples of the free enterprise system in operation, and the Communist nations are looking for vulnerable points of attack. I know that you will bear all this in mind.

It is good to know that this group of distinguished business leaders, educators, and clergymen has undertaken this important task. I am looking forward to seeing continued reports of progress by this Council.

JOHN F. KENNEDY

MAKING A CODE TO LIVE BY

To be meaningful a code of ethics must be written for an individual enterprise or particular industry. If the Council's statement and questions are to be translated into action, a code for a business or an industry must first be hammered out in soul-searching discussions in which company policymakers and managers participate. It must deal concretely with problems a company faces in its day-to-day dealings with all related social and economic groups. It must be explained to, and be understood by all affected personnel. Strong leadership from the top is required for acceptance throughout the organization. Lastly, there must be adequate internal devices for checking compliance.

The long experience of the American Management Association in the study of business ethics, its large library of codes and standards, have been made available to business generally by Council member Lawrence A. Appley, President of the Association. Any company or industry desiring help in the development of a code of ethics should write to Mr. Appley at the Association's headquarters, 1515 Broadway, New York 36, N.Y.

The Business Ethics Advisory Council will continue its endeavors to help our industries achieve even higher ethical goals. For further information about the Council's work, inquiries may be addressed to the chairman, any member of the Council, or to the Secretary of Commerce.

WILLIAM C. DECKER
Chairman, Business Ethics Advisory Council

THE ADVERTISING CODE OF AMERICAN BUSINESS

1. Truth ... Advertising shall tell the truth, and shall reveal significant facts, the concealment of which would mislead the public.

2. Responsibility... Advertising agencies and advertisers shall be willing to provide substantiation of claims made.

3. Taste and Decency ... Advertising shall be free of statements, illustrations or implications which are offensive to good taste or public decency.

4. Disparagement ... Advertising shall offer merchandise or service on its merits, and refrain from attacking competitors unfairly or disparaging their products, services or methods of doing business.

5. Bait Advertising ... Advertising shall offer only merchandise or services which are readily available for purchase at the advertised price.

6. Guarantees and Warranties ... Advertising of guarantees and warranties shall be explicit. Advertising of any guarantee or warranty shall clearly and conspicuously disclose its nature and extent, the manner in which the guarantor or warrantor will perform and the identity of the guarantor or warrantor.

7. Price Claims ... Advertising shall avoid price or savings claims which are false or misleading, or which do not offer provable bargains or savings.

8. Unprovable Claims ... Advertising shall avoid the use of exaggerated or unprovable claims.

9. Testimonials ... Advertising containing testimonials shall be limited to those of competent witnesses who are reflecting a real and honest choice.

Developed and initially distributed by: the Advertising Federation of America; the Advertising Association of the West; the Association of Better Business Bureaus, Inc.

Reproduced by permission of the Advertising Federation of America.

ETHICAL CONDUCT IN THE GOVERNMENT

MESSAGE

FROM

THE PRESIDENT OF THE UNITED STATES

RELATIVE TO

ETHICAL CONDUCT IN THE GOVERNMENT

APRIL 27, 1961.—Referred to the Committee on the Judiciary and
ordered to be printed

To the Congress of the United States:

No responsibility of Government is more fundamental than the responsibility of maintaining the highest standards of ethical behavior by those who conduct the public business. There can be no dissent from the principle that all officials must act with unwavering integrity, absolute impartiality, and complete devotion to the public interest. This principle must be followed not only in reality but in appearance. For the basis of effective Government is public confidence, and that confidence is endangered when ethical standards falter or appear to falter.

I have firm confidence in the integrity and dedication of those who work for our Government. Venal conduct by public officials in this country has been comparatively rare—and the few instances of official impropriety that have been uncovered have usually not suggested any widespread departure from high standards of ethics and moral conduct.

Nevertheless, in the past two decades, incidents have occurred to remind us that the laws and regulations governing ethics in Government are not adequate to the changed role of the Federal Government, or to the changing conditions of our society. In addition, many of the ethical problems confronting our public servants have become so complex as to defy easy commonsense solutions on the part of men of good will seeking to observe the highest standards of conduct, and solutions have been hindered by lack of general regulatory guidelines. As a result many thoughtful observers have expressed concern about the moral tone of Government, and about the need to restate basic principles in their application to contemporary facts.

Of course, public officials are not a group apart. They inevitably reflect the moral tone of the society in which they live. And if that moral tone is injured—by fixed athletic contests or television quiz shows—by widespread business conspiracies to fix prices—by the collusion of businessmen and unions with organized crime—by cheating on expense accounts, by the ignoring of traffic laws, or by petty tax evasion—then the conduct of our Government must be affected. Inevitably, the moral standards of a society influence the conduct of all who live within it—the governed and those who govern.

The ultimate answer to ethical problems in Government is honest people in a good ethical environment. No web of statute or regulation, however intricately conceived, can hope to deal with the myriad possible challenges to a man's integrity or his devotion to the public interest. Nevertheless formal regulation is required—regulation which can lay down clear guidelines of policy, punish venality and doubledealing, and set a general ethical tone for the conduct of public business.

Such regulation, while setting the highest moral standards, must not impair the ability of the Government to recruit personnel of the highest quality and capacity. Today's Government needs men and women with a broad range of experience, knowledge, and ability. It needs increasing numbers of people with topflight executive talent. It needs hundreds of occasional and intermittent consultants and part-time experts to help deal with problems of increasing complexity and technical difficulty. In short, we need to draw upon America's entire reservoir of talent and skill to help conduct our generation's most important business—the public business.

This need to tap America's human resources for public purposes has blurred the distinctions between public and private life. It has led to a constant flow of people in and out of business, academic life, and Government. It has required us to contract with private institutions and call upon part-time consultants for important public work. It has resulted in a rapid rate of turnover among career Government employees—as high as 20 percent a year. And, as a result, it has gravely multiplied the risk of conflicts of interest while seriously complicating the problem of maintaining ethical standards.

These new difficulties and old problems led me to appoint, immediately after my inauguration, three distinguished lawyers to review our existing conflict-of-interest laws and regulations. This panel was composed of Judge Calvert Magruder, retired chief judge of the First Judicial Circuit; Dean Jefferson B. Fordham of the University of Pennsylvania Law School; and Prof. Bayless Manning of the Yale Law School. The proposals put forward in this message are in large measure based upon their work and that of others who have considered the problems in recent years.

The recommendations of this panel were arrived at after careful study and review of the work of other groups, particularly the 1958 staff report of the Antitrust Subcommittee of the House Judiciary Committee under Congressman Celler; the pioneering study in 1951 by a subcommittee of the Senate Committee on Labor and Public Welfare under Senator Douglas; the recent report of the staff of the Senate Subcommittee on National Policy Machinery of the Committee on Government Operations headed by Senator Jackson; and valuable appraisals conducted during the last administration by the executive branch, and by the Association of the Bar of the City of New York.

All of these studies have emphasized the seriousness of the problem encountered. All have recommended that our outmoded and hodge-podge collection of statutes and regulations be amended, revised, and strengthened to take account of new problems. If the proposals have varied in their details, all have underscored the need for legislative and executive action in a commonly agreed direction.

I. STATUTORY REFORM

There are seven statutes of general application termed "conflict-of-interest" statutes. Many others deal with particular offices or very limited categories of employees. These latter usually exempt officials from some or all of the general restrictions. Occasionally they impose additional obligations.

The seven statutes cover four basic problems:

The Government employee who acts on behalf of the Government in a business transaction with an entity in which he has a personal economic stake (18 U.S.C. 434).

The Government employee who acts for an outside interest in certain dealings with the Government (18 U.S.C. 216, 281, 283).

The Government employee who receives compensation from a private source for his Government work (18 U.S.C. 1914).

The former Government employee who acts in a representative capacity in certain transactions with the Government during a 2-year period after the termination of his Government service (18 U.S.C. 284, 5 U.S.C. 99).

Five of these statutes were enacted before 1873. Each was enacted without coordination with any of the others. No two of them use uniform terminology. All but one impose criminal penalties. There is both overlap and inconsistency. Every study of these laws has concluded that, while sound in principle, they are grossly deficient in form and substance.

The fundamental defect of these statutes as presently written is that: On the one hand, they permit an astonishing range of private interests and activities by public officials which are wholly incompatible with the duties of public office; on the other hand, they create wholly unnecessary obstacles to recruiting qualified people for Government service. This latter deficiency is particularly serious in the case of consultants and other temporary employees, and has been repeatedly recognized by Congress in its enactment of special exemption statutes.

Insofar as these statutes lay down the basic law restricting the private enonomic activities of public officers and employees they constitute a sound and necessary standard of conduct. The principle which they embody in varying form—that a public servant owes undivided loyalty to the

Government—is as important today as when the first of these statutes was enacted more than a century ago. However, the statutory execution of this principle in the seven statutes of general application was often directed to specific existing evils which at the time of their enactment were important political issues. As a result large areas of potential conflict of interest were left uncovered.

For example, where some of these conflict-of-interest statutes are restricted to "claims of money and property"—as the courts have said—they do not protect the Government against the use of official position, influence, or inside information to aid private individuals or organizations in Government proceedings which involve no claims for money or property. Yet the danger of abuses of Government position exist to an equal if not greater degree in proceedings such as license applications for TV or radio stations, airline routes, electric power sites, and similar requests for Government aid, assistance, or approval.

Thus, literally read, it would be a crime punishable by fine or imprisonment under these statutes for a postal clerk to assist his mother in filing a routine claim for a tax refund, but it would be permissible for a Cabinet officer to seek to influence an independent agency to award a license for a valuable TV station to a business associate in a venture where he shared the profits.

There are many other technical inadequacies and statutory gaps. Section 434 of title 18, born of the Civil War procurement scandals, prohibits a Government official interested in the pecuniary profits of a business entity from acting as an officer or agent of the United States for the transaction of business with that business entity. By limiting its scope to "business entities" the statute does not cover the many other organizations which deal with the Government. In addition, the concept of "transacting business," if narrowly construed, as would be likely in a criminal prosecution, would exclude many dealings with the Government, such as the clearance or rejection of license applications in the executive branch or before an independent agency.

Similar defects exist in the case of Government officials who have left Government service. Clearly such an official should be prohibited from resigning his position and "switching sides" in a matter which was before him in his official capacity. But for technical reasons the statutes aimed at this situation do not always hit the mark. There is nothing in the criminal statutes which would prevent the General Counsel of the Federal Power Commission from resigning to represent an unsuccessful license applicant who is contesting the Commission's decision in the courts (although such conduct might be grounds for disbarment). And, a Commission employee who was not a lawyer could, in the present state of the law, unscrupulously benefit in such a case from his "inside information" without fear of sanctions.

But if the statutes often leave important areas unregulated, they also often serve as a bar to securing important personal services for the Government through excessive regulation when no ethical problem really exists. Fundamentally, this is because the statutes fail to take into account the role in our Government of the part-time or intermittent adviser whose counsel has become essential but who cannot afford to be deprived of private benefits, or reasonably requested to deprive himself, in the way now required by these laws. Wherever the Government seeks the assistance of a highly skilled technician, be he scientist, accountant, lawyer, or economist, such problems are encountered.

In general, these difficulties stem from the fact that even occasional consultants can technically be regarded as either "officers or employees" of the Government, whether or not compensated. If so, they are all within the prohibitions applicable to regular full-time personnel.

A few examples illustrate some of the difficulties:

Section 281 of the Criminal Code forbids public employees from providing services to outsiders for compensation in connection with any matter in which the United States is interested and which is before a department, agency, or commission.

This section makes it almost impossible for a practicing lawyer to accept a part-time position with the Government. He would be in violation of section 281 if he continued to receive compensation for cases before Government agencies, or even if his law partnership receives such compensation, though he personally has no connection with any case. It is usually impractical for the law firm to withdraw from all transactions involving the Government. And almost all law firms have some tax matters, for example, as part of their normal business. The same prohibition unfairly affects accountants.

In addition, the two existing postemployment statutes raise serious problems in terms of recruiting noncareer personnel (particularly lawyers). Enacted at different times, they employ different terms and are totally uncoordinated in language or in policy.

The criminal statute (18 U.S.C. 284) forbids a former employee for 2 years after his Government employment ceases to prosecute in a representative capacity any claim against the Government involving a "subject matter" directly connected with his Government job. The civil statute (5 U.S.C. 99) forbids employees of an executive department for 2 years after the end of their Government service from prosecuting in a representative capacity any claim against the United States if the claim was pending before "any department" while he was an employee.

These prohibitions are unnecessarily broad. They should be confined to "switching sides." For example, they now prohibit a lawyer who worked for the Department of Labor from subsequently representing a client in a wholly unrelated tax matter which had been before the Treasury during his Government service.

These restrictions prove an even more formidable barrier to the part-time consultant who works in a partnership since he and his partners would be excluded from participation in many if not all claims against the Government—a severe and unnecessary penalty for contributing to public service. It is possible to cite many other examples of excessive restrictions which serve no ethical purpose, but effectively bar Government from using available talent.

It is true that a large number of statutory exemptions passed at various times over the years have mitigated some of the adverse effects of these statutes upon certain specific individuals and certain categories of employees. However, no uniform standard of exemption has ever been adopted by the Congress in enacting these exemptions. Many of the exemptions are inconsistent. Some exemptions are subject to so many limitations as practically to nullify them. Some statutes unqualifiedly exempt categories of employees from all of the conflict statutes. Others exempt them from some but not all of the restrictions. The resulting hodgepodge of exemptions seriously weakens the integrity of the Government personnel system.

To meet this need for statutory reform, I am transmitting to the Congress a proposed Executive Employees' Standards Act—a comprehensive revision of existing conflict-of-interest statutes. I believe that this bill maintains the highest possible standards of conduct, eliminates the technical deficiencies and anachronisms of existing laws, and makes it possible for the Government to mobilize a wide range of talent and skill.

First, the bill closes gaps in regulation of the type discussed above, and eliminates many of the pointless differences in treatment. For example, no longer will some former Government employees be subject to more severe restrictions simply because they once worked for 1 of the 10 executive "departments" rather than in an agency which is not technically a department.

Secondly, the bill overrules existing judicial interpretation that only when a claim for money or property is involved is a former Government employee prohibited from working for a private interest in a matter for which he once had governmental responsibility. The basic issue of integrity is the same if the matter relates to Government regulation rather than to a property or money claim.

Third, the bill establishes special standards for skilled individuals whose primary activity is in private professional or business life, but whose skills are used by the Government on a part-time or advisory basis. By permitting such individuals to carry on private business, even business with the Government, as long as there is no direct conflict between their private and public work, ethical principles are maintained and a wide range of abilities are made available to Government.

Fourth, this bill adds to the traditional criminal sanctions by permitting agency heads to adopt implementing regulation and impose disciplinary measures. Most of the existing laws are criminal statutes. As such they have been strictly construed and, because of their harshness, infrequently invoked. By granting this added flexibility we help to insure more effective enforcement. In addition, the regulations which are adopted will permit more specific adaptation of the general prohibitions tailored to the activities of particular agencies.

Fifth, the bill deals only with employees involved in executive, administrative, and regulatory functions. It does not apply to either the judicial or legislative branch of Government. Existing laws relating to the judiciary are deemed adequate. The adequacy and effectiveness of laws regulating the conduct of Members of Congress and congressional employees should be left to strictly congressional determination.

Sixth, the proposed bill covers the District of Columbia and its employees. However, the District, essentially a municipal government, has its own distinctive problems. I will submit legislation dealing with these problems in the near future.

II. EX PARTE CONTACTS WITH OFFICIALS OF INDEPENDENT AGENCIES

Some of the most spectacular examples of official misconduct have involved ex parte communication—undisclosed, informal contact between an agency official and a party interested in a matter before that official. Such covert influence on agency action often does basic injury to the fairness of agency proceedings, particularly when those proceedings are judicial in nature.

This problem is one of the most complex in the entire field of Government regulation. It involves the elimination of ex parte contacts when those contacts are unjust to other parties, while preserving the capacity of an agency to avail itself of information necessary to decision. Much of the difficulty stems from the broad range of agency activities—ranging from judicial-type adjudication to wide-ranging regulation of entire industries. This is a problem which can best be resolved in the context of the particular responsibilities and activities of each agency.

I therefore recommend that the Congress enact legislation requiring each agency, within 120 days, to promulgate a code of behavior governing ex parte contacts within the agency specifying the particular standard to be applied in each type of agency proceeding, and containing an absolute prohibition against ex parte contact in all proceedings between private parties in which law or agency regulation requires that a decision be made solely on the record of a formal hearing. Only in this manner can we assure fairness in quasi-judicial proceedings between private parties. The statute should make clear that such codes when approved by Congress will have the force of law, and be subject to appropriate sanctions.

III. EXECUTIVE ORDERS AND PRESIDENTIAL ACTION

There are several problems of ethics in Government which can be dealt with directly by Presidential order, memoranda, or other form of action.

First, I intend to prohibit gifts to Government personnel whenever (a) the employee has reason to believe that the gift would not have been made except for his official position; or (b) whenever a regular Government employee has reason to believe that the donor's private interests are likely to be affected by actions of the employee or his agency. When it is impossible or inappropriate to refuse the gift it will be turned over to an appropriate public or charitable institution.

Such an order will embody the general principle that any gift which is, or appears to be, designed to influence official conduct is objectionable. Government employees are constantly bothered by offers of favors or gratuities and have been without any general regulation to guide their conduct. This order will attempt to supply such guidelines, while leaving special problems including problems created by gifts from foreign governments, to agency regulation.

Secondly, I intend to prohibit Government employees from using for private gain official information which is not available to the public. This regulation will be drawn with due regard for the public's right to proper access to public information. A Government employee should not be able to transform official status into private gain, as is done, for example, if a Government employee speculates in the stock market on the basis of advance knowledge of official action.

Third, I am directing that no Government employee shall use the authority of his position to induce another to provide him with anything of economic value whenever the employee has reason to believe that the other person's private interests may be affected by the actions of the employee or his agency.

This regulation is an effort to deal with the subtler forms of extortion; where an employee acquiesces in the gift of an economic benefit, or gives a delicate indication of receptivity. The criminal law deals with outright extortion. Beyond this the problem is too elusive for the criminal law and must be dealt with by administrative regulation, and by the sound judgment of the administrator.

Fourth, I am directing that no Government employee should engage in outside employment which is "incompatible" with his Government employment.

The outside employment of Government employees is one of the most complex and difficult of all ethical problems. It is clear that some forms of employment may have benefits to the Government or society (e.g., teaching in universities); or be beneficial to the employee and not inconsistent with his Government work. On the other hand, some types of outside work may involve exploitation of official position or be incompatible with the best interests of the agency to which the employee owes his first allegiance.

Since "incompatibility" of employment will depend on many varied factors, its definition will be left to agency and department regulation and case-by-case rulings.

Fifth, I will shortly issue an Executive order regulating in more detail the conduct of those officials who are appointed by the President. These high-level officials owe a special responsibility to the Government and to the employees of their departments to set a high standard of ethical and moral behavior. Therefore the Executive order (a) prohibits outside employment or activity of any sort incompatible with the proper discharge of official responsibility; (b) prohibits outside compensation for any activity within the scope of official duty; (c) prohibits the receipt of compensation for any lecture, article, public appearance, etc., devoted to the work of the department or based on official information not yet a matter of general knowledge.

Sixth, in carrying out the provisions of law, I will apply Government-wide standards to the continuance of property holdings by appointees to the executive branch. The law prohibits any conflict of the public and private interests of employees of the Government. The Senate, in the exercise of its power of confirmation, has taken the lead in requiring that Presidential appointees sell their property holdings in cases where retention of property might result in such a conflict of interest. The problem of property ownership by Executive appointees is properly a matter of continuing congressional concern, and I welcome the initiative taken by the Jackson Subcommittee on Conflict of Interest. At the same time, the executive branch has an obligation to insure that its appointees live up to the highest standard of behavior. It is to carry out this responsibility that I will apply general standards governing the ownership of property by Presidential appointees—standards which will insure that no conflict of interest can exist. It is my hope that these regulations will aid the Senate in the uniform exercise of its own responsibility.

IV. THE ADMINISTRATION OF ETHICAL STANDARDS

Criminal statutes and Presidential orders, no matter how carefully conceived or meticulously drafted, cannot hope to deal effectively with every problem of ethical behavior of conflict of interest. Problems arise in infinite variation. They often involve subtle and difficult judgments, judgments which are not suited to generalization or Government-wide application.

And even the best of statutes or regulations will fail of their purpose if they are not vigorously and wisely administered.

Therefore I am instructing each Cabinet member and agency head to issue regulations designed to maintain high moral and ethical standards within his own department. These regulations will adapt general principles to the particular problems and activity of each agency. To aid in the administration of these regulations each agency will establish an ad hoc committee to serve in an advisory capacity on ethical problems as they arise.

Although such agency regulation is essential, it cannot be allowed to dissolve into a welter of conflicting and haphazard rules and principles throughout the Government. Regulation of ethical conduct must be coordinated in order to insure that all employees are held to the same general standards of conduct.

Therefore I intend to designate, in the Executive Office of the President, a single officer charged with responsibility for coordinating ethics administration and reporting directly to the President. This officer will—

> prepare, for Presidential proclamation, general regulations as needed;
>
> develop methods of informing Government personnel about ethical standards;
>
> conduct studies and accumulate experience leading to more effective regulation of ethical conduct, including the formulation of rules in areas which are not yet regulated, such as Government use of outside advisers and the contracting of Government services to private institutions or firms; and
>
> clear and coordinate agency regulations to assure consistent executive policy.

Such an officer will not only provide central responsibility for coherent regulation, but will be a means through which the influence of the Presidency can be exerted in this vital field.

V. CONCLUSION

Ultimately, high ethical standards can be maintained only if the leaders of Government provide a personal example of dedication to the public service—and exercise their leadership to develop in all Government employees an increasing sensitivity to the ethical and moral conditions imposed by public service. Their own conduct must be above reproach. And they must go beyond the imposition of general regulations to deal with individual problems as they arise—offering informal advice and personal consideration. It will often be difficult to assess the propriety of particular actions. In such subtle cases honest disclosure will often be the surest solution, for the public will understand good faith efforts to avoid improper use of public office when they are kept informed.

I realize, too, that perhaps the gravest responsibility of all rests upon the office of President. No President can excuse or pardon the slightest deviation from irreproachable standards of behavior on the part of any member of the executive branch. For his firmness and determination is the ultimate source of public confidence in the Government of the United States. And there is no consideration that can justify the undermining of that confidence.

JOHN F. KENNEDY

The White House, April 27, 1961

TELEVISION CODE

THE NATIONAL ASSOCIATION OF BROADCASTERS

Back in the fall of 1951, a special committee of the National Association of Broadcasters drafted the first Television Code. The Code went into effect in March, 1952—during the first year of full coast-to-coast television. At that time 108 stations were on the air, and 89 of these stations and all networks subscribed to the Television Code.

Today, with 532 commercial stations broadcasting, the Code membership numbers 389 stations, all three networks, and 22 Code Film Affiliates.

PURPOSE OF THE TELEVISION CODE

The Code's purpose is to establish guidelines which Code subscribers can use to determine what is and what is not acceptable for broadcast. In the words of the Code preamble:

> In the voluntary and cooperative adherence to these regulations, broadcasters seek to maintain a level of television programming which gives full consideration to the educational, informational, cultural, economic, moral, and entertainment needs of the American public.

The Code contains guidelines for 14 distinct areas: eight of these areas deal with programming and production;

Advancement of Education and Culture
Responsibility Toward Children
Community Responsibility
General Program Standards
Treatment of News and Public Events
Controversial Public Issues
Political Telecasts
Religious Programs

From a pamphlet published by the Code Authority of the National Association of Broadcasters, 1771 N St., N.W., Washington, D.C. Reprinted by permission.

Six of these guidelines deal with advertising:

General Advertising Standards
Presentation of Advertising
Advertising of Medical Products
Contests
Premiums and Offers
Time Standards for Advertising

HOW THE CODE WORKS

A comprehensive organizational setup has been cooperatively established by broadcasters to make the Television Code a living part of what you see on your television screen. The Code Review Board acts as the appeals court of television broadcast practices. It also serves as the legislative branch to recommend changes in the provisions of the Code, subject to the approval of the National Association of Broadcasters' Television Board of Directors. This is a group of operating television broadcasters appointed by the President of the NAB and approved by the members of the Television Board of Directors.

The office of the Code Authority Director is filled by a former broadcast executive of more than 20 years' experience in network and station broadcasting.

Reporting to him are the heads of the Code Authority in three cities: Washington, New York, and Los Angeles.

In simplest terms: Broadcast executives correspond to a board of directors; the Code Authority is the operating mechanism.

The Code Authority works in a number of ways:

1. It *consults* with stations and networks on questions involving interpretations of Code regulation.

2. It *advises* those concerned with creating material for television by discussing questions of acceptability of material and treatment with film producers, advertisers, advertising agencies.

3. It *maintains liaison* with responsible organizations and institutions, and the public at large to encourage comment from viewers.

4. It *monitors* Code subscribers' broadcast performance to guard against violations.

But one more fact before examining further how the Code works.

Every station and every network has people who are charged with the responsibility of deciding what is or is not acceptable to be broadcast over their station or network.

This activity is variously called "program practices and standards" or "continuity acceptance." The number of people engaged in this work ranges from as few as one or two at some stations to as many as 32 at one network—involving an annual cost of some $400,000.

SOME SPECIFIC PROVISIONS

A number of provisions of the Code are very clear-cut and require no interpretation. For example: "The advertising of hard liquor should not be accepted."

This is a prohibition that represents a multi-million-dollar advertising rejection. And broadcasting is the *only* mass medium which observes this prohibition.

Similarly clear and explicit are the regulations that prohibit profanity, obscenity, and smut, and the one that says, "Contests may not constitute a lottery."

Equally specific are the regulations defining the amount of time that may be devoted to advertising.

This is limited to 13 per cent in prime evening time and rarely exceeds 20 per cent in other times and types of programs. By contrast, the amount of space devoted to advertising in newspapers averages 59 per cent, as reported in the magazine *Editor and Publisher*.

In provisions such as these, the Code's requirements are specific and even quantitative. Like standards that measure physical characteristics—either you can or you can't. It is either this much—which is permitted, or that much—which is not permitted.

Such provisions fall into the relatively narrow black-and-white areas of standards of taste as reflected in the television code. Many more provisions, by far, come within the larger gray area—allowing for individual interpretation, varying from community to community and from time to time.

In establishing guidelines for broadcast acceptability, two factors are considered: Content is one; treatment or manner of presentation is the other.

Is the *subject matter* suitable for presentation on television? And, if it is, is the *treatment* of the subject matter consonant with good taste considering the time of day and audience most likely to view it?

While questions of taste and morality are frustrating problems (and the answer in any single case is rarely satisfactory to everyone), it is essential that the widest possible latitude for judgment be permitted.

As one church group put it:

"Morality must be distinguished from mathematics in its scientific method. Morality is a matter of approximation.

"Moralists are in unanimous agreement on the principles of morality, but they often disagree on the application of the principles to specific cases. . . . Taste is inevitably involved in the matter of judgment."

SOME ACTIONS UNDER THE CODE

In its relatively brief history the Code Review Board has taken some very specific actions concerning some of the broad provisions of the Code itself.

For example, a few years ago a number of stations subscribing to the Code were carrying commercials for a medical preparation used in the treatment of hemorrhoids. The commercials were in good taste and were not shown during hours when they might have been offensive.

Yet because of the nature of the product and the special need that broadcasters recognize for extra care in advertising to a mixed group, it was decided that commercials for such products, along with personal products for feminine hygiene, should no longer be accepted by Code stations.

This decision was made without prejudice either to the product itself or to the advertising treatment of the product. It was a gray area decision that broadcasters invoked in their self-regulation efforts.

The Code Board has also eliminated two once-familiar advertising practices:

There was the "pitchman" technique, which you may recall from television's earliest days. It consisted of a continuous demonstration or sales presentation of perhaps 15 minutes in length. Such program-length commercials were ruled unacceptable by the Board in 1956.

And since the beginning of 1959, the Code has required that dramatized advertising involving statements by physicians, dentists, or nurses must be presented by accredited members of such professions. Thus, actors in laboratory coats, who only *seem* to be doctors, may no longer deliver commercial announcements.

But, in addition to the Code Authority, each station and network considers what it produces and broadcasts in the light of Code regulations.

In the area of programming, for example, there is the Code provision that says, "The detailed presentation of brutality or physical agony by sight or by sound are not permissible."

In the filming of one program in a popular western series, a scene turned up in which a spear was shown striking the victim and protruding from his back as he fell to the ground. After screening the preliminary print, the network decided that this scene was in violation both of the Code and of its own program practices.

The scene was altered. In its final form, the spear was seen being thrown, but the falling body was photographed only from the shoulders up.

Another example of enforcement of Code regulations by broadcasters involved a movie originally produced for theater showing. It contained a disrobing sequence that was considered to be in violation of the Code specification, "The costuming of all performers shall be within the bounds of propriety and shall avoid such exposure . . . as would embarrass or offend home viewers."

The scene was eliminated by the station before the film was broadcast.

ADVERTISING CLAIMS

The terminal responsibility for all advertising—whether in newspapers, radio, magazines, billboards, handbills, or television—goes back to the advertiser. This is the law. The advertiser has access to the facts about his product; he knows what it will and will not do.

But broadcasters, under the Code, have assumed a substantial responsibility in their adherence to a Code regulation urging "that great care be exercised by the broadcaster to prevent the presentation of false, misleading or deceptive advertising."

Verification of some claims depends on the user's personal appraisal—such as "taste better" or "you'll feel proud to own."

Provided they are not misleading or in bad taste or disparage a competitor's product, such commercials are accepted.

Where claims are not self-evident on their face, the advertising agency is asked for supporting proof. Most of the time the claims are supported, and you see the commercial. Quite frequently—through consultations with and suggestions made by the Code Authority or the broadcaster—the advertising agency changes language or action to eliminate questions of believability or accuracy.

In addition, there are other organizations that work to assure standards of accuracy in advertising: Better Business Bureaus, Federal Trade Commission, Food and Drug Administration, American Association of Advertising Agencies. The Code Authority and Code subscribers throughout the country supplement their own efforts by maintaining continuing liaison with such groups.

In these and other ways, broadcasters have, over the years, taken steps to increase the acceptability of commercials to viewers without reducing the effectiveness of the advertising.

Advertisers, through their advertising agencies, have joined in this effort.

There has been an increase in the use of imaginative treatment in television commercials. There has also been a parallel decrease in the reliance on repetition or stepped-up sound to make an advertising point.

ENCOURAGEMENT OF THOUGHTFUL DRAMA

The Code is not to be construed as a limiting instrument—shutting off imaginative and perceptive writing that would illuminate the meaning of life for adult viewers. On the contrary, Code rulings and interpretations attempt to encourage such efforts.

Many of Shakespeare's plays and classic Greek dramas contain language and are based on themes that could be considered offensive by many people today.

For example, Volpone, a play by the Elizabethan dramatist Ben Jonson, was described by one critic as "adroit dirt." The adjoining columnist called it "a treasure of a play."

The problem grows more complex when the drama is the product of contemporary writers, setting familiar scenes in plays with a controversial flavor.

Consider the Code regulations that require avoidance of profanity, elimination of scenes implying the prevalence of drunkenness, avoidance of scenes set in places associated with sexual sin.

Under a strict interpretation of these provisions, Eugene O'Neill's The Iceman Cometh could never have been shown on television. The Code Board ruling on this was made only after extensive consideration. The safest decision would have been "no."

However, the final decision—reflecting the conflict—said:

> The Code Board believes that the play as presented will find widely differing audience responses. Some viewers will find the play to be a rich and exciting performance; others may regard it, because of its language and theme, sordid and offensive . . .
> The Code Review Board believes that this particular presentation is acceptable for telecast, but only under special circumstances.

"Special circumstances" covered, most specifically, time of broadcast, with late evening showings recommended.

An even more difficult decision faced broadcasters in The Power and the Glory—the Graham Greene story of the hunting down of a dissolute priest by an anticlerical government during the Mexican Revolution of the 1930s.

The decision as to its acceptability was made by the network's programming practices department, which viewed the question in the light of the Code and its own policy concerning the treatment of religious subjects and the clergy. A literal interpretation of the Code policy would seem to make this play unacceptable.

Yet, so sensitively drawn was the portrait of the priest, with all his weaknesses, and so profound the message—the Grace of God may be found in the least likely places—that the program was produced and broadcast. Praise for it was virtually universal—not only among general newspapers throughout the country, but in the Roman Catholic press as well.

In the hands of less talented writers than Shakespeare, or Ben Jonson, O'Neill or Graham Greene, and without the most careful attention to production values, dramas featuring drunkenness, procurers, prostitutes, and libertines clearly would not be acceptable.

JUDGING ACCEPTABILITY

The decisions that have been described are typical of the judgments made on a day-by-day basis by the Code Authority and by stations and networks that subscribe to the Television Code.

You may have disagreed with some of these judgments; perhaps you have seen other programs or advertising material on a station subscribing to the Code that you found distasteful or annoying—or both.

Some of it might have slipped by the Code authority or the network's or station's clearance department. This is inevitable in light of the hundreds of hours of television every week and the many sources from which programming and advertising material are drawn.

But—aside from errors in the screening process—it is also inevitable that some material will continue to appear with which you, as an individual, would quarrel. This is bound to occur so long as there are individual differences in taste among people and so long as television does not restrict itself to the wholly innocuous.

In passing judgment on acceptability of material for television, virtually all the needs and ambitions, hopes and fears of people are legitimate areas for portrayal.

Misery and tragedy, cold remedies and detergents, pretty girls and "private eyes," are no less valid subject matter for people watching television than for the same people reading popular magazines or newspapers.

All of which leads to the obvious conclusion: *How* something is treated is the major determinant as to *what* can be treated.

And it is this question of treatment—which draws so heavily on creative resources of writing, acting, and directing—that represents the greatest challenge to those charged with the responsibility for what goes on the air.

For, as the United States Supreme Court put it:

> What is good literature, what has educational value, what is refined public information, what is good art, varies with individuals as it does from one generation to another . . . A requirement that literature or art conform to some norm prescribed by an official smacks of an ideology foreign to our system.

Recognizing the need for flexibility, the Television Code seeks to sanction the aesthetic and suppress the meretricious, to support the honest—while weeding out the sensational.

Clearly, it does not always succeed.

Reflecting as it does the diversity in our society, it does not always please everyone.

But it does provide a standard for the true, the decent, and the reasonable in television.

Depending as it does on intangibles—good manners, good taste, good faith, and good sense—the Television Code enlists the support of broad-casters, advertisers, advertising agencies, program producers, and the public.

Television stations that display the Seal of Good Practice show that they have, freely and voluntarily, pledged themselves to help achieve the true purpose of the Code: Television in the Greater Public Interest.

FIGHT BACK!
The Ungentle Art of Self-Defense

AS RECOMMENDED BY THE
FEDERAL TRADE COMMISSION

————— ▸◂▸◂ —————

HOW CAN YOU AVOID BEING GYPPED?

And, if you have been, what can you do about it?

Here are some answers to both questions. The advice is based on the experience of attorneys for the Federal Trade Commission who have been tracking down business cheats for more than 50 years. Assisted by the vast majority of merchants who are honest, the FTC's gyp hunters have become experts on how fly-by-night and overly eager sellers bilk consumers.

The bait is presented in countless disguises, but always its purpose is the same: to trick you, the buyer, into thinking you are getting much more for your money than you had dared to hope—a bargain too "amazing" to be offered by reputable stores. Thus, you end up paying too much for what you get or not getting what you pay for. And your companion in sorrow is the honest merchant who has had your business siphoned away from him by the cheat.

The first line of defense against the gyp artist should be manned by you, the consumer. No governmental policing is as effective as the chin-pinching purchaser who is willing to shop for what he wants and who is intelligent enough to judge what quantity and what quality he should receive for the price he pays. Just plain old coldblooded shopping makes it tough on the gypsters. And reputable businesses welcome the buyer who gives honest merchandising the favorable consideration it deserves.

The second line of defense is manned by consumers with enough courage to make themselves heard after they have been gypped in their purchases, or even when they have succeeded in avoiding a trap set for the less sophisticated. Certainly it is not enough to silently "chalk up to expe-

A pamphlet issued by the Federal Trade Commission.

rience" a purchase about which you were misled, or simply to congratulate yourself on not having been duped the way others might be. In these United States you can make your indignation heard, and gyp artists do not thrive on such attention. It might surprise you to find out how much good can be accomplished by a citizen with a legitimate complaint who will take the trouble to invite attention to it.

A good starting point is to protest directly to the seller (if you can find him!). Possibly the misrepresentation was done without his knowledge, in which case, he can take steps to assure against its repetition. There is even a chance he might square himself with you.

If, however, the fast-buck operator shrugs you off, you can carry your indignation further by registering your complaint with the organizations in your community devoted to maintaining proper conduct for business. A good example is the Better Business Bureau. And certainly your cause would be served if your complaint, backed by hard facts, went to the newspaper or radio or TV station that carries advertising for the product. It wouldn't take many such letters to deprive the huckster of his innocent readers and listeners. Truth in advertising is too important to these media to risk gaining a reputation for carrying phony ads.

A third line of defense is your local government. This is particularly important because most of the things you buy are marketed only locally, and the seller is not engaged in interstate commerce. The result is that you have to depend not on the federal government but on your city or state for protection. Nearly all of the states have statutes aimed at misrepresentation of products and services. And in some states these laws are enforced with vigor.

Certainly it behooves you to find out what kind of state (or city) protection is available to you. And if none is, you might want to help improve the situation.

Your fourth line of defense is the Federal Trade Commission. Congress gave it the broad responsibility to halt "unfair methods of competition in commerce and unfair or deceptive acts or practices in commerce." Thus, not only were all the known deceptive practices outlawed but any new ones that might be invented. Other responsibilities of the FTC include policing the labeling of furs, woolens and other textile products, and guarding against the sale of dangerously flammable wearing apparel.

With this much authority for the FTC, you might wonder why the federal government could not handle the entire job of protecting consumers from being cheated. There are good reasons why it cannot, the principal one being that Congress never intended to establish the huge Gestapo that would be needed to police every store and salesman in the country. Not only would the cost be prohibitive but businessmen have demonstrated that, with very few exceptions, they are quite capable of policing themselves. Indeed, the FTC provides valuable guidance to them in this self-policing effort.

The FTC's fight against consumer deception is directed at gyp schemes that have an actual or potential impact on the public, as distinguished from actions to settle private controversies. In short, it has neither the staff nor the money to tackle cases that do not have sufficient *public* interest. Also, the FTC has concentrated its force on halting law violators who do at least some of their selling across state lines.

Thus, while the FTC cannot undertake to settle your private or purely local difficulties, it does stand ready to halt important instances of deception—and at no cost to the one who brings the complaint. The reason for this is that the FTC never brings an action on behalf of an individual; instead, it must itself investigate the matter and then act only if there appears to be sufficient public interest in stopping it. Nevertheless, alert consumers perform a valuable service to FTC by inviting its attention to deceptive practices that should be investigated.

The way to do this is simple: just write a letter to the Federal Trade Commission, Washington 25, D.C. The letter should give as many facts as you have available, including any evidence of the chicanery, such as a copy of misleading advertising used to sell the product or the service. (Too many applications for complaint are long on indignation and short on facts that would help the FTC to determine whether the matter warranted investigation.) In writing this letter you have FTC's assurance that your identity will be completely protected. If the deception has sufficient public interest and the FTC is the appropriate authority to tackle the job, your obligation is ended. The FTC will take over the matter from that point on. You will, of course, be advised of what disposition is made of your application for FTC action.

What kinds of action might the FTC take? Depending on the gravity of the law violation, it could be settled by the violator giving FTC assurance and evidence that the improper act would be immediately discontinued. (And this would be no empty assurance because the violator would be in no doubt that a second offense would bring quick formal action.) The FTC, however, might well decide the violation was too serious to be settled by such an assurance of discontinuance, in which case it would issue a formal complaint looking to the issuance of a cease-and-desist order forever prohibiting the respondent from engaging in the illegal act. Should the order be violated thereafter, the FTC would bring action in court seeking a fine of up to $5,000 per day for each violation of the order.

Thus, the FTC provides you, the consumer, with a final defense against many instances of deception in the marketplace. But it is important to remember that you can do a great deal for yourself by following this advice:

1. Shop more before you buy.
2. Bring your complaint first to the seller.
3. Report false advertising to the media carrying it.
4. Report deception to local organizations concerned with better business standards.
5. Write the facts to the Federal Trade Commission.

ANNOTATED BIBLIOGRAPHY

BOOKS

Bibliographical Data	*Annotation*
Bartels, Robert (ed.), *Ethics in Business*, Bureau of Business Research, Ohio State, Columbus, 1963. 135 pp.*	Lectures given to a graduate seminar. Excellent for general background. Includes The History of Ethics in American Business and The Problems of Ethics in Business.
Bowen, Howard R., *Social Responsibilities of the Businessman*, Harper & Row, 1953. 259 pp.*	Somewhat dated, but still interesting. Chapters on Why Are Businessmen Concerned about Their Social Responsibilities? and The Businessman's Conception of His Social Responsibilities.
Bunting, J. Whitney (ed.), *Ethics for Modern Business Practice*, Prentice-Hall, 1953. 261 pp.	Dated, but good sections on Ethics in Chain Store Operation, Ethical Practice in Labor Organization, Ethics and Insurance, and Ethics and the College Program.
Bursk, Edward C. (ed.), *Business and Religion: A New Depth Dimension in Management*, Harper & Row, 1959. 212 pp.	Twelve chapters, each by a different author. Includes Capitalism and Christianity and Cynicism and Managerial Morality.
Conference on Consumer Protection in California, San Francisco State College, 1962, *Proceedings*, San Francisco State College Consumer Research Institute, 1962. 183 pp.	Good sections on Credit Unions in California, State Regulation of Insecticides, Deceptive Packaging, and Small Loans.
DeMente, Boye, *Japanese Manners and Ethics in Business*, East Asia Publishing Co., Tokyo, 1960. 179 pp.	By the editor of *Oriental America* magazine. Chapters on The Importance of Face, The Myth of Politeness, Business Is Not God in Japan, Why Do the Japanese Copy? Excellent coverage.
Dempsey, J. R., S.J., *Ethics for Decision Making*, University of Detroit, 1965. 181 pp.	Chapters on Religion and Ethics, Fairness, Morality and Economics, Justice and Charity.
Drinker, Henry S., *Legal Ethics*, Columbia, 1953. 448 pp.	Excellent, detailed, and specific coverage of legal ethics, including disciplinary proceedings, "quickie" divorces, "collusive" divorces, lawyer's fees, defense of one known to be

* Indicates bibliography.

BOOKS (*continued*)

Bibliographical Data	Annotation
	guilty, etc. A table of cases and committee decisions.
Fagothey, Austin, *Right and Reason: Ethics in Theory and Practice*, C. V. Mosby Co., 3rd ed., 1963. 480 pp.*	Good for philosophical background. Chapters on truthfulness (as it relates to speech), the good as end, and rights and duties.
Fuller, John G., *The Gentlemen Conspirators: The Story of the Price-Fixers in the Electrical Industry*, Grove Press, 1962. 224 pp.	A blow-by-blow account of the prosecution of price fixing in the electrical industry—particularly General Electric and Westinghouse. A very interesting book.
Garrett, Thomas M., *Ethics in Business*, Sheed and Ward, 1963. 181 pp.	Bibliographies at end of chapters. Excellent approach—chapters on Honesty and Truthfulness, The World of the Expense Account, Business Power over Public Opinion, and Professions, Associations and Codes.
Garrett, Thomas M., *An Introduction to Some Ethical Problems of Modern American Advertising*, Gregorian University, 1961. 180 pp.*	Sections on the Ethics of Persuasion. Excellent bibliography, including bibliographies, codes of ethics, books, pamphlets, articles, unpublished materials. Chapters on The Ethics of Consumption and The Power of Advertising. A thesis.
Goodman, Walter, *All Honorable Men*, Little, Brown, 1963. 342 pp.	An account of the scandals in business and politics during the past ten years. Each case examined for its relationship to American society.
Greenwood, William T., *Issues in Business and Society*, Houghton Mifflin, 1964. 545 pp.*	Part V, Ethics, Religion, and Business, has readings on Ethical Aspects of Business Practice and Business and Religion with two cases appended. There are also readings on the ethics of public relations and the businessman in politics.
Hall, Cameron P. (ed.), *On The Job Ethics*, National Council of Churches, 1963. 148 pp.	Sections on bankers, building contractors, top business executives, labor, and public relations. Case studies given.
Hodges, Luther H., *The Business Conscience*, Prentice-Hall, 1963. 250 pp.	Written for popular consumption. Excellent source. Sections on The Ethics of Fair Competition, Business and the

BOOKS (*continued*)

Bibliographical Data	Annotation
	Public, The Value of Ethical Codes, and Good Ethics Start at the Top.
Institute of Practitioners in Advertising, *Subliminal Communication*, 44 Belgrave Square, London, S.W.1, 1958. 32 pp.*	Excellent bibliography. Report of a committee established in December, 1957. Available Harvard and Florida libraries, this country.
Johnson, Harold L., *The Christian as a Businessman*, Association Press for National Board of the Y.M.C.A., 1964. 188 pp.	Cases for the affirmative and the negative on Can the Christian Be in Business? and Why is the Christian in Business? Philosophical.
Johnston, Herbert L., *Business Ethics*, Pitman, 2nd rev. ed., 1961. 300 pp.	Surveys the entire field. Rich in examples and case histories. Chapters on Speech: Its Use and Abuse, and an introductory chapter on defining ethics. Good index.
Key, V. O., Jr., *Politics, Parties, and Pressure Groups*, Crowell, 3rd ed., 1953. 799 pp.	Pages 17–21 deal with Politics and Ethics; pages 479–509 deal with Campaign Techniques, including campaign organization, theory of propaganda, art and strategy of campaigning, channels of propaganda and effect of campaigns.
McGuire, Joseph W., *Business and Society*, McGraw-Hill, 1963. 304 pp.	Chapter 14, pages 271–291, deals with Goals, Values, and Ethics in a Business World.
Milbrath, Lester W., *The Washington Lobbyists*, Rand McNally, 1963. 398 pp.*	Includes sections on Entertainment and Parties, Direct and Indirect Bribery, and Can a Decision Be Stolen or Bought? Very readable.
Mitchell, John E., *The Christian in Business*, Fleming H. Revell, 1962. 156 pp.	A personal account by a business executive of how Christianity and business may work together. Good case histories and examples.
Mitford, Jessica, *The American Way of Death*, Simon and Schuster, 1963. 320 pp.*	A discussion of the ethics of undertakers. Includes chapters on God's Little Million-Dollar Acre, Shroudland Revisited, and The "Nosy" Clergy. Well-documented, challenging account.
Mollenhoff, Clark R., *Despoilers of Democracy*, Doubleday, 1965. 411 pp.	Chapters on Capital Corrosion, The "Honor Code" in Practice, Stockpile

BOOKS (continued)

Bibliographical Data	Annotation
	of Scandal, Lying in State (and Defense), and "This Sordid Situation."
Nossiter, Bernard D., Mythmakers: An Essay on Power and Wealth, Houghton Mifflin, 1964. 244 pp.	Chapter 4, Of Consciences and Kings, provides a good philosophical discussion of the attitudes on ethics in business. Discusses several interesting cases, including the gold situation as related to the Ford Motor Company and American Motors and Romney.
Ogilvy, David, Confessions of an Advertising Man, Atheneum, 1964. 164 pp.	Written in the first person by a Madison Avenue advertising man on such subjects as Should Advertising Be Abolished? and How to Make Good Television Commercials. Entertaining.
Pease, Otis, The Responsibilities of American Advertising, Yale, 1958. 232 pp.*	Excellent chapters on The Weapons of Persuasion, National Advertising and the Good Life, and Public Pressures. Bibliographical essay.
Peterson, Theodore, Magazines in the Twentieth Century, University of Illinois, 1956. 484 pp.	Good chapter on Advertising: Its Growth and Effects.
Quinn, Francis X. (ed.), Ethics, Advertising and Responsibility, Canterbury Press, Westminster, Md., 1963. 165 pp.	Chapters on Advertising of Drugs to the Public: Ethical and Social Considerations; the Moral Imperatives of Television; Ethics and Advertising in the Press; and Ethical and Social Responsibility of Advertising. List of Addresses and Associations. Excellent for over-all picture of advertising.
Schramm, Wilbur, The Process and Effects of Mass Communications, University of Illinois, 1954. 562 pp.*	A collection of essays, including chapters by Merton on Mass Persuasion: The Moral Dimension, and by Lerner on Effective Propaganda: Conditions and Evaluation. Excellent for basic study of communication in all areas.
Schramm, Wilbur, Responsibility in Mass Communications, Harper & Row, 1957. 365 pp.	Part III deals with the Ethics in Mass Communication and Part IV with the Responsibility in Mass Communication. An excellent philosophical discussion.
Selekman, Benjamin M., A Moral Philosophy for Management, McGraw-Hill, 1959. 219 pp.	Part I deals with Moral Responsibility and Its Implications, with the opening section on Business in Search of a

BOOKS (continued)

Bibliographical Data	Annotation
	Moral Philosophy, and Part VI concerns itself with Wanted: A Moral Framework including a section on Abuse and Needed Legislation.
Selekman, Sylvia K., and Benjamin M. Selekman, *Power and Morality in a Business Society*, McGraw-Hill, 1956. 192 pp.	Written for popular consumption. Part I is entitled The Technical "Must" Versus the Ethical "Ought."
Smith, George Albert, *Business, Society, and the Individual*, Richard D. Irwin, Homewood, Ill., 1962. 736 pp. Critical bibliography.	Pages 42–73 deal with How Ethical are Businessmen? Part E discusses the value to the public of pressure selling.
Smith, Ralph Lee, *The Bargain Hucksters*, Crowell, 1962. 216 pp.	Very interesting survey of gimmicks in advertising, including Trickery by Mail, Following the Hearse, Car Buyer, Beware! and The New Smooth Sell and How It Works.
Spurrier, William Atwell, *Ethics and Business*, Scribner, 1962. 179 pp.	Written in letter form. Philosophical. Interesting.
Thompson, Stewart, *Management Creeds and Philosophies*, American Management Association, 1958. 127 pp.	Includes a survey of company creeds, an evaluation of the creed, case-study interviews on creeds, and selected examples of company creeds.
Towle, Joseph W. (ed.), *Ethics and Standards in American Business*, Houghton Mifflin, 1964. 315 pp.	A publication of the School of Business and Public Administration of Washington University. The publication of a symposium. An excellent survey. Chapters on the Protestant, Catholic, and Jewish attitudes toward ethics. Includes codes of ethics and a business ethics check list.
Weir, Walter, *Truth in Advertising and Other Heresies*, McGraw-Hill, 1963. 216 pp.	Written for popular consumption. Chapters on Truth in Advertising, Image Building, and Advertising and Politics.
Wirtenberger, Henry J., *Morality and Business*, Loyola University, 1962. 307 pp.	Author taught course for 10 years at University of Detroit on Morality and Business. Good chapters on How Do We Tell Right from Wrong, Veracity in Human Communications, and Justice in Buying and Selling. Good case histories.

ANNOTATED BIBLIOGRAPHY

PERIODICALS

Periodical	Author	Title, Date	Annotation
Advanced Management Journal	G. D. Fitzpatrick	Good business and good ethics. 30:23–29; Oct., 65.	Frank discussion of the dilemma Christianity presents to the businessman.
Advertising Age		AFA, AAW, ABBB okay nine-point ad ethics code. 35:4; Dec. 14, 64.	Nine-point code condemns disparagement of competitors, bait advertising, false claims, and exaggerated statements.
		Urge for self-respect, not fear, leads admen to police own industry; Commerce Dept.'s ad advisory unit issues long-awaited report. 35:1; June 15, 64.	An evaluation of the Commerce Department's report, *Self-Regulation in Advertising*.
		What's ethical for admen? What is proper conduct in these cases? Deciding may be harder than you think. 35:107, 110; Oct. 19, 64. Discussion, 35: 29–30; Dec. 21, 64.	Cases where proper action from an ethical standpoint in advertising is not easily decided upon.
America	J. W. Clark	Is business socially responsible? *110*: 250–252; Feb. 22, 64.	Should businesses be socially responsible. Pros and cons well supported.
	R. Baumhart	Ethics and Catholic businessmen.	Profile of the 228 Catholics

PERIODICALS (continued)

Periodical	Author	Title, Date	Annotation
		106:436–438; Jan. 6, 62. 106:589–591; Feb. 3, 62. 107:47–52; Apr. 14, 62.	who responded to the 1961 survey made by the *Harvard Business Review*.
American Economic Review	C. E. Warne	The influence of ethical and social responsibilities on advertising and selling practices. 51, no. 2:527–539; May, 61.	Describes five areas where criticism of advertising has taken place: deceptive designations of quality; fictitious price designations; deceptive packaging; built-in obsolescence; oppressive volume and questionable standards in advertising.
Annals of the American Academy of Political and Social Science	A. S. Miller (ed.)	The ethics of business enterprise. 343:1–141; Sep., 62.	The entire issue is devoted to ethics of business. The two articles below are of particular interest to this bibliography.
	W. H. Ferry	Forms of irresponsibility. 343:65–74; Sep., 62.	False ideas of freedom of corporations lead to irresponsibility. "The seductions of public relations and advertising serve unethical ends." Must find a degree of corporate responsibility equal to modern technological society.

Periodical	Author	Title, Date	Annotation
	T. L. Thau	The Business Ethics Advisory Council: an organization for the improvement of ethical performance. 343: 128–141; Sep., 62.	The story of Secretary of Commerce Luther Hodges' Business Ethics Advisory Council, which held its first meeting January 16, 1962.
Antioch Review	Robert E. Fitch	The crisis in American morals. 25, no. 4:509–524; Winter, 65–66.	Author suggests greatest confusion about morality in our society is evidenced by the disappearance of authority, the illusion of the isolation of the individual, and in the caricature of liberty. Pithy.
Atlantic Monthly	L. Hazard	Are big business-men crooks? 208: 57–61; Nov., 61.	Historical background of legal aspects of "free enterprise," New Deal economics. Good for anti-trust.
	C. B. Randall	Free enterprise is not a hunting license. 189:38–46; Mar., 52.	Author was president of Inland Steel. Discusses the need for leadership by the American businessman. A soul-searching article by an outstanding businessman.
Changing Times	E. Peterson, R. H. Levi	Do shoppers need help from the	Peterson: Special Assistant to

PERIODICALS (continued)

Periodical	Author	Title, Date	Annotation
		government? (pro and con discussion). 18:7–12; Aug., 64.	the President for Consumer Affairs; Levi: Washington retail executive and officer of a nationwide department store chain, May Co. In question-and-answer form. Types of complaints, what the government is doing, and labeling. Interesting.
Christian Century	R. E. Gibson	Antitrust and moral confusion. 78:1331–1334; Nov. 8, 61.	Description of the effect of the General Electric scandal on the Pittsfield community, where G.E. was the one industry. Asks why the ministers did not speak out. Holt replies.
	E. J. Holt	Reply. 79:200–201; Feb. 14, 62.	
	K. Watson	The myths of the American way. 80:328–330; Mar. 13, 63.	Our economic system is no longer one in which self-interest and free enterprise operate for the good of all. Our system is not ethical, nor is it free.
Columbia Law Review		The regulation of advertising. 56:1019–1096; Nov., 56.	Eighteen separate articles. Sections on federal, state, and self-regulation.

PERIODICALS (continued)

Periodical	Author	Title, Date	Annotation
Commercial and Financial Chronicle	L. A. Lapham	Industry has obligation to help solve today's problems. 199:2340–2341; June 11, 64.	Industry had better help solve today's problems. If business doesn't help, it will have no one to blame but itself when the government takes over.
Conference Board Business Record[1]	G. J. Fuchs, G. C. Thompson	Corporate directors and business ethics. 18:31–49; Sep., 61.	Actions of boards of directors concerning legal and ethical business conduct of management executives were found to center in "conflict of interest" and adherence to anti-trust laws. Examples of resolutions, policy statements, questionnaires, survey of 130 manufacturing companies.
Conference Board Record	S. M. Mathes, G. C. Thompson	Ensuring ethical conduct in business. 1:17–27; Dec., 64.	Contains several codes, including federal government statement on gifts by contractors, and summary of policies of 186 manufacturing companies.
Consumer Bulletin		Consumers sue for defective products. 47:43; Nov., 64.	Manufacturers are legally responsible for the products they

[1] Periodical's name subsequently changed to *Conference Board Record*.

PERIODICALS (continued)

Periodical	Author	Title, Date	Annotation
			sell, if they cause bodily harm or property damage.
Consumer Reports		New era in consumer affairs; president's special assistant for consumer affairs. 29: 143–144; Mar., 64.	The background and functions of the committee, its federal agency members and the council.
		The docket: notes on government actions taken to enforce consumer protection laws (a regular feature of almost all issues).	Short case summaries of action taken by the federal, state and local officials, including the Agriculture Department, the Food and Drug Administration, and the postal service.
Controller	T. G. Higgins	Ethics for today's business society. 29:192–196; Apr., 61.	Codes are needed. Information on "gray" areas should be available. Effective policing measures are needed. Gives plan of action.
Dun's Review and Monthly Index	J. J. Friedman	Price fixing: what's the answer? 77:36–38; May, 61.	Business leaders complain that the system is too complicated; 75% feel that the electrical scandal could not happen in their companies.
Engineering News-Record		Pentagon clamps down on gifts,	Summary of Defense Depart-

PERIODICALS (*continued*)

Periodical	Author	Title, Date	Annotation
		military procurement personnel prohibited from accepting favors or entertainment from defense contractors. 173:55; Nov. 12, 64.	ment directive concerning gifts and entertainment from defense contractors.
Financial Executive	R. F. Zech	Ethics in business; the responsibility of management. 31:37–39; July, 63.	If business does not police its own ethics, the government will control them by legislation. Management must practice, not just preach, ethics.
Fortune	B. DeVoto	Why professors are suspicious of business. 43:114–115; Apr., 51.	Says that distrust stems principally from advertising. Gives examples to enforce his point. Written in popular style. Concludes that the professor's distrust is worth considering.
	Editorial	The moral history of U.S. business. 40:143–158; Dec., 49.	Gives a brief history of men and ethics in American business over the past two hundred years.
	Editorial	Price fixing case. 63:102; Mar., 61. Discussion: 63:28; Apr., 61.	Electrical case disclosed some clear breakdowns of management responsibility. Reply says laws

PERIODICALS (continued)

Periodical	Author	Title, Date	Annotation
			too chaotic so that those who wish to be ethical do not know how.
	L. Finkelstein	Businessmen's moral failure. 58: 116–117, 194; Sep., 58.	Opinions only, but good opinions
Harper's Magazine	B. Nossiter	Troubled conscience of American business; excerpt from *Myths and Mythmakers in the Modern Economy*. 227:37–43; Sep., 63. Discussion, 227:8; Nov., 63.	Until the businessmen who manage the large companies become "philosopher kings," we need decentralization, and a proper system of checks and balance.
Harvard Business Review	T. M. Hopkinson	New battleground, consumer interest. 42:97–104; Sep., 64.	Unless business becomes more receptive to consumer opinion (besides how much can be sold), government will move in to protect consumer interests. Says what business can do voluntarily.
	R. W. Austin	Code of conduct for executives: proposal addressed to the problems of individual business managers. 39: 53–61; Sep.–Oct., 61.	A lead article. An internally developed code is needed; a professional code of ethics for executives. Gives three recommendations for a successful code.

PERIODICALS (continued)

Periodical	Author	Title, Date	Annotation
	P. W. Chering-ton, R. L. Gillen	Company representative in Washington. 39:109–115; May, 61.	Summary of the duties of the company man in Washington. Gives the political side of ethics. See also *The Business Representative in Washington* (Brookings, 1962) by the same author.
	L. W. Norris	Moral hazards of an executive. 38: 72–79; Sep., 60.	An excellent summary of the problems executives face every day that require not only a sense of ethics but diplomacy as well, such as conflict of interest, freedom to disclose only part of the truth, responsibility to take blame for subordinates, and living up to the image and succeeding as well.
	B. M. Selekman	Businessmen in power. 39:95–110; Sep., 61.	The power of business will increase. With power comes the responsibiity to use that power for the good of all. Covers government, labor unions, corporate duties, and the disparity

PERIODICALS (continued)

Periodical	Author	Title, Date	Annotation
			between Judaeo-Christian morality and economic reality.
Journal of Accountancy	H. M. Turnburke	Ethics examination for CPA candidates. 109: 70–72; Apr., 60.	Florida's State Board of Accountancy shocked to find that 38% of applicants for licensing failed one or more of the ethical questions asked.
Journal of Business	R. C. Brooks, Jr.	Neglected approach to ethical business behavior. 37:192–194; Apr., 64.	Many different approaches suggested. Suggests that a voluntary breaking down of powerful units can be an ethical act superior to using marked power wisely.
	A. Lentz, II. Tschirgi	Ethical content of annual reports. 36:387–393; Oct., 63.	Analysis of 219 annual reports of business firms reveals that many businesses show a concern for their customers, stockholders, employees, and community that is not entirely economic.
Journal of Communication	E. J. Kottman	Semantic evaluation of misleading advertising. 14: 151–156; Sep., 64.	Experimental study designed to test concept of "misleading advertising." Concludes that

PERIODICALS (continued)

Periodical	Author	Title, Date	Annotation
			it does not mean same thing to all people.
Nation	F. J. Cook	Corrupt society; with foreword by the editors. *196*: 453–497; June 1, 63.	Good on case histories, electrical scandal, TV quiz shows. Detailed account of packaging, highway contracting, embezzling, burglarizing by policemen, backstabbing by executives on the way up, expense accounts, call-girls, student cheating, Billie Sol Estes.
New Republic	T. K. Quinn	Corporation conscience. *144*: 11–12; June 5, 61.	There are only individual consciences which are often overruled when participating in collective behavior; no solution except greater role for federal government.
Printer's Ink	P. R. Dixon, E. W. Kintner	Will self-regulation work? Two views at AFA meeting. 275:13; June 2, 61.	Dixon says that tough policing by government is the backbone of voluntary compliance with the law; Kintner says individuals are doing a good job with self-regulation;

PERIODICALS (continued)

Periodical	Author	Title, Date	Annotation
			federal government must be fair as well as firm.
		Sales ethics; truth and taste needed? 279:25–28; June 1, 62.	A clean-cut policy statement by management, indoctrination of salesmen, and meticulous controls needed to solve problems of ethical salesmanship. Steps taken by G.E. and Westinghouse to clean house.
Redbook	S. Blum	Honesty and dishonesty. 124:46–48; Dec., 64.	Results of questionnaire mailed to several thousand. Respondents reacted to cases of malpractice by checking "I wouldn't blame him a bit," "I don't like this," etc. Reactions interesting.
Sales Management	B. Mills	Should you blow the whistle on your competitor? 88:37–40; Apr. 20, 62.	Should a businessman report to the Federal Trade Commission any illegal acts of competitors? FTC's chairman P. R. Dixon says yes; most executives cautious; because of "gray" areas in federal regu-

Periodical	Author	Title, Date	Annotation
			lations, they are living in glass houses.
		The business inquisition; why it's happening; what must be done. 86:35–38; May 19, 61.	Factors in rising resentment against many business practices. Degree of government regulation inversely related to degree of self-regulation imposed by business.
University of Washington Business Review	J. Fletcher	Situational ethics: a note for business management. 20: 18–32; Oct., 60.	Says pietism, moralism, legalism are folk attitudes which corrupt effort to apply ethical standards to decision-making in business. Judge each situation separately. Challenging.
Vital Speeches	Henry Ford II	Business ethics in 1961. 27:454–457; May 15, 61.	Given before Minnesota Junior Chamber of Commerce. A thoughtful comment on recent scandals in business.
	S. J. Insalata	Deceptive business practices; address Feb. 21, 63, Annual Dinner, Better Business Bureau of Beloit, Wis. 29:473–475; May 15, 63.	Outlines some areas of remedial action open to industry and to state and federal law.

ANNOTATED BIBLIOGRAPHY

DOCUMENTS[1]

Source	Annotation
"Are We Swatting Flies or Draining the Swamp in the Sherman Adams Case?" *Congressional Record*, 85th Congress, 2nd session, Vol. 104, Part 9, June 24, 1958, pp. 12001–12006.	An exposition by Senator Neuberger on the Sherman Adams case.
House Concurrent Resolution No. 175, 85th Congress, 2nd session, "Proposing a Code of Ethics for Government Service."	Introduced to Senate, July 10, 1958, C.R., Vol. 104, Part 10. Passed by Senate, July 11, 1958, C.R., Vol. 104, Part 10. One of many efforts to establish a code of ethics for all governmental employees.
Congressional Record, Index, 85th Congress, 2nd session (1958), Vol. 104, Part 16, pp. 225–226.	This index cites a long list of speeches, bills, editorials, and resolutions concerning ethics, including an address by Edward R. Murrow (A6695) and an article by Richard Nixon (A6168). This series of sources is excellent and too detailed to cite here.
Donald E. Hayhurst, *Protection of Consumers in West Virginia*, Bureau for Government Research, West Virginia University, 1959. 43 pp.	An example of a state pamphlet. Discusses consumer problems, West Virginia laws, and enforcement agencies. Points to omissions in state laws concerning adulterated drugs, misbranded foods. West Virginia only state without meat inspection laws.
"Ethics in Congress and the Regulating Agencies," *Congressional Record*, 86th Congress, 2nd session, Vol. 106, Part 5, Mar. 22, 1960, pp. 6256–6260.	A dialogue about ethics in government between Senator Proxmire and the House Committee on Interstate and Foreign Commerce.
"Law Can Help Improve Ethical Conduct of Public Officials," *Congressional Record*, 86th Congress, 2nd session, Vol. 106, Part 5, Mar. 28, 1960, pp. 6665–6666.	A reprint of an article by William S. White from the Washington *Evening Star* of Mar. 23, '60, entitled, "Honesty Not Induced by Laws—Codes of Behavior for Public Officials Described as Likely to be Futile."
"Nomination of James R. Durfee to be Associate Judge of the U.S. Court	A general discussion of ethics led by Senator Proxmire of Wisconsin, pro-

[1] Chronologically arranged.

DOCUMENTS (continued)

Source	Annotation
of Claims," *Congressional Record*, 86th Congress, 2nd session, Vol. 106, Part 6, Apr. 10, 1960, pp. 8164–8188.	voked by reports that Durfee had accepted hospitality from airlines while chairman of the C.A.B. The discussion includes excerpts from the Washington *Post*, a reprint of "The Age of Payola" by William Attwood from *Look*, and "A Study of Gratuities and the Public Employee" done by the Library of Congress for Senator Proxmire.
"A Public Interest Code for American Business," *Congressional Record*, 87th Congress, 1st session, Vol. 107, Part 14, Sep. 7, 1961, p. 18447.	Senator Javits' speech before the N.Y. State Society of Certified Public Accountants. A recommended code of 10 points is given.
Hearings before a Subcommittee of the Committee on Commerce, U.S. Senate, 87th Congress, 2nd session, on Senate Joint Resolution 159, "Quality Stabilization," Apr. 9, 19, 25, May 24, 25, 1962. 472 pp.	The resolution would have amended the Federal Trade Commission Act to promote quality and price stabilization. The owner of a brand, name, or trademark could control sales.
Code of Federal Regulations, Title 3, The President, 1959–1963 Compilation.	Memorandum of May 2, 1963, Presenting Conflicts of Interest on the Part of Special Government Employees (annotated), 834–848. Memorandum of May 21, 1963, Standards of Conduct for Employee Organizations and Code of Fair Labor Practices, 848–854. Memorandum of February 9, 1962, Preventing Conflict of Interest on the Part of Advisers and Consultants to the Government (annotated), 818–827. Executive Order 10939, To Provide a Guide on Ethical Standards to Government Officials, 469–470.
Advertising Advisory Committee to the Secretary of Commerce, *Self-Regulation in Advertising*, U.S. Department of Commerce, 1964. 105 pp.	Says there are four main types of self-regulation: by individual advertisers, by individual industries, by advertising trade groups, and by advertising media. Excellent discussion of how each type is operating. Very specific, e.g., shows how the Chicago *Daily News* and *Sun-Times* self-regulate

DOCUMENTS *(continued)*

Source   Annotation

their advertising in such areas as trusses, tear-gas protective devices, books for adults, free health lectures, and mushroom growing. Strong statistically.

Secretary of Defense, "Standards of Conduct," *Cumulative Pocket Supplement to the Code of Federal Regulations as of January 1, 1965*, Title 32, National Defense, Part 137, U.S. Government Printing Office, 1965.

Details the new, stringent regulations pertaining to personnel under the Secretary of Defense. Discusses gratuities, conflict of interest, regulations concerning advisors and consultants, and other factors concerning defense employees.

Annual Report of the Federal Trade Commission, 1965. U.S. Government Printing Office, n.d. 64 pp.

Survey of all activities of the Commission. Excellent for perspective on hearings and litigations.

MATERIALS AVAILABLE FOR PURCHASE[1]

The Advertising Association, 1 Bell Yard, London, W.C.2, England
The British Code of Advertising Practice.
British Code of Standards—The Advertising of Medicines and Treatments.
How Advertising Disciplines Itself. 1s 6d
Advertising Investigation Department leaflets (write for list): *The Hair; Advertising for Slimming; Advertising for Cosmetics;* etc.

The Advertising Council, Inc., 25 West 45th St., New York, N.Y. 10036
A private, nonprofit group supported by American business and advertising. Conducts national advertising campaigns on domestic, noncontroversial problems, such as "You won't get tomorrow's jobs with yesterday's skills," "USO is there only if you care," and "Every litter bit hurts." Only the Annual Report available.

Advertising Federation of America, 655 Madison Ave., New York, N.Y. 10021
The Advertising Truth Book (Ethics). $1
Truth About Advertising series (write for list): *How Advertising Shapes Decision; How the FTC Works; Broadcast Media Programming;* etc.
Questions and Answers about Advertising.
John Crichton, President, *Why Advertising Will Have to be Better.*
AAAA, one of the series of releases known as "Repros."

American Bar Association, 1155 East 60th St., Chicago, Ill. 60637
Canons of Professional Ethics.
Canons of Judicial Ethics.

American Business Press, Inc., 205 East 42nd St., New York, N.Y. 10017
Code of Publishing Practice.

American Dental Association, 222 East Superior St., Chicago, Ill. 60611
Principles of Ethics.

The American Medical Association, 535 North Dearborn St., Chicago, Ill. 60610
Principles of Medical Ethics.

The Association of National Advertisers, Inc., 155 East 44th St., New York, N.Y. 10017
Proof-of-Performance Affidavits—Verifying Appearance of TV Commercials. $2
Using the B.A.R. Monitoring Service to Verify the Appearance of TV Commercials. $2.50
Gilbert H. Weil, *Legal Rules of the Road to Honest Advertising.*

Direct Mail Advertising Association, Inc., 230 Park Ave., New York, N.Y. 10017
Standards of Ethical Business Practice of the Direct Mail Advertising Association.

---

[1] Only representative items are listed, to demonstrate what materials are available (materials of this nature go out of print quickly). Students are urged to write for lists of releases. Items with no prices are generally free, although not necessarily so.

Adventures in Selling—18 separate direct mail case histories, $1 each (write for list), such as: #12. *Ford Motor Company: Mercury develops dealer traffic with multimillion dollar campaign to prospects.*

Federal Communications Commission, New Post Office Building, Washington, D.C. 20554

Broadcast Application and Hearing Procedures. Inf. Bulletin No. 1-B, January, 1965.

Federal Trade Commission, Washington, D.C. 20580

Antibiotics Manufacture, Economic Report on, June, 1958. $1 (Write Supt. of Govt. Docs.)

Fur Products Labeling Act, Rules and Regulations Under the, Amended May 15, 1961.

Guides. Available on a variety of subjects, such as: *Cigarette Advertising,* September, 1965; *Deceptive Pricing,* January, 1964.

Federal Trade Commission Business Advisory Service to Help Businessmen Comply with the Law.

Here Is Your Federal Trade Commission.

Trade Practice Rules. Available on a variety of subjects, such as: *Tobacco Distributing Industry,* 1962; *Residential Aluminum Siding Industry,* 1962.

National Association of Broadcasters, Public Relations Service, 1771 N St., N.W., Washington, D.C. 20036

Radio Code of Good Practices. free

The Television Code. free

Seal of Good Practice. free

National Association of Manufacturers, 277 Park Ave., New York, N.Y. 10017

Code of Business Practices.

Moral and Ethical Standards in Labor and Management.

National Association of Purchasing Agents, 11 Park Place, New York, N.Y. 10007

N.A.P.A. Standards of Conduct, officially adopted by the N.A.P.A. Executive Committee, June 11, 1959.

National Better Business Bureau, Inc., 230 Park Ave., New York, N.Y. 10017

Fact Booklets 15¢, 8 for $1.00 (write for list): *Advertising; Furs; Life Insurance; Jewelry.*

Making Self-Regulation a Reality: Report on Operations, 1964.

Deceptive Vending Machine Promotions, November, 1964.

Facts You Should Know about Your Better Business Bureau.

Outdoor Advertising Association of America, Inc., 24 West Erie St., Chicago, Ill. 60610

What You Should Know about Outdoor Advertising.

Recommended Operating Practices.

The Society for the Advancement of Management, 16 West 40th St., New York, N.Y. 10018

The Ethical Challenge of Modern Administration. 35¢

Motivation—What Makes Sammy Run? 35¢

Integrity, The Touchstone of Good Management. 35¢

SUGGESTED SPEECH SUBJECTS

Informative Speeches: Round One:
Organizations Concerned with Business Ethics

1. The Significance of the *Good Housekeeping* Seal of Approval
2. The Significance of "Commended by *Parents' Magazine* for use as advertised therein"
3. The Significance of *McCall's* "Laboratory and Use Tested"
4. The Pure Food and Drug Administration
5. The Federal Trade Commission
6. The Better Business Bureau
7. Mrs. Esther Peterson, The Assistant Secretary for Labor Standards
8. The Advertising Policies of *The New Yorker* magazine[1]
9. The Advertising Policies of the *Reader's Digest*
10. The Television Code of the National Association of Broadcasters
11. The Radio Code of Good Practices of the National Association of Broadcasters
12. The Standards of Ethical Business Practice of the Direct Mail Advertising Association
13. The Recommended Operating Practices of the Outdoor Advertising Association of America
14. The Advertising Acceptability Department of The New York *Times*
15. The Advertising Federation of America (AFA)
16. The Association of National Advertisers (ANA)
17. The American Association of Advertising Agencies (AAAA)
18. Recommended Standards of Practice for Advertising and Selling Automobiles of the National Automobile Dealers' Association
19. Self-Regulation by the Liquor Industry
    The Distilled Spirits Institute, Its Self-Imposed Restrictions
    The Standards of Advertising of the U.S. Brewer's Association
    The Statement of Advertising Principles of the Wine Institute
20. The National Association of Purchasing Agents Standards of Conduct
21. The Principles of Ethics of the American Dental Association
22. The Canons of Ethics of the American Bar Association
23. Principles of Medical Ethics of the American Medical Association
24. The 1957 AFL-CIO Ethical Practices Code
25. The 1950 National Association of Manufacturers Code of Moral and Ethical Standards

Informative Speeches: Round Two: Areas of Unethical Practices

26. The Art of Deceptive Packaging
27. The Advertising Tactics of Small Loan Companies
28. The Actual Rate of Interest Charged by Small Loan Companies
29. The Television Quiz Show Scandals of 1959

---

[1] Write for "A Code of Publishing Practice," The New Yorker, 25 West 45th St., New York, N.Y. 10036.

30. The Use of "Less Than a Dollar" ($1.99, $2.98) Prices in Salesmanship
31. The Methods by Which Collusion of Prices Was Effected in the Electrical Industry in 1961
32. Ethics in Selling Insurance
33. "Quickie" Divorces
34. "Collusive" Divorces
35. The Ethics of the Expense Account
36. Unethical Practices During the Recent Presidential Campaign
37. Lavish Entertainment by the Washington Lobbyist
38. Legislation Pertaining to Washington Lobbyists
39. The Strange Language of the American Undertaker
40. How the Grieved Are Pressured into Lavish Funeral Costs
41. Advertising by Patent Drug Companies
42. Trickery by Mail
43. The Tactics of the Automobile Salesman
44. Recent Legislation Affecting the Tobacco Industry
45. Fraudulent Real Estate Advertising
46. The Damage Suits by State and Private Companies against the Electrical Industry Following the Convictions of 1961
47. Thalidomide, Was Its Release Unethical?
48. Madison Avenue, the "Home" of the Advertising Industry
49. Pressure-Selling Tactics by the Door- to-Door Salesman
50. The Soliciting of Funds by Agencies Whose Charitable Nature Can be Challenged

Informative Speeches: Round Three: General

51. Biblical Statements Concerning Usury
52. Protestant Attitudes Toward Ethical Practices in Business
53. Roman Catholic Attitudes Toward Ethical Practices in Business
54. Jewish Attitudes Toward Ethical Practices in Business
55. Japanese Attitudes Toward Ethical Practices in Business
56. Morality in Labor Relations
57. The *Consumer Bulletin* (monthly)
58. The Code of Ethics of Professor Robert W. Austin of Harvard University
59. The Baumhart Survey of Business Ethics Reported in the *Harvard Business Review*
60. The *Consumer Bulletin Annual* (yearly)
61. *Consumer Reports* (monthly)
62. The *Buying Guide* Issue of *Consumer Reports* (yearly)
63. The Fair Trade Laws
64. The Denver Better Business Truth Emblem Plan of 1961
65. The "Truth-in-Advertising" Law in the State of ———
66. President Johnson's Committee on Consumer Interests
67. The Volume of Advertising in the United States
68. The Ethics of Subliminal Advertising
69. National Legislation Pertaining to Advertising
70. The Ethics of Mass Communications

71. The Ethics of the American Labor Union
72. Speech: Its Use and Abuse in Advertising
73. The Consumer Packaging Bill Sponsored by Senator Philip Hart of Michigan
74. The Robinson-Patman Act
75. United States v. Aluminum Company of America (148 F. 2nd 416)

Informative Speeches: Round Four:
Investigations by the Federal Trade Commission[2]

76. [1952] Benrus Watch Company (establishment of prices)
77. [1952] C. Howard Hunt Pen Company (14-carat gold pen points)
78. [1952] National Health Aids, Incorporated (drugs as food)
79. [1955] Drew and Company, Incorporated (oleomargarine as butter)
80. [1955] Reddi-Spred Company (oleomargarine as butter)
81. [1956] Carter Products (Carter's Little Liver Pills)
82. [1956] Travelers Health Association (terms and conditions of insurance)
83. [1957] Loesch Hair Experts (baldness, hair care)
84. [1957] VitaSafe Corporation (additional shipment of capsules)
85. [1958] Double Eagle Refining Company (reclaimed oil)
86. [1959] Drug Research Corporation (the Regimen case—"calories don't count")
87. [1959] Liggett and Myers Tobacco Company (sales promotion)
88. [1960] Exposition Press Corporation (royalties)
89. [1961] Colgate-Palmolive Corporation (the sandpaper shave)
90. [1961] Helbros Watch Company (sales promotion)
91. [1962] Carter Products (Rise shaving cream)
92. [1962] Mary Carter Paint Company (durability of paint)
93. [1962] Mueller (price discrimination)
94. [1964] National Bakers Services, Incorporated (Hollywood diet bread)
95. [1965] Brite Manufacturing Company (failure to disclose foreign origin)
96. [1965] Libbey-Owens-Ford (the GM case—no glass in the windshield)
97. [1965] Stauffer Laboratories, Incorporated (exercising device)
98. [1964] Merck & Company, Inc. (complaint, television advertising of throat lozenges)
    [1965] initial order to cease and desist
    [1966] final order to cease and desist
99. [1958] Borden Company (complaint, no differentiation of labels)
    [1963] final order to cease and desist
    [1964] Court of Appeals sets aside order to cease and desist
    [1966] Supreme Court reverses Court of Appeals, remands
100. [1959] Fred Meyer, Inc. (complaint, price discrimination in hosiery)

[2] Initial research may be begun under the following headings:

Business Periodicals Index	Readers' Guide
Television Advertising, Ethics	Advertising, Fraudulent
Television Advertising, Fraudulent	Advertising, Ethics
Advertising, Fraudulent	Trade Cases (Chicago: Commerce
Advertising, Ethics	Clearing House, yearly)

Federal Trade Commission Decisions; Findings, Orders, and Stipulations (Washington, yearly)

[1963] final order to cease and desist

[1966] Court of Appeals upholds Trade Commission

Note: At the time this book went to press, the government document entitled *Federal Trade Commission Decisions* had been published through 1962. Therefore, all complaints and orders to cease and desist before 1962 may be found in those volumes. Those after 1962 may be found in the *Federal Register*. Also, FTC complaints and orders to cease and desist issued after 1962 may be located by using the *Trade Regulation Reporter Transfer Binders* for 1961–1963 or 1963–1965 and by using *CCH Topical Law Reports* in looseleaf binders for 1966. Cases on which orders to cease and desist have been followed by litigation in the Court of Appeals or in the Supreme Court can have court rulings located by using the *CCH Trade Cases*. Reference to the official case as published by the Government Printing Office may be facilitated by the government documents' librarian. All cases listed above except No. 98 are cases on which litigation has occurred, and therefore the court decisions can be secured through the *CCH Trade Cases*. Students should work their way back from the court decision to the FTC orders to cease and desist and finally to the complaint. Caution: Cases on which the FTC complaints have been issued but on which the order to cease and desist is still pending will not appear in *Federal Trade Commission Decisions* until the order to cease and desist has been issued.

Persuasive Speeches: Round One

1. The "cut-rate" drug store is an asset to a community.
2. The chain store is an asset to a community.
3. Television should solicit advertisements for hard liquor.
4. Television should abolish beer commercials.
5. State laws should require small loan companies to state to the borrower the actual yearly rate of interest.
6. Contractors and purchasing agents should be prohibited from receiving gifts from customers.
7. The Quality Stabilization Bill would result in price fixing.
8. The proposed rise in steel prices, which was curtailed by President Kennedy, was ethical and responsible, and should have been permitted.
9. The businessman must become more interested in politics in order to become more aware of consumer interests and therefore more ethical.
10. The indiscriminate use of insecticides has resulted in unethical practices.
11. When a lawyer agrees to defend a client whom he believes to be guilty, he is not committing an unethical practice.
12. The end of a business practice is more important than the means.
13. The top executives in the electrical industry were unaware of the price fixing done by their subordinates in the years before 1961.
14. Federal legislation should provide for an investigation of all identical bids submitted to the government.
15. Codes of ethics are valueless in establishing better business practices.
16. The present method of rating television programs has resulted in an unethical treatment of the American public.
17. The questionable ethics in American politics sets a poor example for ethics in business.
18. Washington lobbyists greatly control the legislation passed by Congress.

19. A good Christian can be a good businessman.
20. The American undertaker runs a highly ethical business.
21. Physicians should be permitted to advertise.
22. The prices charged by American drug companies are unethically high.
23. Cigarette advertising is not unethical.
24. Sound ethics is not only good public relations; it is also good business.
25. The best way for a young businessman to enter his profession with high ethics is to find an ethical employer.

Persuasive Speeches: Round Two

26. Price fixing is a widely accepted practice in business.
27. Testimonials as used in advertising are likely to be untruthful and therefore unethical and should be abolished.
28. College newspapers should be permitted to publish tobacco advertisements.
29. The decline in American business ethics is in keeping with a general decline of American morals.
30. Sabbaticals would permit businessmen to gain a perspective and therefore be more likely to maintain high ethical standards.
31. A business executive should be made responsible for the unethical practices of his subordinates.
32. "Cheesecake" should be abolished from advertisements.
33. The powers of the Pure Food and Drug Administration should be increased.
34. A businessman should report unethical business practices by his competitors to the appropriate governmental agency.
35. Business can impose its own regulatory practices without the assistance of further governmental legislation.
36. The Better Business Bureau is doing an excellent job of controlling unethical business practices.
37. The average used-car dealer does not hesitate to indulge in unethical practices.
38. The techniques by which the tobacco industry associates smoking with youth and health are unethical.
39. The charging of interest by Christians is irreligious.
40. Most businessmen feel that they are more ethical than businessmen in general.
41 The liquor industry has done an excellent job of self-regulation.
42. There was nothing unethical about the television quizzes of 1959 because the American public should have known that television was just putting on a good show.
43. Madison Avenue is not responsible for unethical advertising because advertisements are subject to the approval of the client.
44. The Fair Trade Laws would benefit the individual consumer.
45. The staff of the Federal Trade Commission should be substantially increased, so that it can prevent unethical practices by business.
46. The Federal Communications Commission should be permitted to withdraw the license of any radio or television station which permits fraudulent advertising.

47. The prosecutions of the electrical industry in 1961 have resulted in a definite decline in price fixing among American businessmen.
48. There is little evidence to support the charge that "call girls" are used to entertain prospective clients of businessmen.
49. The business executive is often faced with the dilemma of being ethical and losing profits or being unethical and gaining sales.
50. Chambers of Commerce have made businessmen aware of the importance of their ethical image.

Debate Propositions

1. *Resolved:* that the ethics of Christians are incompatible with business enterprise.
2. *Resolved:* that the federal government must enforce ethical practices because business is incapable of self-regulation.
3. *Resolved:* that American industry should agree on a code of ethics and hire its own staff to make certain that the code is enforced.
4. *Resolved:* that cigarette advertising should be abolished.
5. *Resolved:* that the general tenor of ethics of the American businessman is commendable.
6. *Resolved:* that the powers of the Federal Communications Commission should be increased so that it can withdraw the license of any station convicted of using fraudulent advertising.
7. *Resolved:* let the buyer beware!
8. *Resolved:* that the only way to make business ethical is to abolish the profit motive.
9. *Resolved:* that lobbying should be greatly curtailed.
10. *Resolved:* that the neglect of national advertising by the Hershey Company proves that a good product will sell itself.

Discussion Subjects

1. How can the business community properly balance the profit motive with consumer interests?
2. To what extent is a businessman responsible for the unethical practices of his subordinates?
3. Is Judaism (or Christianity) incompatable with capitalism?
4. Are codes of ethics of value to American business?
5. Is it ethical to insert sex artificially into an advertisement?
6. What are the more common unethical practices in American business, and how can they be eliminated?
7. Would a watchdog committee appointed by American industry be successful in enforcing more ethical practices?
8. Can improved legislation make business more ethical?
9. What is the significance of the convictions in 1961 of executives of the electrical industry?
10. To what extent are the advertisements in the "pulp" magazines unethical?

III

TEACHER
EDUCATION

SELECTED READINGS

THE AREA OF TEACHER EDUCATION is very broad; thus the material included in this unit covers a wide area. There is much more to training the teacher than the academic subjects he takes. To begin with, the caliber of persons attracted to teaching affects teacher education, so that the recruitment procedures, salaries, and the status of the profession are relevant to this unit. Second, the college in which the teacher trainee enrolls and its curriculum are highly important to his training, so that the complete spectrum of the student's college life is also relevant. Third, the relationship between the teacher and the several accrediting agencies forms a facet of teacher training. This means that the way in which the teacher is initially accredited and how he maintains that accreditation through short courses, institutes, and advanced degrees pertains to teacher education. Indeed, attracting the proper persons into the profession and keeping them proficient once they have become teachers seems more important than the four or five years of college work they take as undergraduates.

Students are encouraged to interview administrators and professors at their colleges to supplement their library research. They should take advantage of their visits home and to other communities to consult with school superintendents, principals, teachers, and public officials. They should seek out the persons responsible for teacher institutes, for teacher accreditation, and for teacher curriculums, and consult them first hand. Observation of classes in progress at the university and of student teachers at work should be of major assistance. The student should try to attend the regional and state meetings of the teachers' associations. By such personal contact with his subject, the student will make this unit become as vital and real as it deserves to be.

Every effort has been made to include material on both sides of controversial issues. The editors of this manual have not taken sides. It must be said, however, that the critics of the status quo seem to write more vigorously and more interestingly than its defenders. Any bias that may be detected, therefore, must be attributed to the research materials available.

THE ACADEMIC PREPARATION
OF SECONDARY SCHOOL TEACHERS

The Reports of Four Committees of the Twenty-nine College Cooperative Plan

───── ▸◄◆►◄ ─────

INTRODUCTION

These four reports have the aim of offering to prospective secondary school teachers a guide to appropriate preparation in the subjects they are planning to teach. The four committees which drafted the documents suggest, rather than prescribe, and while they make no claims exhaustively to have studied their topics, they hope their efforts will serve for the present to offer guidance to students who are considering careers in teaching and to colleges which wish to provide sound undergraduate academic preparation for future teachers.

The authors of these reports are professors at member colleges of the Twenty-nine College Cooperative Plan, a group of northeastern liberal arts colleges and universities which joined together in 1952 for the purpose of encouraging students into careers in teaching, particularly in elementary and secondary schools.[1] Representing principally four-year liberal arts colleges without professional schools of Education, the Plan has retained close contact with a variety of fifth-year graduate training programs, especially

The Academic Preparation of Secondary School Teachers, Harvard University Press, 1962, pp. i–iv, 1–24. Reprinted by permission of the publisher, distributor for the Harvard Graduate School of Education.

[1] The members, now totalling thirty, are: Amherst, Barnard, Bates, Bennington, Bowdoin, Brandeis, Brown, Bryn Mawr, Colby, Colgate, Connecticut College, Dartmouth, Hamilton, Harvard, Haverford, Holy Cross, Lafayette, Massachusetts Institute of Technology, Middlebury, Mount Holyoke, Pembroke, Radcliffe, Sarah Lawrence, Simmons, Smith, Swarthmore, Vassar, Wellesley, Wheaton, and Williams. It should be noted that the reports that follow are endorsed by the individuals representing these colleges, not the college governing boards as a whole.

Master of Arts in Teaching programs and similar plans for prospective elementary school teachers. The Plan, which originated through the initiative of various members of the Harvard faculty, has been closely allied with the fifth-year programs at Cambridge, and representatives meet annually at Harvard to discuss problems and decide policy. At the 1961 meeting of this group the suggestion to draft the following reports was made. Undergraduates interested in secondary school teaching had continually asked their advisers in the colleges to suggest relevant programs of preparation. The college representatives therefore decided that a published guide available to students would be desirable. The question faced by the four committees appointed by the representatives was simply this: in your judgment, what should be the course of study for a prospective secondary school teacher in order best to prepare himself in his discipline, if one assumes four years of undergraduate work and a fifth, graduate year of training? The four committees each met several times during 1961 and 1962; their findings were discussed by a general meeting of college representatives and committee members at Cambridge in January, 1962. Revisions were then made, and a final draft was prepared in the spring of the same year.

A number of cautions should be entered at the start. By suggesting studies for prospective teachers which are organized in a five-year sequence, the members of the Plan are not necessarily endorsing the general notion that all teachers need as much (or as little) as five years of preparation. They are suggesting studies within a five-year framework because this is a common one, if not the only one, that is reasonable and realistic for their particular students, organized as their several colleges are. Members agree that they have no particular brief for the Master of Arts in Teaching programs or for any others, and that, with the lack of evidence of any "best" way of preparing teachers, they favor a variety of entrees into teaching.

Another caution is that these committees are not designing programs for college "majors." They are, rather, stating minimal goals in as general language as possible. They feel that students and their colleges need variety for vigor, and that a too strict program might be stultifying.

Most important is the caution that the contents of these reports are tentative. The committees were made up of distinguished men and women; the reports are the opinions of these scholars, debated and refined. But in no way were the activities of the committees full-scale investigations, and in no way do they wish their suggestions to be considered the be-all and the end-all of teacher preparation. As the various footnoted objections within the reports show, there were differences of opinion; these were recorded, not resolved. The lack of appendices, statistical summaries, and the solicited opinions of high school teachers is evidence of the limited and tentative nature of these reports. The four documents represent the best current advice from experienced college teachers who are deeply concerned with their responsibility to prepare secondary school teachers.

Cautious though the members of the Twenty-nine College group may be, they were emphatic at their meetings on several common points. All four committees underscored the essential requirement of a liberal education. A clear definition of this now hackneyed phrase did not emerge from these documents any more than it has from the pens of other proponents, but the committees' intent was clear. All prospective teachers should have some acquaintance with all of the central academic disciplines and the start on a profound understanding of one or more. All should be sensitive both to the rigor of statistical analysis and to the intuition of artistic appreciation. All should have the basic skills of computation and expression. All should have been vigorously exposed to the process of logical thought and critical insight. The committees were emphatic that the *sine qua non* of all liberal education, particularly for teachers, is the ability to communicate orally and in writing. The most valuable abstract scientific finding, it was argued, is useless without its discoverer's ability to inform others of it. And at the same time it was urged that mathematics provide for the liberally educated its particular tool of analysis and communication in a form useful to society. The strong feelings of the committees on these points leave an obvious message for the liberal arts college *in toto* and not just to that portion of its students who are preparing to teach in the secondary schools.

No less important was the form in which the four committees were organized. There were not separate committees for English, the modern foreign languages, and the classics; all, rather, were joined in a single Committee on Language and Literature. While the various languages receive their due in the report, the point is clear that the problems of language and written expression are common ones across subjects now quite arbitrarily divided in American colleges and secondary schools. The word "grammar" is notable by its absence: language is conceived, by the committee, to be formal grammar and much more, a larger field that the competent teacher must grasp. The Committee on the Social Studies restyled itself History and the Social Sciences; its point was not to debate what a "science" or "social science" was but rather to affirm that *both* history and the social sciences are required in the training of a secondary school social studies teacher. Its report and the minority views appended to it are provocative in this regard. The Committee on the Natural Sciences faced a similar problem of definition since the strands of chemistry, biology, physics, and the earth sciences, with their essential unity and overlap as well as their very real specialization, are as complex as the overlaps of history, sociology, economics, and psychology.

Serious omissions, of course, are the lack of reports on art and music. The members of the Twenty-nine Colleges decided in 1961 to prepare reports only for those fields in which the overwhelming majority of their student wish to teach, but they are aware of the implications of their neglect of the arts and music. Stepchildren these subjects are in many American secondary schools, and stepchildren, the members agree, they should no longer be. Reports from committees in these fields may be prepared in later years; their absence from this present volume is not meant to imply disinterest or neglect.

What should be taught to teachers in order that they may teach children? This question, which is essentially the one dealt with by the four committees, really puts the cart before the horse: until one has decided what the children are to learn, how can one prescribe the content of teachers' preparation? This nagging question plagued all the committees as will be immediately evident: each group had to find a balance between suggestions for training for present school curricula and training for some ideal, theoretical school. Prescribe training to provide teachers for the *status quo*, and one implies unintentionally that the *status quo* is satisfactory or even desirable. Prescribe training for some ideal school, and one prescribes unrealistically and less usefully for our college students. Furthermore, decisions on the curriculum of the ideal school would take far more basic work than the assembled committees of the Twenty-nine Colleges were able to afford. Accordingly the four reports are in the form of a self-conscious and often unhappy compromise. Each committee tried not to stand pat on the *status quo*, but at the same time attempted to be realistic. The results are hardly perfect in their authors' eyes, but provide, in their view, constructive, if temporary and tentative, advice to the teachers of two or three years hence, persons now undergraduates in the cooperating colleges. The results are *not* construed to be blueprints in vague form of ideal curricula for the secondary schools.

Another problem faced by the committee members was the disorder in the structure of their various disciplines and the confusion this leaves in both secondary school and college curricula. Not only has the volume of accumulated knowledge increased, but the neat disciplinary forms in which it has been packaged are breaking down. When is physics physics and not chemistry? Where does sociology stop and history start, and where does literature overlap the latter? Suggesting realistic courses of study in the existing departments of the Twenty-nine Colleges was as difficult a venture for the committees as identifying realistic secondary school curricula for which to prepare.

With these foregoing cautions and emphases in mind, then, are the reports to be read. That they prove useful for undergraduates and their colleges is their authors' hope.

THEODORE R. SIZER

December, 1962

LANGUAGE AND LITERATURE

I. SOME PRELIMINARY CONSIDERATIONS

In order roughly to define the mandate of this committee, it is necessary first to observe that, particularly in English (the largest of the disciplines under consideration), high school teachers are drawn from institutions and programs of several different kinds. Many high school teachers of English, especially in the East, are graduated from liberal arts colleges that make no provisions for courses in pedagogy: in order to obtain certification, these graduates must spend a year in a School of Education. A larger number of teachers, particularly in the Mid- and Far West, are graduated from teachers' colleges or state universities with credit for many courses in pedagogy. (At Ohio State University, for example, all English majors planning to teach in secondary school must enroll in the School of Education.) A third group, of uncertain but increasing size, is composed of those who have had strong liberal arts training in college together with a minimal program in pedagogy (say, two or three semesters) and some practice teaching. This committee, it is clear, can concern itself only with the first and third of these groups: we address ourselves to the training of undergraduates in liberal arts colleges that may or may not offer a few courses in Education. We must accordingly assume that most students with whom we are concerned will have at least one year of post-graduate study before they begin to teach. Some of our recommendations, therefore, can be distributed over a five-year period if necessary; some of them (see "Language," below) may have to be so distributed.

This committee, in the course of its very limited deliberations, found itself more than once discussing two peripheral but important questions that arise from the situation of the liberal arts undergraduate who goes into high school teaching. The committee has neither the information required to suggest even a tentative resolution of each problem nor the time to get such information. But we believe that the questions should be posed for general, long-range consideration.

1. To what extent do honors and major programs of the liberal arts colleges so distinguish between the superior and the average student as to imply that a career in secondary school teaching is appropriate only for the second-best? Is it true that honor candidates, whether in English or a foreign language, are customarily encouraged by training and example to go on to the Ph.D. rather than the M.A.T. (Master of Arts in Teaching)? Does the pre-professional training of some honors and major programs discriminate in favor of those, especially men, whose capacities are more relevant to the scholarship and teaching of the college than of the high school?

What kinds of careers do they encourage? What discriminations among students do they make?

2. To what extent, on the other hand, is it proper or necessary to warn the woman undergraduate who wants a career in education that her chances for employment and advancement may be greatest in secondary school or junior-college teaching? Is this a problem too large—too entangled with social and economic considerations—for any academic advisory group to face? Worse, is it a problem that can only be exaggerated by public discussion?

In brief, the educational practices of some of our colleges and universities seem to encourage the promising young man to turn away from a career in high school teaching; the staffing practices of those same colleges and universities seem to discourage the promising young woman from turning to any teaching career except that in the secondary school: to put our two problems in this form is doubtless to oversimplify. But the simplification may emphasize certain features of the situation before us that qualify any confidence we may feel in the power of curricular standards and reform.

II. ENGLISH LANGUAGE AND LITERATURE

Because it involves the largest number of teachers and students, we consider first and by itself undergraduate training of the future high school teacher of English.

A. LANGUAGE

The high school teacher of English must spend a great deal of time introducing pupils to and instructing them in the language they already "know"; we therefore believe that the preparation of this teacher should include some study of the history and the structure of the English language. We are encouraged in this recommendation by recent and continuing developments in the study of linguistics. These developments, indeed, may lead to the day when all undergraduate students of language and literature may be enrolled in a general course in the structure of language from which they will severally move into courses in the history of the languages in which they are majoring—French, Russian, English, or any other. Such a course cannot arrive on any campus tomorrow, and it will be many years before most colleges can add experts in modern linguistics to their faculties. We recognize, too, the painfulness of yet one more requirement in an undergraduate curriculum, for we know well that our future high school teachers need all the time they can get to read widely and deeply in the literature they will present. It seems reasonable to us, however, that at least within the assumed five years of training (undergraduate and one year of graduate study), the future high school English teacher should be informed of the history and structure of the English language.

B. COMPOSITION

Although the high school English teacher has always been as much concerned with his student's writing as he knew how to be, the recent furor about the subject suggests that he may have to be even more deeply concerned with it in the future. It does seem clear that whether or not they must ask for more writing from their pupils, most high school teachers do not know enough about the practice of writing. It seems true, furthermore, that a good many high school teachers have had no formal training in rhetoric or general principles of composition since their freshman year in college and sometimes not since high school. The undergraduate training of the future high school English teacher must therefore include as much practice and study of composition as the curriculum can support.

To assist this general aim, we believe that all undergraduate courses in English should be strongly fortified with writing. Exactly how much formal instruction in rhetoric should be required will of course depend upon the practice of individual departments of English. Mere learning of "rules" or the arid application of "patterns" can of course do little to prepare a teacher to give effecive help to puzzled, clumsy, inarticulate high school students. On the other hand, one of the most pressing problems of the English teacher is where to learn the convention of usage and what attitude to take toward those conventions. Some training in formal rhetoric (together with the historical study of English) will assist the teacher to mediate with firmness and confidence between the increasingly widespread belief that usage is as mutable as the stock market and the belief that what is "correct" can be found only in certain models of the past. Above all, the undergraduate prospective teacher should establish for himself an awareness of the relation between his experience and his language. The more disciplined, criticized writing he can do, the sharper will be his sense of this critical relation. He must have passed through the discipline to which he will ask his students to submit.

C. LITERATURE

Most high school graduates do not want to read, do not enjoy reading, and, in short, simply do not read. Everyone can offer a set of large and important reasons for this unhappy situation, but it is possible to suggest some corrective measures within the undergraduate major program itself. Let it be said at the outset that the study of literature is, and should be, exacting. We wish to suggest that the goal of easy mastery of literature may be too common among high school teachers of literature: such a goal (many textbooks openly flaunt it) breeds contempt for books and, of course, breeds also an all-too-willing obliviousness of texts that cannot be easily mastered. Again, the notion that a work of literature can be "solved" like a cryptogram is as misleading and as stultifying as the older notion (which it has largely displaced) that the way to understand a work of literature is to find in it a moral or learn something about its author's life. This committee agrees that the undergraduate training of the future teacher should be as various as the enormously varied subject before him. The English major should be a compound of period courses, genre courses, single-figure courses. But every course must be shaped by the most relevant approach to the works it puts before its students. These students must be shown how to isolate a work so that they may meet it as fully and as openly as possible. Some works must be explained by and disengaged from special and detailed historical backgrounds. Others must be explained by and disengaged from special techniques of analysis—for example the sorting out of patterns of metaphor. Still others must be explained by and disengaged from detailed biographical information. And still others, especially many major works, must be approached by a combination of these methods. The undergraduate student of literature must experience throughout his training *both* the enormous variety *and* the traditional continuities that make his subject central in all our humanistic values. The experience of this combination cannot come about by moral exhortation alone: frequent short and incisive papers should accompany every course in the literature curriculum. Such training may not perfectly equip the future teacher to be satisfied with the material he must present, say, to pupils of the ninth grade but, even there, it should assist him to encourage in his pupils those habits of reading and attention that will keep them from sliding off the stories and other works before them into reverie or something vague called "background." We also believe that the future English teacher should know at least one foreign language well enough to teach with some awareness of idiom, etc., the translation of a work from that language.

III. FOREIGN LANGUAGE AND LITERATURE

There is of course no need to urge a stronger position for the study of language and the practice of composition (certainly at least of oral composition) in the undergraduate foreign language programs. Some achievements here, in fact, have given fresh insights and techniques to the study of English. College teachers of foreign languages, moreover, are agreed that the main emphasis of the literature courses should be not on coverage but on variety of matter and on critical approach. The so-called "century" courses may not be, as their titles suggest, a survey of all the major and minor writers; they may in fact combine genre and period simply by emphasizing for each century the most vigorous genre in it (e.g., the drama in

17th-century France). The introductory course is likely to be a survey in the conventional sense, but it must be remembered that most foreign-language departments are not large enough to offer a full range of courses each year, and the survey is the only practical way in which to give a student a sense of the span of the literature he is studying and to prepare him to enter any of the less extensive courses that can be open to him in any later year.

In general the committee believes that any foreign-language major must involve a study of literature texts. The committee also suggests that certain recent innovations in high school curricular organization strongly indicate that in the future foreign-language teachers may be called on to teach in translation those texts in the high school English (or "Humanities") courses that were originally not written in English. It is hoped that all teachers will make sure, when teaching a translation, to let their students know that the work before them *is* a translation and, it may be, not always the most perfect translation conceivable.

The study of Greek and Latin in college entails few survey courses; nearly all courses concentrate on a single figure (Ovid, Cicero, et al.). Moreover, the period in which archeology and philology were the principal concerns of teachers of the classics is probably past: historical considerations of the text are now more likely to be subordinated to literary considerations. The committee believes that the college classics major ought to provide the future teacher with a strong sense of the varieties of material that could be used in introducing students to Latin, including medieval texts and paying special attention to lyric poetry and narrative prose. In many high school Latin programs pupils still pursue a course of study (Cicero and Vergil) that lacks such variety: it is as if 9th and 10th grade English classes were to limit themselves to a study of Burke's speeches and *Paradise Lost*. The aim of the student of classics, we believe, should be to meet Greek and Latin literature directly, freely, and with enjoyment—and without relying on side effects for justification (e.g. "mental discipline," "assistance to the study of English," etc.).

IV. SOME MINIMUM RECOMMENDATIONS

As a *minimum* requirement the prospective high school teacher of English should have taken courses[2] involving the following (the study of these subjects being, if necessary, completed in a fifth year):

Prose Fiction.
Intensive Reading of Poetry.
Advanced Composition.

[2] For the sake of clarity, all committees have used the term "year course" to mean a full year's work in a subject, whether the particular college is on a semester or quarter system. Accordingly, "half-year course" and "quarter-year course" have meaning in this light. Presumably a student would carry four or five "year courses" a year.

The Structure and History of Language.

The Works of Shakespeare.

The Major Figures of American Literature.

Sufficient knowledge of a second language to allow the judging of a translation.

Sufficient knowledge of history and the social sciences so that the prospective teacher of English could also teach some courses in Social Studies.

For the prospective teacher of Foreign Languages:

Proficiency in the spoken language. The prospective teacher should have fluency and authority in class.

Solid grounding in major periods of foreign literature (e.g., classical drama in French, the age of Goethe in German, the era of Cervantes in Spanish).

Training in composition.

Sufficient background in the history and culture of the country to provide a context for literature.

A year of study abroad is a welcome enrichment of any undergraduate preparation in a language major. While it does not constitute a requirement, it does enable the prospective teacher to acquire skills and knowledge not ordinarily obtainable through academic formation on this continent. A few summer schools, such as Middlebury, may offer some degree of equivalent experience.

For the prospective teacher of Classics (primarily Latin):

Training in Composition.

Familiarity with the literature and thought of the First Century, B.C. and the Augustan Age.

Enough reading in history and culture, including archeology, to provide a context for literature.

The committee is aware that its discussion of English is both more comprehensive and more specific than its discussion of foreign languages. The fact is that the largest problem in the high schools now and for the future is, we believe, the study of English in all its branches.

GEORGE BECKER, Swarthmore College
KONRAD BIEBER, Connecticut College
G. ARMOUR CRAIG, Amherst College
W. NELSON FRANCIS, Brown University
HAROLD C. MARTIN, Harvard University
ELIZABETH NYE QUINN, Mt. Holyoke College
WYLIE SYPHER, Simmons College

MATHEMATICS

In this report, we shall be concerned mainly with the problem of training mathematics teachers for high schools. We should like to speak first, however, on two matters which are not strictly within our mandate.

We wish to underscore the point that every teacher should have a liberal education. It is easy for this idea to be missed, when representatives of various fields argue (as of course they should argue) for thorough study of the prospective teacher's specialty. For a number of reasons, however, we believe that the case for broad liberal education is especially strong when the student intends to be a teacher.

In the first place, teachers exert both a personal and an intellectual influence on their students. Thus the teacher's cast of mind tends, for better or worse, to propagate itself. If a mathematics teacher feels for literature an indifference or antagonism born of ignorance, this may be conveyed to the student. The same applies to an English teacher who feels the same way about mathematics or science.

In the second place, if the faculty of a school is to cooperate as a group, then it should not be an uneasy coalition of technical specialists; most of its members should have a sympathetic understanding of the work of the school as a whole; and this is more likely to come from substantive education than from abstract preachment.

Finally, it is a fact that the leaders in the school world are drawn mainly from the classroom. It hardly seems practical for them to get the broad educations that they need, late in their careers, on a remedial basis.

These remarks apply with special force to prospective elementary teachers, who seem to be expected to know everything. If there is a major gap in the teacher's training, the students suffer for it. Poor and insufficient mathematical training seems to be especially prevalent. An excessive number of elementary teachers are so ignorant of mathematics that they regard it with an antagonism due to fear. The present college mathematics curricula are not an ideal solution of this problem; work is now being done on the design of more appropriate courses. Meanwhile, however, as a minimum, prospective elementary teachers should be urged to study enough mathematics in college to solidify their basic skills and to realize that mathematics is a science—even an art—and certainly more than a mere clerical chore. If an undergraduate program includes little or no mathematics, the resulting gap is much too big to be filled in a Master of Arts in Teaching program. The study of mathematics takes time. And it is surely worth the time of an elementary teacher, because it forms about a fourth or a fifth of her job. In many cases it is not practical for a liberal arts college to offer special courses for prospective elementary teachers. Standard courses, however, if the student actually studies them, will free the special graduate courses from the impossible remedial task which they now face.

Our recommendations for prospective high school teachers are only slightly different from the usual undergraduate major. We recommend merely certain shifts of emphasis. We believe that the main objective is to produce a really thorough understanding of the sort of mathematics that is taught—and is coming to be taught—in the high schools themselves. The order of presentation varies, and there are some innovations now widely used. But the following is a fair, rough outline:

Ninth grade. Introduction to algebra.

Tenth grade. Geometry.

Eleventh grade. Algebra, trigonometry, analytic geometry.

Twelfth grade. Some of the following: Trigonometry, solid geometry, probability theory, abstract algebra, analytic geometry and calculus.

As basic undergraduate preparation for the teacher we recommend the following:

(1) A three-semester sequence in analytic geometry and calculus.

(2) Two semesters in abstract algebra.

(3) Two semesters (total) of probability and statistics.

(4) Two semesters of geometry, beyond the analytic geometry already mentioned.

(5) Two semesters of elective courses.

These courses have been selected with due attention both to mathematics considered as a science in itself and to the mathematical needs of the natural and the social sciences. All of them (except perhaps the last) are recommended as direct contributions to the mastery of the high school curriculum.

(1) Analytic geometry and calculus is fundamental in any case. It applies to almost any program in the eleventh and twelfth grades.

(2) Study of abstract algebra is obviously a preparation for teaching more elementary forms of the same subject-matter in the twelfth grade. It applies in a less obvious way to the work of the ninth grade. Here the point is that while many elementary algebra courses aim to produce skills on a largely behavioral level, most of the new ones attempt more logical treatments, and these call for a sort of understanding, on the part of the teacher, that is best acquired in a course in abstract algebra. Almost any college mathematics course reinforces the manipulative skills of algebra, but the elucidation of the concepts is another matter; and the concepts should be clear in the mind of the teacher, no matter what the method and spirit of the ninth-grade course may be.

(3) Probability and statistics are among the most important applications of mathematics. In scattered schools, they are now taught in the twelfth grade; and this would probably be done more widely if the teachers were prepared for it.

(4) Tenth-grade geometry is in a rather peculiar position: the usual un-

dergraduate courses throw rather little light on its fundamentals. (Courses in "advanced Euclidean geometry," for example, make a rather small contribution to this problem.) There is a good deal of debate on the question whether the tenth-grade student should be asked to have a thorough logical understanding of geometry. Some believe that the treatment of geometry should be largely intuitive. But in any case the *teacher* should have such a thorough logical understanding; and we believe that this requires a two-semester sequence. This should include material on the foundations of geometry (in the commonly understood sense of the term) but should go beyond this so as to elucidate not just the very beginnings of the subject, but the later material ordinarily taught in schools. It should include collateral material (for example, non-Euclidean geometry) which brings the elementary theory into sharper focus.

The program proposed above differs from the usual undergraduate major chiefly in two ways.

First, the stress on analysis is reduced; we have not recommended a course in advanced calculus or even a course in differential equations. This is because we believe that these courses are not sufficiently close to the high school curriculum to justify giving them high priority in a minimum program. (In fact, most junior-level courses in differential equations are devoted mainly to the study of techniques of calculation; conceptually, some of them actually represent retrogressions from the preceding calculus course.) We urge, however, that the elective courses include a course in advanced calculus, of a sort which would reinforce conceptual grasp of elementary calculus. Every high school teacher who is qualified to teach calculus is likely to be asked to do so, but the converse is lamentably false. In the specific recommendations above, analysis has been somwhat neglected, on the ground that various other topics deserve priority. But if calculus is thought of as part of a high school teacher's job, this neglect needs to be remedied.

All of the courses that we have described, with the possible exception of geometry and probability, are now commonly taught; and the latter two are not intended to be "trade school courses" in such a sense as to be foreign bodies in a liberal arts curriculum. We believe that they should be taught, at least in alternate years, if enrollments and staff resources make them practicable. We believe, moreover, that a net increase in the number of courses offered can be avoided by dropping from the curriculum various courses now commonly taught but not really needed. For example, we do not need separate courses in trigonometry, the theory of equations, "advanced Euclidean geometry," or solid analytic geometry. The material that is really needed from these courses is included in the ones recommended in this report.

The preparation recommended here is rarely achieved by the present generation of high school teachers. Ideally, however, it should be regarded as minimal rather than maximal; and the student who completes it has by no means reached a point of diminishing returns. The demands made on high school teachers have increased very sharply in the last decade, and it seems very likely that they will increase further in the next. Already a few schools have reached a point at which their natural next step is to offer a *second* year of calculus at the end of accelerated programs. And in the great majority of schools it appears that the limits of student achievement are being set not by the students but by the staff.

It will be observed that we have not attempted to discuss the problems of preparing teachers for the junior high school. It is reasonable to suppose that the minimum preparation for this level could be less than for the senior high school; but the junior high school curriculum is now in such a rapid state of evolution that it is not plain to us just what the minimum might be. (For a recent discussion of this problem, see "Recommendations of the Mathematical Association of America for the Training of Teachers of Mathematics," *American Mathematical Monthly*, volume 67 (1960), pp. 1–10.)

Finally, we emphasize that our recommendations for prospective teachers do not depend, in any significant degree, on the merits of the various new high school mathematics curricula which have recently appeared. We believe that the sort of preparation we have described is needed for teaching *any* sound high school program. The teachers' knowledge should in any case be broad enough and deep enough so that curricular reformers in the next few decades will not face a prior problem in teacher-training.

N. C. ANKENY, Massachusetts Institute
of Technology
JOHN G. KEMENY, Dartmouth College
EDWIN E. MOISE, Harvard University
CLETUS O. OAKLEY, Haverford College
HELEN G. RUSSELL, Wellesley College

NATURAL SCIENCES

Rapid advances in fundamental scientific knowledge and in the impact of scientific results on social affairs are putting increased responsibility upon science teachers at all levels, from the early grades through the university. The effects are particularly significant for secondary school teachers (grades 7–12) with whom most of our young people have nearly all of their study of sciences.

The young person of today, on reaching junior high school, has already begun an informal science education through instruction in the elementary school, as well as from popularly written articles, from television, and even from some of his toys. Subsequent instruction in the secondary school offers the opportunity to extend and guide interest through an introduction to scientific ways of working and thinking that will form a dependable, enlightened basis for his later contacts with the expanding influence of science on the life of everyone. If he goes no farther in his study of science, it should give him something dependable, although introductory, for his maturer intellectual life. If he does elect further scientific study, this beginning should be designed as a stimulating base for further study.

Apparently some students in the 10th, 11th, and 12th grades can learn more than previously believed. Many can handle reasoning that was earlier considered beyond their maturity and respond enthusiastically to the genuine intellectual challenge of scientific problems. In this connection it should be noted that colleges and universities are giving greater attention to the placement of students who have had advanced science courses in high school.

Scientists of today are making serious efforts toward a new era in science education. Scientific societies have directed, through the efforts of selected groups of teachers and professional scientists, the production of new textual materials, laboratory exercises, and films directed toward secondary school education. These materials emphasize science as an intellectual and exciting human activity. Special opportunities for summer study in advanced science work have been made available for secondary school teachers. Already these efforts are beginning to change the character and content of secondary school science teaching. The future teacher must be trained through college courses which have this new spirit and emphasis on dynamic science.

The science teacher has a responsibility for creating a program of active student inquiry. He must aid the student to make observations both in the world about him and in the laboratory. He should encourage the student to develop an inquiring mind as to why thus and so happens or how it might be explained. He must provide stimulating opportunities for his students' synthesis of knowledge provided by field trips, laboratory experiments, reading and class discussions. He must teach his students how to think logically about scientific phenomena as a basis for sound judgments. He should be ready to encourage the independent projects of his more interested students. The teacher must inculcate in students a sense of strict honesty in gathering and interpreting data. Necessarily we expect the future teacher's undergraduate program of study to provide breadth and depth in his knowledge and training, which both directly and indirectly focuses upon his preparation for teaching.

The unity of the world and the growing interdependence of the classical subdivisions of science require that the academic background of the science teacher have breadth. The methods, concepts, and equipment of physics and chemistry are used by the biologist to probe the structure and functioning of cells and organisms. The chemist must use his knowledge of physics, and the physicist must use his of chemistry. Astronomy, geology, meteorology, and oceanography are linked as earth sciences, in which facts and concepts from physics, chemistry, or biology are frequently used. Mathematics, in addition to being studied for its own value, is needed as a tool for evaluation in all sciences. New information, new perspectives, new methods of approach all call for a broad background of study in the sciences. In addition, the prospective teacher needs the self-confidence and competence that result from study in depth of one phase of science. Thus we conclude, as have the several committees of the American Association for the Advancement of Science (1946, 1960), that approximately one-half of the course work in college of a future science teacher should be concerned with science and mathematics.

Of central importance is our belief that as a result of his total collegiate study the secondary school science teacher must be capable of continued scholarly growth. Therefore, we believe that independent study of a problem is desirable to put the student "on his own." Such an investigation may open whole new areas of study for the student and extend a growing knowledge of the general field and an awareness of the methods used by scientists.

If the science teacher is to hold the respect of his colleagues, his students and the community, he should have a cultural background including training in English, the arts, languages, and social sciences.

A successful science teacher must give to his work a genuine enthusiasm and zest that carries over to his students. He must feel and exhibit the stimulation of learning, of interrelating ideas, the excitements of provoking new discoveries by the pupils, and the pleasure of creating in them the fascination that he finds in a subject. These assets stem both from his own personality and from the perspectives of his scientific background. Supporting them, however, there must be the steadiness and security that come from good professional training including practice teaching.

Since practice teaching and other educational requirements must obviously be met, a nice fit is required in the planning of a program which shall satisfactorily embody the aims of breadth, depth, and professional experience. While a four-year program can be devised, five years is desirable to develop a beginner who is an apt apprentice.

The prospective teacher is entering a respected and very important career. Many opportunities exist for increasing responsibilities for those who wish them. Successful teachers gain satisfaction from helping younger students to learn of the world and to become responsible for their own interpretations of phenomena. Student interest in our subjects, possibly to the extent of choosing a career in their further study or teaching, is very gratifying. A teacher has the opportunity to continue being a student and interpreter of the exciting exploration of the world. Also, continuing contact with those extending the forefront of knowledge adds to the joys of being a teacher. To us, serving as science teachers is a rewarding life of great social importance.

GENERAL RECOMMENDATIONS

1. To meet satisfactorily the prospective secondary school teacher's need for breadth and depth of subject matter, as well as for professional experience, the fifth year of study, i.e., one year beyond the baccalaureate degree, is highly desirable, in fact almost a necessity.

2. In solving the dilemma of choice among breadth, depth, and professional experience, much of this last may best be left for the fifth year. In many undergraduate programs little time and supervision is available for practice teaching and postponement of this experience until after the acquisition of a good deal of knowledge may have a distinct advantage.

3. As academic distinctions become less sharply defined, the required areas of study are not usefully spelled out in terms of specific courses and hours. It is more important that the future teacher gain an understanding of the nature or structure of the subjects to be taught and an appropriate attitude toward them. It is strongly recommended that this be planned for in each of the areas of study by obtaining training, whenever possible, with specialists who are actively interested in research and who are themselves good teachers. This may serve as a guard against teaching students later a mass of unrelated facts which are to be memorized and, upon command, regurgitated.

4. Between one-third and one-half of the undergraduate program should, if possible, be arranged with respect to the student's eventual plan for teaching. Ordinarily one year of beginning study in each major field—chemistry, physics, biology, and mathematics—is essential for the teacher of natural sciences. Furthermore, it is highly desirable that these introductory courses be taken as part of the undergraduate program. Geology, astronomy, and meteorology are also potentially rich resources for any teaching, and especially for teaching general science or the earth sciences. Here we are faced with a persistent problem in designing programs for future science teachers: how much breadth and how much depth? There is no precise answer. We recognize the need for breadth of introductory study in several sciences as a basis which further study and reading can extend. Yet we acknowledge the competence and confidence that result from study of one science to some depth. Ordinarily the student can achieve some breadth as well as some depth; we warn against excesses of either breadth or depth.

5. The allied work required as support for the major should include more than one of the related sciences—as, for example, chemistry and physics for the biology major. Whatever the major, we emphasize the great value of experience with an independent laboratory problem.

6. The undergraduate program recommended here is one that demands early planning if the fifth year is to be used effectively. Many liberal arts students who take the fifth year of preparation for teaching do not decide to do so until they are juniors or seniors; for them some compromises or additional study may be necessary. It is therefore recommended that students who have any possible interest in teaching secondary school science be encouraged to consult with their advisers while they are still freshmen and sophomores.

7. The importance of mathematics for future teachers in any of the various fields of science is emphasized. A year of calculus is recommended, and also a half year of statistics especially designed for science students, if possible.

8. Summer study at institutions with a specialized scientific focus is highly recommended for the future teacher. For example: for the biologist, there are positions in hospitals and biological industries, as well as marine and inland summer laboratories; for the physical scientist, there are positions in various government, university and industrial laboratories, or with field expeditions. By such experience, horizons are expanded for research, and wider intellectual contacts are made.

9. Prospective teachers will be wise to begin during their undergraduate program to make a card file on the sources of various teaching materials, films, sourcebooks, identification keys, etc. A teacher can never know of too many such sources.

10. Some study of the history and philosophy of science in the preparation of the prospective teachers is desirable, but such courses will be more significant when taken after previous study of the science. Incidental reading, perhaps during the summers, would also be helpful in filling what is often a serious gap in the knowledge of the prospective teacher of the development of scientific ideas, their rationale, and their impact upon the thought and behavior of individuals and groups.

ADDITIONAL RECOMMENDATIONS FOR PREPARATION IN THE EARTH SCIENCES

The earth sciences, here considered as geology, astronomy, meteorology, and oceanography, provide splendid opportunity to arouse an interest in science. Through them students can learn to observe and to question as a means of increasing their knowledge; to visualize things in three dimensions, with the aid of models and then in imagination; and to work with abstractions.

For the prospective teacher of the earth sciences, the college program should include, as a *minimum*, a year course in either astronomy or geology. We do not consider a semester of astronomy and a semester of geology as adequate. Study in meteorology or oceanography is desirable, if such courses are available. In addition, the prospective teacher should read widely and, if possible, hear a series of lectures by experts actively engaged in research in the various earth sciences, if necessary through the use of tapes, films, or television. A major in geology or astronomy with some study in other aspects of the earth sciences is one practical program for a future science teacher.

Since meteorology unfortunately is taught in only a limited number of colleges, and oceanography in even fewer, it is recommended that there be available for tomorrow's science teachers a generous reading list covering the two fields, revised frequently and listing books which present the fundamentals clearly. This would emphasize the effective use of libraries to the ultimate benefit not only of the prospective teacher but also of his students.

ADDITIONAL RECOMMENDATIONS FOR PREPARATION IN THE PHYSICAL SCIENCES

Unless a more radical change than we can foresee takes place, the typical physics teacher, like most other science teachers, will find it necessary in the future, as he has in the past, to teach one or more other subjects. If about six per cent of the high school population is taking physics in any given year, and we hopefully envisage fewer and smaller sections per teacher than are now customary, a full load of four physics sections of twenty-five students each would be available for a teacher only in a school with more than 1700 students.

We therefore do not believe that we should necessarily expect every prospective physics teacher to complete an undergraduate major in physics. We do believe that adequate preparation can be given in a five-year program if the student majors in physics or chemistry or mathematics. In such a case two years each of physics, chemistry, and mathematics, two additional years of advanced courses as part of a major in one of these fields, and a year of biology or geology should be completed by the end of the fifth year.

ADDITIONAL RECOMMENDATIONS FOR PREPARATION IN CHEMISTRY

Beyond the informational content of a college course in chemistry there is its greater value in developing in students an appreciation of its theoretical basis, its evolutionary character, and its value as a cultural discipline. A realistic four-year course of training for secondary school chemistry teachers should be built around a minimal chemistry major (general, analytical, organic, and physical) with the inclusion of as much physics (and the necessary mathematical background) and other science courses as can be accommodated to the general liberal arts requirements and the Education courses needed for certification. The fifth year should then be devoted to further courses in chemistry and other sciences, or in part to Education and practice teaching if these requirements have not already been satisfied.

ADDITIONAL RECOMMENDATIONS FOR PREPARATION IN BIOLOGY

With the inevitable changes that are coming into high school biology teaching, the teacher must do his part to develop young people's understanding of the living world around them. He must know as many plants and animals in the field as possible, and he must understand how to go about their identification. He must also know how to grow and experiment with microorganisms for their usefulness in short-term experiments. He must know how to use a microscope with ease, and how to study the cellular anatomy of plants and animals. He must have grasped the significance of what we currently know of genetics and its all-pervasive importance. He should be able to recognize the dynamic aspects of living matter by functional studies on plants and animals, and he should study human physiology for its place in physiological thought, rather than solely as a basis for exhortations in hygiene. Most important of all he must have developed a "feel" for the changes that are always going on in living organisms, some in response to changes in the environment, some resulting from internal regulation of growth and metabolism.

The biology teacher will need to study physics and chemistry (including organic) not only for their theoretical value but also for their practical help in the use of simple apparatus, the making of solutions, and the performance of chemical tests. Without the concepts of biochemistry and biophysics he will be unable to understand and appreciate the significance of developments in molecular biology.

Furthermore, the secondary school teacher of biology should have gained through his reading or courses an understanding of the economic, social, and political implications of today's knowledge of the biological sciences in areas of human concern such as world food supplies, population increases, radiation hazards, space travel, and problems of health and disease. In short, secondary school biology should provide a sound basis for an appreciation of the role of the life sciences in all aspects of human life.

GORDON S. CHRISTIANSEN, Connecticut College
HARRIET S. CREIGHTON, Wellesley College
CHARLOTTE HAYWOOD, Mt. Holyoke College
L. DON LEET, Harvard University
WALTER C. MICHELS, Bryn Mawr College
CHARLES H. SMILEY, Brown University
FLETCHER G. WATSON, Harvard University

HISTORY AND THE SOCIAL SCIENCES

Although its mandate is to make recommendations for the specific subject-matter appropriate to the training of social studies teachers, the committee feels it is important to make clear at the outset its reaffirmation of the desirability of a broad liberal arts education. Though it cannot be denied that mastery of the subject field is essential to successful teaching, it is equally true that the acquisition of skill in critical thought and an appreciation of the variety of the human experience are also needed. This is especially so for work in the social studies, where the curriculum has become, all too frequently, doctrinaire, and either superficially descriptive or overgeneralized. These tendencies can be counteracted whether in the teaching of existing courses or in the revision of the curriculum only by teachers who have had a broad and rigorous intellectual training. It is assumed, therefore, that every prospective teacher will have at least a basic acquaintance with the natural sciences, mathematics, philosophy, foreign language, literature, and the fine arts. The committee has deliberately kept the amount of study recommended in the social sciences down to a level which would make that possible.

Furthermore, the committee also feels it is necessary to emphasize that general intellectual ability is no less desirable a trait in a teacher than is knowledge of particular subject-matter. Thus, it has strived to avoid a rigid prescription of undergraduate training lest it thereby preclude an intellectually capable student from seeking the Master of Arts in Teaching or another, similar degree merely because he has not taken the required courses. Such an approach is justifiable also for the sake of preserving the diversity inherent in the facts that candidates come to Master of Arts in Teaching Programs with differing subject-matter backgrounds and may elect a great variety of courses during their graduate year. Again, however, it must be said that sound knowledge of the subject field is also requisite to effective teaching. The inference is that, where an intellectually able student with limited training in the social sciences is accepted for Master of Arts in Teaching candidacy, extra study may be required of him.

For these reasons, the committee has defined its task to be the recommendation from among the varied offerings of the Twenty-nine Colleges and a university such as Harvard of a pattern of courses which the Master of Arts in Teaching candidate should elect *over his five-year period of training* in order to prepare himself for the role of a secondary school social studies teacher, assuming either the continuance of the existing curriculum or his participation in its reform and improvement.

With these points in mind, then, the committee's specific recommendations for the subject-matter training of the prospective teacher are as follows.

Within the five years encompassed by undergraduate study and the year of graduate work, social science M.A.T. candidates should have fulfilled these requirements as a basic minimum:

(1) They should have had 3 full courses (one-year courses or their equivalents) in history including introductory courses, one of which should be in United States History.

(2) They should have had 3 full courses (one-year courses or their equivalents) divided between 2 social sciences other than history (anthropology, economics, political science, sociology, human geography).[3]

(3) They should have acquired thorough grounding in the ideas and institutions of an area other than the United States and western Europe—either as part of recommendations (1) and (2) or in addition to them.

(4) They should have written one or more research papers on an historical or social science problem.

Each of these recommendations deserves further elaboration and more specific connection to the committee's basic assumptions.

1. THE HISTORY REQUIREMENT

Any decision about subject-matter preparation of a teacher depends in part on knowledge of the courses he will be required to teach. We are here concerned with the "fifth-year" graduate who takes a position as a social studies teacher in a junior or senior high school. Although there exists no careful study of the instructional duties of such a position, the committee felt it possessed sufficient evidence[4] to warrant making the following generalizations: (1) American history is the subject most frequently taught by social studies teachers in both the junior and senior high schools. This will

---

[3] Though the majority of the committee did not agree, Professor Feldmesser contends that psychology is a social science which is fully as relevant as anthropology, economics, political science, sociology, and human geography and should therefore have equal standing with them in this recommendation. Professor Pennock wished to record the following dissent: "In view of the fact that, according to the information supplied to the committee, the prevailing pattern of secondary school requirements includes study of American government, community civics, and problems of democracy during the eighth, ninth, eleventh and twelfth grades, it appears to me that we should recommend specific training directed toward the teaching of these courses as we have in the case of American history and the study of non-western cultures. The fact that the work in these high school courses is notoriously often at a rather superficial level provides further justification for such a requirement. My personal recommendation, then, would be that the social science requirement should include at least one-half course designed to give some sophistication in the theory and practice of politics, and to combat the formalistic and purely descriptive mode of instruction that so often prevails in the high school courses in this subject."

[4] The committee had available data from U.S. Office of Education surveys and a survey made by Professor Bolster.

likely continue to be so in the predictable future since laws in 46 states require courses in American history in the senior high school and many of them prescribe it in the junior high school as well. (2) The obligations in content fields other than American history are difficult to predict because of the large number of different topics encompassed in the "social studies." In the high school, a survey course in World History, though increasingly offered on an elective basis, is second in frequency to American history, followed by courses in "Problems of Democracy." Many high schools also offer elective courses in special areas of history (e.g., Far Eastern History, Latin American History) and in sociology, economics, and American government where the staff includes a faculty member able to teach such courses. The law of one state (Pennsylvania) now prescribes a course in world cultures as a requisite for a high school diploma and it is possible that this type of course will become popular as an alternative to world history. In the junior high school, content is even more variable than in the senior high, with a tendency to offer "fused" courses in "social studies," "correlated courses" in English and social studies, and courses in "community civics." (3) Most "fifth-year" graduates teaching in senior high school are required to teach in two related content areas. (4) Graduates are normally required to teach students of all levels of ability, but the majority of their pupils are in the average and above-average categories. Some, however, are given the opportunity to instruct the "advanced placement" classes in the senior high school after they have had a few years of classroom experience.

Thus history's dominance of the secondary school curriculum as well as its position as a major social science demand its study by the prospective social studies teacher. Since it is certain that nearly all Master of Arts in Teaching graduates who remain in classroom teaching more than a few years after receiving the degree will be asked to teach content from the area of American history, knowledge at least equivalent to that available in a college survey course in United States history should be obtained by all candidates. Moreover, there is distressingly frequent evidence that American history teachers are being forced to defend their teaching against attacks by pressure groups, whose goal is to use the social studies curriculum as a propagandizing agent for super-patriotic, ultra-conservative political and economic views. It seems axiomatic to the committee that the teacher's best defense against such attack is the kind of thorough knowledge of the American past available in rigorous, analytic courses.

For a number of reasons specific requirements beyond United States history are difficult to define. Adequate preparation of junior high school teachers, for example, is complicated by the existence of the "English-social studies combination" which purports to combine content from these two areas. Frequently novice teachers whose subject matter background is chiefly in history are assigned to such courses in their apprenticeship or offered positions teaching them upon graduation. In such cases it is essential that history training be supplemented by instruction in language arts, with special emphasis on the teaching of composition.

Another difficulty is presented by the unsatisfactory nature of the world history offering in the high school. In its present form this course faces the teacher with the immense problem of surveying within a single academic year sufficient portions of the total recorded human past to enable the high school sophomore to comprehend the historical development of the significant nations and problems of the contemporary world. Such a task is patently impossible, and in his attempt to cope with it the teacher all too frequently doles out large collections of half-true, half-understood generalizations to students who thereby come to dislike history. The most promising means of improving this unfortunate situation seems to lie in a much more rigorous selection of content than is now practiced. This will require much thought to develop intellectually sound criteria according to which the selection may be made. The committee wishes to encourage the small number of high schools which are attempting this type of reform, but it also believes that the presently typical history course will remain prominent for several more years. Its recommendations thus seek both to prepare new teachers to participate in the much-needed revision of this course as well as to cope more adequately with an inherently objectionable situation.

With the foregoing considerations in mind, then, the committee proposes the following generalizations as guides to the selection of history courses: (1) Introductory courses should be taken in undergraduate college since they are closed to graduate students in many fifth-year programs. (2) The canons of general education as well as the nature of the secondary school curriculum make it mandatory for students concentrating in some form of American studies to take also at least a basic course in European history or culture. (3) Depth of study in some specialized area of history (e.g., American, modern European) is highly desirable to develop some acquaintance with the more complex materials of the discipline. This recommendation is also warranted by a growing tendency for high school history courses for advanced students to include within their scope detailed analysis of historical problems. (4) Both American and European history majors should consider taking courses as they are available in the history of Latin America, Africa, the Near East, India or the Far East as a means of fulfilling the recommendation to study an area beyond western Europe and the United States.

2. THE REQUIREMENT IN THE OTHER SOCIAL SCIENCES

Although the social sciences other than history have had relatively little significant impact upon the secondary school curriculum, there are a number of reasons why considerable knowledge in at least one of them should be required of all prospective social studies teachers. Both their methodology and their concepts are increasingly valued throughout the world as an aid in more adequately understanding human society; indeed they are even being increasingly applied to the writing of history.[5] Moreover, the social sciences have become basic to the advanced study of education and they are being relied upon as aids in the making of both public and private decisions.[6] Finally, they are themselves likely to be taught more often in the future as part of the high school social studies curriculum.

In regard to the social science requirement, the committee recommends that the following standards should apply: (1) To provide breadth, introductory courses in more than one area of social science are recommended and these too should be taken in undergraduate college. (2) Beyond the introductory level specialized concentration in one area of social science is desirable as a means of providing acquaintance with the methodology and some of the advanced thinking of the social scientist. At the same time the prospective secondary school teacher should recognize that highly technical courses are not especially relevant to his training since he is aiming to develop not the refined tools of the research scholar, but rather helpful insights into the nature of human society. (Highly technical courses appear to the committee to be prevalent in the field of economics, though they exist in other behavorial sciences as well.) (3) Courses in social science, especially those in cultural anthropology, provide a possible means of fulfilling the recommendation regarding the study of an area outside the United States and western Europe.

3. THE REQUIREMENT FOR STUDY OF AN AREA OUTSIDE WESTERN EUROPE AND THE UNITED STATES

The rationale for this recommendation rests heavily on the committee's conviction that there is far too much parochialism in American popular thought. Though broad perspective and tolerance would seem implicit in the very concept of "liberal education," there is considerable evidence that graduates of both secondary schools and colleges in the United States in fact frequently have an essentially naive and limited image of the world. Careful study would be required to ascertain the exact relationship between the parochial viewpoint and the content of formal education, but it seems reasonable to predict that social science training which emphasizes the western tradition exclusively would reinforce a culture-bound outlook. For this reason the tendency of Master of Arts in Teaching candidates to concentrate their content preparation overwhelmingly in western history

[5] Cf. H. Stuart Hughes, "The Historian and the Social Scientist," *American Historical Review*, LXVI, No. 1, October 1960.

[6] Cf. for an explication of this idea Daniel Lerner (ed.), *The Human Meaning of the Social Sciences* (New York, 1959).

should be resisted.[7] The same course of action is also justified as a response to recent agitation for state laws requiring courses in the nature of world communism. Since there is good reason to suspect that they are frequently sponsored by ultra-conservative forces, they are likely to consist solely of propaganda unless those who write and teach them have at least sufficient content background to organize comprehensive and analytic studies. For this purpose collegiate study of the world beyond western Europe and the United States, particularly of the history and society of Russia, would be advantageous.

Finally, aside from its intrinsic rewards, which can be immense, exposure to a non-western culture is one of the best means of gaining perspective on United States history. The increasing need of the teacher of United States history will be to define American values and history in the larger context of America's relations with her European past and her non-western neighbors. The study of American foreign policy will alone demand great breadth and depth of understanding, knowledge, and insight. Here, Islamic, Indian, and Far Eastern studies all have the advantage of introducing the student to culture worlds of vast importance and to more adequate comprehension of policy problems in our contemporary society.

4. THE RESEARCH PAPER REQUIREMENT

The committee accepts as given the proposition that adequate teaching of the social studies requires familiarity not only with their significant data and generalizations but also with the methodologies according to which they operate. The argument favoring the encouragement of critical thought in the curricula of all schools is so obviously applicable that it does not need reiteration here. What does warrant further consideration is the proposition that, though related, the methodologies of the historian and the social scientist are different and that the nature of these methodologies affects the content of these disciplines in ways with which the teacher should be familiar. Consideration of these topics would be of value to the prospective social studies teacher not only as an aid to understanding the content he will teach, but also as a means for facilitating sharp thinking. While formal courses in historiography and philosophy, particularly those covering the nature of the scientific method, are highly desirable, the first-hand experience of grappling with some social science problem requiring substantial research according to the canons of a social science discipline is even more valuable. No matter what its form or length, a suitable study would necessarily involve a rigorous analysis of a problem, the rational defense of a solution to it, and scrupulous attention to excellence and skill in

[7] An informal survey of the 1961–1962 group of social science M.A.T. candidates at Harvard has revealed that as a group they have taken in undergraduate college a total of 1,959 full courses in western history and only 7½ courses in non-western civilization.

expression and communication. In the committee's opinion it is more important to emphasize these objectives than to prescribe whether such a paper be written within or outside the requirements of a course.

It should be understood that the committee's proposals are to be construed as minimal. They describe the beginning and not the end of competence in the social sciences, and no teacher possessed only of the knowledge they demand is likely to be truly superior. Obviously then, prospective teachers who can arrange their programs in such a way as to build substantially on these foundations while still in college should be encouraged to do so. For clearly an important assumption on which the social science committee operated is one of the basic premises of most Master of Arts in Teaching programs themselves: depth of knowledge of subject is an indispensable element of outstanding teaching.

ARTHUR S. BOLSTER, JR., Harvard University
ROBERT FELDMESSER, Dartmouth College
FRANK FREIDEL, Harvard University
EDWARD V. GULICK, Wellesley College
EDWARD C. KIRKLAND, Bowdoin College
J. ROLAND PENNOCK, Swarthmore College
GEORGE R. TAYLOR, Amherst College
BENJAMIN ZIEGLER, Amherst College

WHAT STRANGLES
AMERICAN TEACHING

The Certification Racket

L Y D I A S T O U T

Has the certification of teachers for the public schools become an obstruction rather than an aid to good education? There is reason to believe that the abuses which Lydia Stout finds in the Florida system are paralleled in many other states. A faculty wife at the University of Florida in Gainesville, Mrs. Stout taught in the public schools of New Hampshire and New Jersey and has served for the past three years as an unpaid lobbyist for an independent group on the certification issue.

The most stubborn obstruction to good schooling in the United States is the hierarchy which the educationists themselves have established. Their influence has a restricting effect 1) on teacher-training courses, with the emphasis on theory or method as opposed to content, 2) on the lawmaking bodies where, by means of lobbying and other wirepulling tactics, they have gained so much power, and 3) on the prestige of the organized groups within the teaching profession itself.

Teacher training, from the point of view of students or teachers, is humiliating. Every state has its own code of laws or regulations governing the education and certification of teachers. Usually those requirements specify that the students planning to teach shall, while obtaining their college degree, pursue some general and some specific courses in education (that is, pedagogy or the how-to courses), and obtain some experience in practice teaching. Ostensibly those regulations were intended to keep poorly qualified teachers out of the classrooms, and parents and the public have been led to think that is what they do. State departments of education enforce the regulations and issue certificates which teachers must have before they can be hired. But colleges of education, when left to themselves, often require a great many more credits in how-to courses than the law specifies. As a result, the teacher-training programs have become top-heavy and tragically wasteful while the quality of the education being given to the pupil has been progressively downgraded.

In Florida even a kindergarten teacher must now take more than half of her whole college curriculum in education courses, and in order to obtain the highest pay and rank must have a doctor's degree. The certification requirements are backed up by a rigid pay scale. With some thirty thousand teachers in Florida, each of whom has probably had to take ten courses in a college of education, and with a demand for two thousand or more new teachers each year, the education colleges must teach several hundred classes in pedagogy just to satisfy the state requirements. The teachers' colleges then become big business and the cornerstone of the powerful empire that the educationists have built for themselves. Other devices are the automatic pay raises for advanced degrees, restrictions on reactivation of certificates, and the limiting of scholarships to prospective teachers. These require brief explanations.

Many older teachers hold life certificates from "normal schools," but such long-term certificates are no longer issued or honored. The theory is that a teacher constantly on the job does not keep sufficiently informed in the most recent educational theories and therefore forgets how to teach. The most competent of university faculties can boast not more than a half-dozen professors who could actually be certified to teach in public school, and not even Albert Einstein could legally have taught first-grade arithmetic! College graduates who have fulfilled the so-called requirements are now given a "graduate" certificate and required to return to college periodically to take summer courses in the latest theories (the victims call it "sipping at the same old soup"); otherwise their certificates will expire. These refresher courses often work a real hardship on women teachers with families and on others who are physically exhausted from teaching, but they do help swell the enrollments in education classes and keep the summer-school machinery running at full capacity.

Florida, like many other states, has a law, written by a professor of education, which provides automatic rank and pay raises for teachers who obtain advanced degrees in education! In substance, the law states that a teacher with a bachelor's degree is placed in Rank III and receives the minimum teaching salary. The teacher with a master's degree is placed in Rank II and automatically receives $400 to $600 a year more salary. Likewise the teacher with a doctor's degree[1] is placed in Rank I with another in-

---

[1] Even with a doctor's degree in education, a teacher may have fewer course credits in subject matter than are required for a bachelor's degree in liberal arts.

crease of $400 to $600. Merit has nothing to do with the teacher's rank and salary—they are simply a matter of obtaining the advanced degrees, and the pay increase is dependent upon the teacher's returning to college and taking graduate work.

Even as an undergraduate the prospective teacher has had to pursue so many courses in educational theory and so few in any scholarly field that he has little choice but to take his degree in education. His desire for financial betterment naturally helps fill the classrooms of the professional pedagogues in the universities. The University of Florida offers 125 graduate courses in teacher training. The dean of that college of education justifies this situation by saying that "*If you know enough about how to teach, you can always pick up enough facts to face a high school class.*"

Meanwhile the National Education Association and other agencies are insisting that the federal government must make large contributions toward improvement of the schools. The staggering sum of $4.5 billion has been suggested, much of it to go for increases in teachers' salaries. But unless the certification laws are changed, any federal money that is poured into salaries in expectation of attracting better teachers to the profession will be wasted, because genuinely superior teachers will refuse, as they do now, to submit to ridiculous certification requirements. Obviously it is going to take drastic measures to alter a system on which the public has been so thoroughly misled.

THE EDUCATIONIST LOBBY

In order to see the educationists in operation, one has to go to the Legislature to watch them actually legislate themselves into business. The account that follows tells of the political stratagems of the departments of education and the state educational associations in Florida, but Florida is controlled by pretty much the same kind of educational politicians as Ohio or any other state.

Prompted by a desire to get at the facts, I helped form a Committee of Parents and became its chairman. We succeeded in getting a bill introduced into the 1955 session of the Florida Legislature. The most important provision of the bill was to permit arts and science students to meet certification requirements with a minimum number of credit hours in how-to-teach courses specified by the State Department of Education. The Senate passed this bill thirty-four to one, the one vote being that of a senator who had promised the president of Florida State University that he would oppose it.

The educationists, marshalling their forces and campaigning the state, solicited letters and telegrams from teachers and parents in opposition to the bill. They thus succeeded in keeping the measure from reaching the House floor for debate. Their argument was that such legislation would lower the standard for teachers and would make the shortage more critical, though just how it would do so was never explained. Our experience with this bill taught us the lesson that we want desperately to pass on to other parents and legislators: that control of the school system has been taken over by people who are concerned only with their own aggrandizement and who have no sincere desire to advance the cause of better education. With those people in control, and all advice coming from them, we shall never have good schools *no matter how much money we pour into them!* The teacher shortage has been created by and for the colleges of education, and the certification requirements are being used to operate a closed shop.

The colleges of education, in their efforts toward self-expansion, depend on two powerful auxiliaries, the Florida Education Association (FEA) and the State Department of Education, to do the actual lobbying in the Legislature. The State Department of Education is headed by the State Superintendent of Public Instruction. The department supposedly is an executive branch of the state government, but in Florida the Superintendent appears to have plenty of money with which to lobby for more state money, much like the farmer who bought more land so he could grow more corn to feed more hogs so he could buy more land, and so forth. However, our Superintendent, who is a product or a convert of a college of education, has charge of the actual issuing of the teachers' certificates, and it is not unusual to find that former teachers, or *experienced teachers from other states,* must take more than a solid year of professional education courses before they can teach in Florida schools.

Our Florida Education Association is similar to organized groups of teachers found in other states and is also the state counterpart of the National Education Association. The FEA serves the same trade-union type of purposes as NEA and uses its enormous slush fund—in 1957 it was $240,-000, collected as dues from teacher members—for lobbying or any other purposes which will "protect the interests" of those teachers. Teachers are not required to belong to these state and national organizations but are generally pressured into doing so. Like any other trade union, the FEA has some legitimate aims, such as better salaries and working conditions, but for the most part the money is used to further the ambitions of the educationist. The executive secretary of FEA and his assistants constitute what one legislator called "the most powerful lobby that ever walked the halls of the State Capitol."

These three branches of the educationist hierarchy work hand in glove. Invariably the laws and regulations which are drafted by professors of education are railroaded through the Legislature by the FEA. The State Superintendent then carries out those laws and regulations in accordance with the interpretations which he or the other educationists choose to put on them. By this system of coordination, the triple alliance has been able to dictate school policies all the way from certifying teachers and specifying the curriculums down to selecting and buying all textbooks, planning and approving the school building programs, running the buses and cafeterias, and dictating new school legislation.

SCHOLARSHIPS LIMITED

The triple alliance is assisted in this lobbying by a number of other groups, among them the Continuing Educational Council, the Citizens Advisory Council, the Course of Study Committee for Public Schools, the Junior College Council, the Classroom Teachers' Association, and other special organizations for county superintendents, principals, and school board members. Despite their important-sounding titles, they serve as "fronts" and execute the commands of the FEA, impress the Legislature, and confuse the issues for outsiders. They are particularly effective in the committees of the Legislature which deal with education.

An illustration of their performance occurred in 1955, when a scholarship bill was amended so as to make the Legislature a party to channeling students into the classrooms of the colleges of education. This scholarship bill regularly provides each of 1050 students with $400 a year during undergraduate years. According to the original law, the scholarships were available to meritorious students in any field of learning. A student had only to sign an agreement that for each year he received the $400 he would, upon graduation, teach a year in Florida schools or refund the money.

Early in the 1955 session, the Superintendent, as is the custom, presented the bill which would appropriate this scholarship money. Routinely passed by the Senate, the bill then went to the House, where it was held up until nearly the end of the session. When affairs had become so rushed that small items could be given little attention, an assistant to the Superintendent sent an amendment to the House Committee on Public School Education, and the committee then hurriedly approved the bill as amended. The bill then went to the House, where it was passed at once and returned to the Senate and given final approval. Not one of the legislators I talked with was aware that the amendment restricted *all the scholarships to students enrolled in colleges of education*. Even students already receiving those scholarships and not enrolled in education colleges were required to transfer or were taken off the list for the following year.

Several members were so enraged about the manipulation of this deal that another bill was introduced in the 1957 session designed to remove the restriction. Somehow this bill was "lost" after it passed the Senate but before it reached the House committees, so it never got to the floor of the House. The railroading of the amendment is but one of many instances which showed the educationists' methods and power.

When Representative Pratt introduced a bill providing for three lay citizens—to be appointed by the governor—to serve on the eleven-man

Course of Study Committee for Public Schools, the Superintendent objected strenuously. The bill was reviewed by the House Committee for Public School Education, and several legislators spoke out about the need for citizens to take an interest in school matters and pointed out that youngsters are getting inferior preparation in mathematics and science. Representative Maness said that the Legislature should call on the people who foot the big bills to take a look at what is being taught. Several others spoke in favor of Pratt's bill because it would give citizens at least some voice in school programs. But the bill was defeated by lobbyists of the FEA.

MICKEY MOUSE COURSES

It has come to be taken for granted that colleges of education, with rare exceptions, attract the poorest students. Only the most naïve can bear up under the equivalent of fifteen to twenty repetitious and often meaningless "Mickey Mouse" courses, as the students themselves call them. The college of education at the University of Florida requires of its students a score of only 400 on the Graduate Record Examination for entrance into its graduate department, while all other branches of the university require a score of 500. The low level of ability required to get a degree in education is a standing joke in colleges and universities. Other departments, such as engineering, science, and liberal arts, routinely advise their poorest students to look for easier berths in the colleges of education. These castoffs from the other colleges obtain certificates and stay with teaching indefinitely because their trade union (FEA) has seen to it that they can draw just as much pay as the best teachers.

As another example of the way those laws operate, take the case of a family man for whom jobs other than teaching are available. To him, the equal salary scale for men and women teachers with the same certification rating provides little attraction, because a man has a struggle to support a family on a salary that is adequate for the spinster schoolma'am or working wife. Consequently, the few men now entering the teaching profession are the athletic coaches and vocational teachers who receive substantial salary supplements. But in due time their jobs become blind alleys, and if they seek greater opportunity, they must find it in the higher pay and prestige of the school administrative positions.

Again and again I have heard teachers and former teachers complain of unpleasant or undesirable working conditions. One of them said, "I couldn't complain about my salary, but it was the other things that made teaching unattractive. We rarely have principals nowadays with liberal-arts backgrounds, and so they just don't believe in the kind of standards we need in our schools." When I began checking, I found that in order to qualify for a certificate in supervision, a person must earn twenty-four to thirty credits in special education courses and must hold a master's degree. Those requirements alone are sufficient to keep qualified liberal arts graduates out of principalships *because one cannot get an M.A. degree requiring thirty to thirty-six credits in liberal arts if he has to take so many courses in education.*

The result, as pointed out by a professor of physical education, is that 60 per cent of the principals in Florida schools are majors in physical education and were formerly the coaches. Many of the others are graduates in agricultural education. No wonder a local school board member complained, "It is useless to change principals hoping to get a better one, because all the new candidates have had the same educationist background."

The new look in the school system, brought about by administrators of characteristic ex-athlete caliber, explains why the emphasis in Florida schools has all been transferred from scholarship to activities and why we find these administrators in their trade journals and elsewhere making statements such as: "The trouble with the ninth grade is that some people still think English, algebra, science, and foreign language should be included." Older teachers, fighting to maintain high standards, admit that they have their backs to the wall. In Gainesville, when the physics teacher resigned from our high school, her letter to the school board stated that her reason for quitting was that the principal had turned her physics laboratory over to the student activities and driver-training groups.

NO CREDIT FOR EXPERIENCE

No small part of the difficulty with certification laws has been the way the State Superintendent's office administers them. Perhaps I chose a bad day to visit the certification office, but when I arrived, there were two people, a man and a woman, talking about obtaining certificates. I couldn't help overhearing them and sensing the annoyance and irritation in the atmosphere. "I'm just not going to take any more of those courses," said the man as he walked out. When the woman picked up her papers to leave, I followed her and got her story. She said, "I've taught elementary school for thirty years. When I retired in Oklahoma, my husband and I came to live in Florida. I don't need to work, but I love to teach. My degree was in liberal arts with a major in Latin, which I have never taught. All my experience has been in elementary schools, and I have a master's degree in education. Last fall I started teaching before receiving my certificate and was astonished to find, when it came, that I was certified to teach nothing but Latin. Then because I was teaching outside my field (I was teaching an elementary grade), I was given only a temporary certificate, good for one year, and told that I would have to take *twenty-four credits in education.*

Early in the 1957 session of the Legislature, the Superintendent made the grandiose announcement that he would never be a party to any legislation that would "lower standards for teachers." But just four years previously he *had* lowered requirements in *subject matter*, so colleges of education could require students to take more of their teacher-training courses.

Last year a new organization called the National Teacher Accreditation Association was formed. This is an organization of institutions that train teachers, but its purpose evidently is to make sure that certification requirements operate to the maximum advantage of the colleges of education in those institutions. The Superintendent declared that Florida has joined that association and that it (the NTAA) is "going to seek to put out of commission some liberal-arts colleges by not accrediting their graduates to teach." One cannot help wondering why a State Superintendent of Public Instruction is interested in putting any educational institutions out of business. Does he fear competition from those colleges, or is it just because he cannot hold the certification club over the heads of all their teachers?

Recently newspaper and magazine articles and programs on the air have begun to scrutinize the educationists and have put them on the defensive. In spite of the criticisms, the Superintendent continues to make it clear that he and his cohorts intend to stick to their guns. Immediately after Sputnik I, the Superintendent's office released a story to the newspapers, placing the blame for poor schools squarely on the shoulders of parents because they are not taking sufficient interest in school problems. But that story is haunted by the ghost of Representative Pratt's bill, which the Superintendent fought and defeated because it would have placed just three lay citizens on the eleven-man Course of Study Committee for Public Schools.

At a state meeting of school board members a representative of the Superintendent gave them to understand that it was they who have been at fault all along because they have not paid enough attention to curriculums. That is a hollow argument because, on the recommendation of the Superintendent's own agents, every school board has one or more specialists on its payroll who are known as "coordinators of curriculum." Immediately after Christmas the Superintendent released another item, this time blaming pupils because they have not been taking more courses in science and mathematics. He insisted that the schools have been offering nine to twelve years of mathematics, with equally adequate science courses, but that pupils just have not been electing those courses. But he did not mention that the State Department of Education requires for graduation from high school only three years of English, one year of mathematics (which may be general math, similar to that of the eighth grade), one year of science (which may be general science, similar to what pupils already had in grammar school), two years of social studies, and two years of physical education. Neither did he mention the educationists' constant preachings that pupils should be allowed to elect their own courses without interference.

The educationists are seeking desperately to escape the blame for short-comings in the school system. Undoubtedly they will next point at Washington, and the federal government will be blamed for not appropriating a few billion more for buildings and salaries. Everything possible is being done to divert attention from the real cause, certification, and to make us believe that dollars are a cure-all. But higher salaries, per se, will do little more than give the hierarchy a stronger hold on the schools. As long as all the teachers and administrators in elementary, high, and junior college schools must be processed through a system that attracts the least capable people and indoctrinates them with an overdose of pedagogy and the myth that you need not know a subject in order to teach it, there will be a continuous downgrading of education at every level.

CHANGES IN TEACHER EDUCATION
Influences, Directions, Implications

JAMES M. HANLON

————————————

Dr. Hanlon is associate professor of education, Marquette University, Milwaukee, Wisconsin.

In teacher education, change seems to be the order of the day. But unexamined change is no more worth making than the unexamined life is worth living. It seems to me, therefore, that we owe it to ourselves to look very carefully at the forces which are influencing change in teacher education, the direction in which these forces are leading, and the implications this direction has for teacher education organizations and personnel.

Each of us, of course, must make his own assessment, and we may well find ourselves disagreeing with one another in any or all of these areas. We will probably disagree also in our judgments about the value of specific changes. This is all to the good, since it is obviously important that all facets of the dialogue receive thorough attention. In the interests of continuing this very important discussion, I would like to offer the following comments about current influences, directions, and implications.

INFLUENCES

At least five major forces are influencing teacher education today:

1. *The drive toward professionalism.* Teaching is experiencing today the same growing pains experienced by medicine as it grew toward professional status. The debate over unionism, for example, is a symptom of these pains. From all sides, however, the demand for professional prac-

The Journal of Teacher Education, 14:25–28; March, 1965. Reprinted by permission of the National Education Association-National Commission on Teacher Education and Professional Standards.

tices acts, including licensing by the profession under standards set by the profession, is growing in size and volume. The professionalization of teaching seems to be as inevitable as the integration of the schools. The demand for professional practice acts and licensing will therefore sooner or later be met.

2. *Accreditation.* The current debate over accreditation in general, and NCATE in particular, is accomplishing something very important. It is bringing into the open very frank discussion about what constitutes minimum standards for teacher education. There are without doubt some serious flaws in NCATE organization and procedure. The desire to set minimum standards, however, is not only laudable but essential—and there seems little doubt that we are coming closer to agreement on the nature of these standards.

3. *State certification requirements and local pay scales.* By 1960, over one-third of the states required advanced study for a permanent or higher grade teaching certificate. Moreover, several states require both advanced study and some years of satisfactory service for the permanent or higher grade certificate. The trend seems to be toward more, not less, study and experience for advanced certificates.

The existence of salary scales for teachers is an explicit recognition of the desirability of study and experience. Many scales now grant an increment for thirty semester hours of advanced study and an additional increment for thirty hours beyond the first thirty. Others grant an increment for the master's degree, another for thirty hours of study beyond the master's degree, and still another for the doctorate. More graduate work, coupled with experience, will therefore be demanded for and by teachers in the future.

4. *Research in education and related fields.* Education is in a very definite sense one of the youngest of the social and behavioral sciences. It is young in the sense that it has had the benefit of scientific study and experiment for but a brief span of years. The amount and varied nature of the research which has been accomplished in those years, however, constitute a testament to its vigor and potential.

Furthermore, research in education is being accelerated and expanded, thanks to grants from foundations and the U. S. Office of Education. Research is being conducted in the areas of curriculum, methods and materials of instruction, teacher-pupil interactions, classroom climate, evaluation, over- and underachievement, and a host of other areas. As a matter of fact, so much research is being reported that it is just about time for the National Education Association or some similar body to set up a committee for continuing synthesis so that this research can be assimilated by teachers and put to use in the classroom.

Research in fields related to education is also being accelerated and expanded. Advances have been made in anthropology (the works of Hall and Spindler, for example), in psychology (the works of Allport and

Maslow), and sociology (the works of Loomis and Hunter). Knowledge of these advances, together with their implications for teaching, is essential to the education of every teacher. Certainly the results of all this research are bound to influence teacher education, and to influence it increasingly.

5. *Experimental programs in teacher education.* Experiments are being conducted in practically every phase of teacher education, ranging from the general education of teachers (the Temple University experiment, for example) to the professional education of teachers (the Arkansas experiment), from undergradute programs to graduate programs, from small phases of a program to entire programs. As the results of these experiments are pooled and evaluated, we will be no firmer ground for proposing changes. There is already enough evidence to warrant much wider and more exact experiment in some areas, and certainly enough evidence to warrant changing some parts of our programs without further experiment.

DIRECTIONS

An assessment of the trends in the drive toward professionalism, the trends in accreditation, and the trends in certification and pay scales, together with an evaluation of the results of research in education and related fields and the results of experimental programs in teachers education, leads me to believe that teacher education is moving toward the following developments:

1. *A preeducation program.* This program will be similar in concept to prelaw and premedicine programs, but will be different in structure. It will be four or five years in duration, depending upon the time of the student's decision to enter teaching, and will be patterned somewhat as follows:

a. *A broad liberal arts background.*
   This background, however, may be quite different from the concept of liberal arts found in many of our colleges and universities. It is becoming apparent that analysis in many subject areas does not produce a synthesis of these subjects into the carefully evaluated world view demanded by teaching. The preeducation liberal arts program, therefore, may resemble more the honors program concept than the traditional liberal arts separate-subject program.

b. *Scholarly study of one subject field.*
   The broad liberal arts background, with its attendant careful construction of a world view, will include scholarly study in depth of one discipline. Here the student will learn the techniques needed for continuous extension of knowledge in the discipline of his choice.

c. *Thorough grounding in the social and behavioral sciences.*
   Anthropology, economics, political science, psychology, and sociology

will be studied as part of the basic liberal arts program. It will be possible, therefore, to devote the time allotted to education courses to appropriate materials instead of covering matter from these related fields and calling this education.

d. *A basic sequence in education.*

This sequence will probably consist of a maximum of twenty-four semester hours and will be taken toward the end of the preeducation program. The student will be introduced to the historical, philosophical, psychological, and sociological foundations of education, drawing here upon his knowledge, understanding, and skills gained in the earlier parts of his program. He will then study methodology. The sequence will end in a supervised teaching experience.

This education sequence will combine theory and practice. All courses will be laboratory courses, and the student will be gaining experience in schools beginning the first week of the first course. The sequence will be designed with one end in view—to prepare the student for his first year of actual teaching experience.

2. *An internship program.* For the first two or three years of his career the teacher will be considered an intern, in the same sense as the medical intern. He will practice his profession, but under the close supervision of a critic teacher *and a supervising teacher from his college or university.* These will be his inservice years. He will be attending lectures and seminars *designed cooperatively by his school and his college or university.* These will be in the area of diagnostic and remedial techniques in his teaching areas, test construction, etc. The school and the college or university will therefore be full partners in this phase of the professional program. When it is completed successfully, the student will have earned his master's degree.

During this internship the student will be given a chance to look at areas of specialization, including administration, guidance, and supervision, even as the medical intern looks at obstetrics and surgery. He will be tested in terms of his potential for these fields. He will receive guidance to help him decide whether to remain in the classroom or to become a specialist.

At the end of his internship, the student will take a state examination administered by the profession for a state license to practice as a teacher, just as the general practitioner in medicine obtains his license.

3. *Expanded professional studies for specialists.* As a doctor of medicine goes on to years of advanced study if he wishes to become a psychiatrist so will specialists in education, after they have been screened and accepted, be required to complete an additional period of study in the area which they have chosen. Part of the screening will be recommendation by the school in which the student was an intern. The programs will lead to the Ed.S., Ed.D., or Ph.D. degree.

The programs in these areas will be distinctly professional, demanding high intellectual output, outstanding skill, and definite levels of professional ethics and dedication. These programs also will culminate in field experience and/or an internship. *When the program has been completed, a state examination administered by the profession will be taken for a license to practice.*

4. *A program of continuing education.* Colleges and universities engaged in the business of teacher education will sponsor several types of continuing education programs, including regular courses, intensive seminars, and demonstration workshops. These programs will be provided for the general practitioner as well as the specialist. Some will deal with professional subjects, including up-to-date techniques, newest testing devices, and the last word in research in education and related fields. Other programs will deal with the humanities, the sciences, politics, economics, religion, and the arts, so that teachers may remain conversant with the changes daily taking place in this dynamic world. In other words, these programs will help teachers to keep themselves current in all the areas they must master if they are to be truly competent teachers.

5. *Closer cooperation between the schools and the colleges and universities.* Good hospitals and good schools of medicine go hand in hand. In the same way, good elementary and secondary schools and good schools of education cannot exist without each other. There is some evidence to suggest that we are moving toward both of these goals.

IMPLICATIONS

If this assessment is at all correct, if we are in fact moving in these directions, then it seems to me that the following implications now confront us:

1. *Colleges and universities must decide now on their commitment to teacher education.* A school of education of the type called for here will cost millions of dollars to build and maintain. Not every college and university can afford a complete commitment to teacher education of this type. Others may not care to make the commitment. Still others may wish to make a partial commitment, in terms of preeducation, and enter into a partnership with universities which have the facilities for a complete school of education.

Teacher education has nothing to lose and a great deal to gain if those who cannot or care not to enter the field on the scope indicated will say so quite frankly *now*. Similarly, those who can and wish to make the commitment must make that commitment clear *now*. Schools have a large stake in teacher education. It is only just that they be given the opportunity to develop and have a say in selecting the schools of education with which they choose to cast their lot. They cannot do so unless colleges and universities first declare their intentions.

2. *Schools and colleges and universities must begin to plan for an active*

partnership. Many college and university professors have not seen the inside of an elementary school or a high school in years. Many elementary and high school teachers have not taken an advanced course in years. Committees of teachers and professors working on common problems are rare. The day when such practices can be tolerated is just about over. Interaction must be sought by both sides at every opportunity. This also must begin *now*, for the sake of both. If the partnership is coming, let us seek it in good faith now, before the need for haste is upon us.

3. *Information about teacher education must be disseminated more widely.* Practitioners of teacher education have been much too reticent. Critics have been loud in condemnation, but we have been soft in justification. Professors in our colleges and universities who are not engaged in teacher education do not understand the problems of teacher education. Neither does the general public understand the problems. In a time of change, this is neither wise nor prudent. We must explain, justify, and document every move we make, whether it be for the sake of experiment or a more or less permanent shift in direction. In other words, we must end what appears to many to be our self-made isolation.

THE EDUCATION
OF COLLEGE TEACHERS

————▸◂◆▸◂————

The debate over the appropriate preparation of college teachers is as old as graduate education itself. There has never been a time in the past 80 years when the question was not the subject of interest and argument.

The intensity of the discussion today stems from the acute need for more college teachers. In 1956, the National Science Foundation estimated full-time (or equivalent) faculty at 196,000. The Foundation estimates that by 1970 this figure will rise to 495,000 if we succeed in keeping pace with our needs. In the period between now and 1970 we must not only find enough new teachers to cover enrollment increases, but must replace all present college faculty who retire or move on to different fields. Considering these added burdens, it is possible that the total new faculty to be recruited by 1970 would be between 300,000 and 400,000.

How many new college teachers will actually be trained between now and 1970? Dale Wolfle predicted that 135,000 Ph.D.'s, only half of whom would enter college teaching, would be produced between 1954 and 1970. The Association of Graduate Schools has estimated 235,537 for the same period. The latter prediction comes within reaching distance of estimated needs, and would be encouraging if it were not for the fact that in the past quarter century only 60 to 70 per cent of the Ph.D.'s from leading universities became college teachers. And most present-day observers believe this percentage will drop in the face of vigorous recruiting efforts from government and industry. That means that there will be a sharp decline in the proportion of college faculty members holding the Ph.D. One authoritative source predicted a decline from the current 41 per cent to about 20 per cent by 1970. Perhaps many institutions could absorb a

Summary of a discussion by the Trustees of The Carnegie Foundation for the Advancement of Teaching, reprinted by permission from the Fifty-third Annual Report, 1957–1958, pp. 11–26.

higher student load with no increase in number of faculty. But even with allowance for such absorptive capacity, the task ahead is of serious dimensions.

If the graduate schools do not produce enough college teachers to meet the demand, the teachers will be produced by other means. Great numbers of youngsters will flood into our colleges and universities whether we are prepared or not. And these youngsters will be taught—taught well or taught badly. And the demand for teachers will somehow be at least partly met—if not with well-prepared teachers then with ill-prepared, if not with superior teachers then with inferior ones.

The dilemma of the graduate schools is clear. If they attempt to meet the demand by rapid expansion or by lowering of standards, they risk diluting their product. If they follow their natural inclination to raise standards and to offer a higher quality of graduate education, they are likely to restrict their output rather than increase it. And if this occurs, the preparation of college teachers will to a considerable degree be taken over by institutions other than the graduate school. The dilemma is acute because most graduate school people are frankly dubious of the capacity of any other instrumentality to produce good college teachers.

There is no mystery as to which other institutions will move in to take up any slack left by the graduate schools in the production of college teachers: the schools of education are looking with lively interest on the prospect. Meeting an unfulfilled national demand in teacher preparation is not a new experience for the teachers colleges. The normal schools, out of which the teachers colleges developed, were themselves the product of such a demand. They sprang up in the nineteenth century when the liberal arts colleges were not preparing (and had no inclination to prepare) a supply of elementary and secondary teachers adequate to the nation's needs.

Let us set aside for the moment the question of what *should* happen. Most sensible observers are in agreement as to what probably *will* happen. The graduate schools will increase their output substantially, but not nearly enough to meet the demand. In some fields a good deal of this output will be siphoned off by industry and other non-academic competitors. Of the Ph.D.'s produced by the graduate schools who do go into academic work, most will go either to one of the leading universities or to one of a select few liberal arts colleges. The less influential universities, most of the liberal arts colleges, and all of the junior colleges will get their teachers through other channels. Some will be individuals who have obtained the Master of Arts degree in graduate school. Many others will have obtained the M.A. or Ph.D. degree in a school of education, graduate school of business, or other institution. Some observers go so far as to predict that within a couple of decades the graduate school will no longer be the dominant factor in the preparation of college teachers.

If these predictions are even approximately correct, they suggest a desirable line of action for the graduate schools. First, the graduate school should re-examine its own procedures and organization to determine the feasibility of increasing its output substantially. Second, the graduate school should accept the fact that even with expansion it will not meet all the needs, and it must admit that the unmet needs are legitimate. Some critics believe, perhaps without justification, that the graduate schools, sitting at the rarefied pinnacle of our higher education, cannot see far enough down through the haze to discern the needs of institutions such as the junior colleges. To the extent that such an attitude exists, it is ultimately destructive of the position of the graduate schools themselves. Even though the graduate schools cannot meet all of these needs, they can show a sense of responsibility about them and collaborate with other institutions in dealing with them, playing their part where they have a part to play, and lending moral support and intellectual guidance beyond that.

It is not easy to say just how far the graduate schools ought to go in meeting the pressures of numbers themselves. The first-rate professor in the first-rate graduate school is doing one of the most important jobs in our national life—training our most gifted students for the highest responsibilities of scholarship. It is an exacting job, and he is under heavy pressure to do it well in the national interest. If he does not have time left over to think about the junior colleges, it is not wholly surprising.

It is vital that we preserve ideals of excellence in graduate schools. The pressure of numbers must never lead us to swamp the first-rate in the second-rate nor to substitute quantity for quality.

To sum up, there are many levels and kinds of college teacher preparation, none of which should be neglected. There is a whole spectrum of legitimate demands. No one kind of institution must meet them all. All must be met.

What are the realistic possibilities of expanded output on the part of the graduate schools? There are two kinds of possible action: expansion of graduate school facilities, and better use of existing facilities through improvement of the practices of graduate education. Let us look first at the problems of expanding facilities.

Expansion in graduate education is an expensive process, involving such costly items as laboratories and libraries and a heavy investment in faculty. It is not only expensive but slow. It takes time to build a faculty capable of graduate teaching.

Perhaps the best hope at the moment is to strengthen the so-called "marginal producers"—graduate schools which have already laid a sound base for their future development but have not become major producers of graduate students. There are a number of institutions which have quite strong faculties and offer Master's degrees in a few fields, but do not offer the Ph.D. Some of these institutions already have the most important basis on which to build a graduate school: good faculty members, a good library, good laboratory facilities. All that they need is a judicious further strengthening of their faculty. Even if only one department is ready to offer the Ph.D., that department should be encouraged to do so without awaiting a more general graduate level development in the institution. Such departments may occasionally make fruitful alliances with the graduate school of a neighboring university. Another suggestion is that professors in separate four-year institutions, many of whom are fully qualified to supervise dissertations, take on a certain number of graduate students from neighboring graduate schools. Since most professors like to have at least some graduate students, the arrangement would have advantages on both sides.

In the effort to expand graduate education it is important to keep in mind the various regional compacts which have been developed for sharing of strength among institutions. Such regional collaboration could lead to a sounder and more rapid strengthening than might otherwise occur.

RECRUITMENT

The colleges must look forward to an increasingly competitive situation in recruitment of college teachers. Industry and government have shown ingenuity and aggressiveness in recruiting from the same pool of talent which must supply the colleges. If the graduate school is not to take the leavings, it will have to develop a recruiting ardor which has not characterized it to date.

Undergraduate colleges do relatively little to interest students in a teaching career, yet it is generally agreed that they could do this very effectively. The undergraduate college can inform the ablest seniors of scholarships and other opportunities in graduate work; acquaint them with the nature of American higher education; inform them of career possibilities in the field of their major; and acquaint them with the academic profession—a measure as effective in discouraging the unfit as in persuading the fit.

The college has an advantage over all competitors in that its natural recruiting agents—the teachers themselves—are in daily contact with students. Much informal evidence suggests that the teacher can be highly effective in recruiting. It is an impressive experience for the student to be singled out by his professor as a potential colleague.

Once the student is in graduate school, the most important means of winning him to a teaching career is to stimulate his intellectual interest in the subject of his choice. Many men now on college faculties had no conscious plan during their early graduate years to enter teaching, but were simply engrossed in a particular subject. It is almost certainly an advantage in gripping the student's interest if the graduate department exposes him early to actual dealing with the subject matter outside the classroom; i.e., in the laboratory, in "apprentice" teaching, or through active research. Autobiographical testimony of scientists and scholars suggest that it is often this sort of experience which first stimulates career plans.

Recruiting efforts must take into account the financial difficulties so common among graduate students, and these hardships cannot be considered separately from the long-term economic rewards of the profession. If the eventual economic rewards of a field are adequate, young people will put up with the momentary hardships. It is only when they see the deprivation as permanent that they tend to avoid the field.

College teachers themselves often point to the low public esteem of college professors as a deterrent in recruiting, but this is arguable. Studies of public attitudes toward various professions have always placed college teaching high on the list in terms of prestige.

Campus life has great attractions, and many individuals now on college faculties are there because of these attractions. Yet in the actual circumstances of graduate life, the student may live miles from the campus in an unattractive neighborhood and may experience no sense of community with other graduate students or with the university. A wife living in the slums while her husband is doing graduate work may not be the most vigorous proponent of an academic career.

When the graduate student observes the academic career as exemplified on his particular campus, he may encounter other discouraging conditions: prospects of slow advancement; indications that the "community of scholars" is really a collection of petty kingdoms; heavy teaching loads; low faculty morale; inadequate fringe benefits. The college which corrects these conditions is in a strong position to attract young people into academic life.

Many have emphasized that the recruitment efforts for college teaching should not be limited to graduate students. Much might be done to use the talents of retired professors, to raise the barriers on minorities, to draw married women with appropriate professional preparation back into the field after they have raised their families, and to borrow qualified professional men from industry and government. The possibilities offered by any one of these paths are limited, but all are worth exploring.

Those industries which have had to recruit large numbers of young men for scientific or advanced technological work have much to gain by collaborating with the universities—which are, after all, the sole source of such talent. Such industries should send their young men back for study until they get their Ph.D.'s, send their Ph.D.'s back for part-time teaching, and in other ways collaborate with the universities in the interests of both. The universities on their side should help industry where in-service courses are needed. The greater use by industry of research and professional personnel will almost inevitably lead to the need for such collaboration simply because such personnel will require continued intellectual stimulation.

PROPOSALS FOR REFORM OF GRADUATE EDUCATION

The graduate schools have been the subject of vigorous criticism for years, and this criticism has not stemmed from outsiders—it has originated within the system. There is ample reason for reform of graduate education.

One of the most familiar criticisms is that graduate education takes too long. Unfortunately there does not exist any wholly satisfactory data on how long it does take. The Association of Graduate Schools reports data from 30 member schools indicating an elapsed time to completion of Ph.D. requirements of 5½ years for the humanities and social sciences and 4¾ years for the natural sciences. Evidence from other sources suggests that these data are probably on the conservative side for the country as a whole.

The ablest leaders in higher education are in agreement in deploring excessively prolonged graduate work. All too often the marathon wrecks nerves, places a heavy strain on family life, and diminishes the likelihood that the individual will have a creative and valuable intellectual experience. Graduate training should be a vital experience and not an endurance contest.

It is possible to speed the process of graduate education. Most competent observers agree that the Ph.D. should take in the neighborhood of three years beyond the A.B. "Dilution" need not be a consequence: true scholarship need be neither exhausting nor interminable. Some first-rank departments in some institutions have always turned out their Ph.D. students in three years. Here are some of the suggestions which have been made for reducing the time required for the Ph.D.

1. More careful selection to insure that the student has the ability, the motivation, and the fortitude to carry him through a rigorous course without breakdowns or postponements.

2. Better counseling for the graduate student: early identification of his deficiencies, and a program for correcting them; early notification to those not likely to make the grade; a wise fitting of each student's program to his capacities; and realistic advice for those who wish to work part-time or to interrupt their graduate study.

3. More fellowships to avoid interrupting or lengthening graduate study with part-time or full-time work.

4. Acceleration for able students, beginning with elementary school. This is not a direct means of shortening graduate study, but it is a means of insuring that the student is not middle-aged before he receives his Ph.D.

5. Reorganization of graduate study. This might involve such measures as reducing the amount of course work, eliminating meaningless requirements, reducing the emphasis on "stuffing" the student with information, reducing the number of fields required for general examinations, excusing

the student from courses on which he can pass qualifying examinations, and freeing the dissertation of pretentious scholarship.

A good many critics believe that graduate education today is altogether too loosely organized and permissive, that it lacks well-defined objectives and invites students to dawdle. Critics point to the contrast in medical and legal education, in which tightly knit programs designed to produce definite intellectual results absorb the student's entire time and offer few choices.

Many believe that full-time study is our best hope for the reform of graduate education, and argue that graduate education should be a central and consuming experience for the student, not a part-time one. They do not object to limited amounts of teaching or other work which is part of the student's education, but oppose work which teaches him nothing and leaves him exhausted for his studies, or work which delays too long the completion of his degree requirements. The problem is a financial one in a high proportion of cases, but sometimes it is simply the competition of exciting alternatives that draws the student away from full-time study.

Some of the time lost in graduate school is spent making up for inadequate undergraduate preparation, and the deficiencies run all the way back to high school and elementary school. The corrective would be a vigorous raising of standards for the academically talented beginning as early as possible in the educational system.

So much for the problem of speeding up graduate education. Another familiar criticism is that training for research is overemphasized at the expense of training for college teaching. The conflict is a real one. The graduate school is uniquely the place where individuals may be introduced to the highest standards of scholarly investigation. It is also the primary producer of college teachers. It is inevitable that there should be some conflict between the two objectives.

Let us give research its due. The graduate school has a heavy responsibility to produce the finest kind of scholar. The university is, after all, a "citadel of learning," and the advancement of knowledge is one of its proudest goals.

The graduate school cannot resolve the conflict by turning out a certain number of creative researchers and in addition producing a certain number of college teachers. It must seek to inculcate scholarly research interests and standards in every man it turns out. Properly conceived, research training is simply a means of allowing a man to dig deeply into one subject so that he can understand what it means to know a field in depth. Without such knowledge he will not be able to understand or interpret the research of others, nor to distinguish between sound and meretricious scholarship.

But the critics do not deny the important role of the graduate schools in training for research. They simply assert that this has got out of balance with other legitimate objectives, chief among them being preparation for college teaching. Although good teaching is at the heart of good higher education, every graduate student knows that his future promotions will be determined more heavily by his writing than by his productiveness as a teacher.

Fortunately, it is possible to find a middle path between the extreme proponents of research and the extreme proponents of teaching. Every future college teacher should have the kind of graduate education which prepares him in some measure for both scholarship and teaching. Love of learning is a prerequisite for both productive scholarship and productive teaching. Every college teacher needs a taste of research training if he is to inspire future researchers. In order to keep abreast of what is going on, to appraise critically and interpret wisely, the teacher must be something of a scholar, though not necessarily an original researcher. But the graduate school must be sufficiently flexible in its approach so that it can encompass the training of some individuals who will be primarily scholars and others who will be primarily teachers. Any graduate department can achieve such flexibility without undergoing a major reorganization.

Any discussion of the role of research in graduate education leads to the question of the dissertation. A sound conception of the dissertation recognizes that it should be a trial run in scholarship and not a monumental achievement. Some graduate departments have magnified the thesis beyond reason, both in size and in emphasis upon it as an original contribution. There is no demonstrable relationship between the size of the dissertation and its quality. Some believe that the emphasis on an original contribution to knowledge is the most important factor in forcing students into more and more abstruse and narrow topics.

The important thing to keep in mind is that it is not so much what the individual can "prove" or "contribute" that counts in a dissertation; it is what the individual shows of how his mind works, of his literacy, of his quality of thought. Students must not be encouraged in the pretentious habit of trying to put everything they know into the thesis.

Some critics have attacked the whole notion of research training implicit in the dissertation by pointing out that a high percentage of Ph.D.'s do not make any published contribution after the thesis. Whether or not the facts are accurate, the argument is irrelevant. Published contributions are only one desirable consequence of research training. Other consequences are scholarly judgment, critical acuity, knowledge in depth, and the capacity to teach in an inspired fashion.

The criticisms of graduate education are more numerous than the constructive proposals for reform. However, there is a variety of proposals for a sounder Ph.D. program. One such is that advanced by the Committee on Policies in Graduate Education (Association of Graduate Schools). This committee proposes that the Ph.D. program should take no more than three years. The first two years would include all courses, leaving the third for the dissertation. Before admission the candidate would be required to prove that he could write respectable English and that he had mastery of one foreign language. He would be required to pass both foreign languages by the end of the second year; if he failed to do so he would be dropped or placed on probation. The faculty adviser would assist the student in developing a program suitable to him, excusing him from courses he did not need. Research and writing on the dissertation would be completed in a single year—a year which would be free of other courses.

There have been various proposals for introducing greater flexibility into graduate education. It is not unfair to say that today the imagination of the graduate faculty is dominated by the image of one kind of product—the research scholar. Much recent criticism has insisted that this should be supplemented with another image—that of the teacher. But these two images do not exhaust the possibilities. There are excellent students in the leading graduate schools today who have not the slightest intention of going on either to research or college teaching but instead look forward to careers in government or industry. Some graduate departments have found it extraordinarily difficult to admit that these students exist, and even more difficult to deal with them.

The most common recommendation for dealing with at least some of these deviants from the traditional graduate pattern is to revitalize the Master of Arts degree. Many universities have awarded the M.A. as a consolation prize for individuals who could not achieve the Ph.D. Others have awarded an M.A. automatically to individuals who complete a certain amount of time on their way to the Ph.D. It is not surprising that the prestige of the degree has fallen. Whether it can be restored is an open question.

Since neither the junior colleges nor the majority of four-year colleges are going to have the bidding power to attract as many Ph.D.'s as they would wish for their faculties in the competitive years ahead, there is much to be said for refurbishing the M.A. for those who want to teach at this level. This is alarming to some observers, who point out that the first two years of college are in many ways the most important and require the best teachers. But for the institutions with low bidding power, the choice will not be between an M.A. and a Ph.D. but between a good M.A. and a bad one, or between a good M.A. and no M.A. at all. Even today a quarter of college teachers do not have even the M.A. degree. In other words, the attempt to develop a sound M.A. is an attempt to provide these particular colleges with a better product than they will otherwise get. And many observers have pointed out that the Ph.D. is not, after all, the only avenue to good teaching. Teachers may be excellent and even productive in research without that magic degree.

It goes without saying that a refurbished M.A. should be rigorous; should involve a thesis and not just courses; and should be regarded as a terminal degree in its own right—a respectable route to certain kinds of college teaching with adequate prestige, promotion, and salary value of its own. The Committee on Policies in Graduate Education has suggested a program for the refurbished M.A. lasting a year and a half and involving a 75–125 page essay. They believe that the subject in which the student takes his M.A. should be named on the M.A. diploma.

Next to rehabilitating the M.A., the most familiar recommendation for introducing flexibility into the graduate program is that there be two kinds of Ph.D.—one for teachers and one for scholars. But the reaction of experts to the proposal is that one of the two degrees would inevitably be downgraded, and holders of that degree would be treated as second-class citizens in the eyes of university faculties.

Others have suggested that the present Ph.D. be kept just at it is with both teachers and scholars taking it, but that future teachers be required to supplement their Ph.D. with a "Certificate of Proficiency" requiring extra tasks (e.g., a teaching internship under supervision). This suggestion is nicely balanced by one which proposes that the present Ph.D. be kept just as it is, but that future researchers be required to go on to a more advanced degree. It is doubtful whether either of these suggestions will make any headway. Both have the great disadvantage of lengthening a process that has already grown unbearably long. To keep a scholar in leading strings for any period after the present Ph.D. program would only postpone his coming to maturity.

As far as the Ph.D. is concerned, there is already room for considerable flexibility if the academic department wishes to introduce that flexibility. Many departments already do a good deal to take into account individual differences in professional objectives. One thing is certain—no responsible person wishes to separate the research and teaching features of the Ph.D. But within that framework it would be useful to give far more explicit emphasis to different kinds of objectives and the ways in which the program could be varied to meet these objectives.

SPECIFIC PREPARATION FOR COLLEGE TEACHING

No one knows how to teach the future college teacher to impart knowledge. No one is even sure whether there are formal ways of doing this. More is involved than the communication of facts. The teacher must impart knowledge in such a way that the students see it as full of questions; he must quicken the intellectual processes of the student.

When people assert that there should be some kind of specific preparation for college teaching (other than subject matter preparation) they generally have in mind one or more of the following objectives.

1. Acquaintance with the skills, techniques, and methods of teaching.

2. Familiarity with the important ideas and issues in educational philosophy.

3. Teaching experience.

4. Understanding of the scope and nature of American higher education. Every faculty member believes it is his right to participate in decisions of importance to higher education, yet few understand the nature of higher education outside their own departmental activities.

The most prevalent faculty attitude toward all of these various measures is simply indifference. In most graduate departments, no steps of any kind are taken to prepare the graduate student specifically for his role as a college teacher. In a good many departments, however, the matter is given informal attention: a few faculty members see that the teaching assistants get informal help in learning their trade and that students receive part-time teaching assignments in summer or regular terms. Least common of all are formal courses to prepare students for college teaching—but such courses appear to be increasing. One study of 50 leading graduate schools shows that 78 per cent gave one or more (up to 24) courses in higher education, consisting either of courses that describe and analyze higher education or of courses in teaching methods. Some institutions which do not have courses have graduate seminars on problems of teaching. Some graduate school professors are actively opposed to such formal arrangements and believe that all significant objectives can be achieved through less formal activities.

There remains to be discussed one other means of preparation for college teaching—actual teaching experience. The most familiar vehicle for such experience is the traditional teaching assistantship, but it is universally agreed that this is not as meaningful an educational experience as it might be; and in any case, teaching assistantships are not required of all graduate students. If they were required and were a more significant learning experience, they might be a powerful factor in preparation for teaching.

Some observers argue for something substantially new in the way of apprentice teaching: supervised teaching linked with seminars and discussion groups. The teaching fellowships at the University of Chicago offer an example of an apprentice experience: the student is expected to devote about half time to work as "apprentice teacher" under the supervision of a department member; he helps prepare courses and exams, takes over teaching the class for a few weeks, handles a section on his own, and participates in a seminar on the problems of college teaching.

Many believe that the college which first employs a new Ph.D. is in a unique position to contribute to his education as a teacher, and has a positive responsibility to do so. Yet few colleges do anything. Here are some of the possibilities that have been discussed.

1. The employing college might set up an internship or apprenticeship

system, giving new Ph.D.'s a year of training under supervision, possibly also giving them seminars in higher education.

2. The college might employ the new Ph.D. in the regular rank of instructor but require that he enroll in a seminar on college teaching and accept supervision at the departmental level.

3. The college might take steps to encourage young teachers to increase the breadth and depth of their learning and experience. Adjustment of teaching loads and provision for summer study are among the ways of doing this. The first five years after the Ph.D. are vital in the creative life of the faculty member.

THE IMPROVEMENT OF TEACHERS

Increasing the effectiveness of present college teachers could be almost as significant a step toward solving the teacher shortage as recruitment and pre-service training. The statement that we have 200,000 faculty members is, after all, a very inadequate picture of our present resources. Many of the 200,000 are well-prepared and effective teachers; some are ill-prepared and ineffectual. Every one of the former is a tower of strength for higher education; the latter really should not be included in the total since they are not assets in any sense of the word. Any program which moves teachers from the second to the first category is as profitable as a recruiting program.

Well-designed programs for the further education of college teachers may be especially important in the years ahead, when the demand for teachers will draw into the profession many who are substandard in preparation for their jobs. Even under normal conditions of demand there are too many teachers who never complete the requirements for their Ph.D. or never continue their personal growth beyond graduate school.

Perhaps the most important requirement for the continued improvement of college teachers is that the *improvement of teaching* be a positive and widely shared value in the college. This should be reflected in a promotion policy which rewards good teaching as well as original research. Some colleges have prizes or awards for good teaching. Others have experimented with faculty committees on the improvement of teaching—a useful device for helping younger teachers.

Another requirement is that the college administration, including department heads, be continuously alert to opportunities for continued intellectual growth on the part of faculty members. This will be reflected in the policy on sabbaticals and leaves of absence for continued study or creative research.

The final requirement is arrangements which make it financially possible for the teacher to undertake continued study or research. This may require fellowships for further graduate study or for creative work. It may involve laboratory facilities, access to library collections, or travel. It certainly suggests a reasonable teaching load which allows some margin of time for self-development.

CONCLUSIONS

For 80 years the graduate schools have been debating the same issues and wrestling with the same problems. The issues have not changed, the problems have not been solved, and the battle lines have remained the same from one generation to the next. It now appears that circumstances will force at least a partial resolution of some of the issues.

Since the graduate schools have been the traditional producers of college teachers, and since they are powerful sources of strength in our higher education, it is desirable that they participate in framing any changes which occur, lending their prestige and wisdom to the task of shaping these changes. The alternative is that the changes will occur without their participation, without their advice and assistance, and perhaps in directions contrary to their wishes.

The graduate schools are not facing a blank wall. There are many possible paths which they may test out. Let us review some of the lines of action which may prove fruitful for the graduate school. In doing so, we must caution against easy generalization. Graduate schools differ greatly from one to another; a promising solution for one may not be for the next one. Many ideas which are promising enough to deserve a trial may in the long run prove fruitless or even damaging.

1. The graduate schools should accept the statistical facts concerning the number of college teachers needed in the decades ahead, and should make a reasonable effort to meet the demand within the limits of their own resources. If there are legitimate demands still unmet (and this is a certainty) by their own rate of production, then they should collaborate willingly with those institutions which must take up the slack.

2. Both the undergraduate college and the graduate school can play a more imaginative and effective role in recruiting future college teachers.

3. Efforts should be made to reduce the length of time required for the Ph.D. degree through better counseling, more fellowships, early admission or advanced placement of able students, and reorganization of graduate study.

4. The dissertation should be regarded as a trial run in scholarship and not as a monumental original contribution to knowledge.

5. The universities should throw their prestige and strength behind all efforts to raise standards for the academically talented student in elementary, secondary, and undergraduate education.

6. Every graduate department should give some thought to the extent to which it is preparing its young people for college teaching. Departments may differ as to the positive steps which they wish to take—some will be

satisfied with informal efforts along these lines; others will wish to institute a seminar, a requirement for supervised teaching, or formal course work. The precise pattern followed is less important than the question of whether they admit the relevance of the task and are willing to give *some* kind of serious thought to it.

7. A vigorous effort should be made to revitalize the Master of Arts degree and make it a terminal degree for teaching.

8. All institutions of higher education should accept responsibility for the continued intellectual and professional growth of faculty members.

CAMPUS-WIDE PREPARATION
OF TEACHERS
An Exercise in Collaboration

ERNEST L. BOYER

———————→◄●►◄———————

Dr. Boyer is executive dean for university-wide activities, State University of New York, Albany, New York. He was director of the Joint Commission to Improve the Education of Teachers in California, 1960–1962.

A recent conference over the luncheon table at a resort in Santa Barbara marked another milestone on the road to better teaching in California. Attending the meeting were a professor of English, a mathematician, a historian, a professor of Spanish, a biologist, an economist, a director of teacher training, a school superintendent, two deans of education, and several education professors from California state colleges.

The story behind the luncheon began when the Board of Directors of the California Council on Teacher Education (a group named to advise the State Superintendent of Public Instruction) met with officers of the Western College Association to look for ways to arrest the growing tension between "academicians" and "educationists" on the campusus of the colleges and universities in California.

This meeting of arts and science leaders with their counterparts in education was strategically timed. Post-Sputnik anxiety had crescendoed, and on many campuses the clash over the nation's schools in general and the training of teachers in particular had become embarrassingly nonprofessional. At the very time when wise men should have led the state in a constructive appraisal of both the ends and means of education, college people

The Journal of Teacher Education, 14:271–274; September, 1965. Reprinted by permission of the National Education Association-National Commission on Teacher Education and Professional Standards.

were locked in an interprofessional struggle that pitted department against department and prejudice against prejudice.

THE TASK

Meeting in this climate of discord and distrust, the executives of the Western College Association and the California Council on Teacher Education resolved to seek statemanship. After sifting alternatives, the WCA and CCTE officials agreed to begin the process by sponsoring jointly a blue ribbon team staffed by both professionals in education and leaders in the liberal arts. As conceived, the members of this interdisciplinary committee would meet together over an extended period and seek, first of all, to build bridges of understanding *among themselves*. Further, the executives agreed that if the experiment went well the study team would then seek ways to balance off—statewide—the rival and frequently acrimonious claims of general education, the academic major, and training in the arts of teaching.

So it was that six California professors of education and a similar number of liberal arts professors came together to improve the quality of teacher training in California by improving the relationship among those who train. The beginning session was marked by caution and reserve, for, after all, the task assigned was substantial and the path uncharted. But, fortunately, decency dominated as reservation yielded to cordiality. Delegates quickly discovered that beneath prejudices and vested intellectual interests lay convictions shared by academicians and educationists alike. Indeed, during the very first session, basic agreements were identified which were to form the foundation for all future talk and action. These declarations read in part as follows:

1. *Members of this Commission are in complete agreement that the preparation of good teachers is the function of the college or university as a whole. For it needs the best that the institution can contribute for each prospective teacher toward his full development as a person, toward his broad, liberal education, toward solid foundations of the subject matter he will teach, and toward his professionalization as a school worker.*
2. *As we ponder the education of elementary teachers, particularly, we concluded that we simply cannot satisfy the twin goals of producing a liberally educated person (which a teacher is, first of all) and a professionally trained worker in a four-year program. We are forced, therefore, to call for a five-year minimum of preparation for all teachers.*
3. *In a five-year program, or in longer programs for that matter, prospective teachers cannot be prepared to perform all their classroom functions in the fashion of veterans. The attempt to do so leads to a proliferation of professional courses and the requirement of so many units in Education as to imperil the desired amount of preparation in non-professional sub-*

ject matter. Experience in teaching will improve skill in teaching, especially when it is supported by such means as further professional study, in-service workshops, and local supervision.

4. We believe uncompromisingly in the critical importance of preparation in academic subject matter to provide an essential part of the equipment of all teachers.

5. Our great concern for the general and liberal education of every teacher is paralleled by equal concern for his professional preparation. It should be achieved as compactly and as economically as possible; nevertheless, again uncompromisingly, time must be found for what is essential.

6. The development of a program for the education of teachers, including balancing and harmonizing of the general education, specialized subject preparation, and professional education sectors, is the function of each college or university as a whole.

We urge the formation in each college or university of an institution-wide policy body—committee, council, or whatever mechanism may be suitable—to study the program as a whole and coordinate the process of its improvement.

Encouraged by early rapport and the ease with which these agreements had been reached, the group moved quickly to consolidate gains. In quick succession, the Joint Committee selected a name,[1] outlined a plan of action, and secured funds to finance the venture.[2]

THE PROCEDURE

The first major thrust beyond the conference room was directed toward college presidents and deans. Commissioners reasoned that full administrative support was not only helpful but essential if this statewide venture was to succeed. This conviction led to a commission-sponsored conference for all chief campus officers in California. At this conclave, members of the Joint Commission reviewed the basic agreements they themselves had reached and candidly called for improved relations among liberal arts and education departments at colleges across the state. The response was encouraging.

Next, faculty support was solicited. Every California institution accredited to train teachers was invited to send delegates to one of four regional faculty conferences. Two hundred twenty-one college and university professors from forty-seven institutions of higher learning answered the call. At these sessions, teachers from a score of academic departments met together;

[1] The first official name, "The Joint Commission on the Improvement of Teacher Education in California," was later changed to the more euphonious title, "Joint Commission to Improve the Education of Teachers in California."

[2] Grants from the Rosenberg Foundation, San Francisco, and the Ford Foundation, New York, assured the future of the Commission and made it possible for its influence to be extended across the state.

spoke critically, yet constructively, about present practices in teacher education; and speculated about new kinds of programs that might be designed cooperatively during the days ahead. Most professors agreed that the preparation of teachers was indeed the responsibility of the college or university as a whole, and everyone urged the Commission to continue its effort to weld together all of the partners into a working unit.

But all this ferment was only preliminary to the main campaign. Clearly, platform declarations, statewide conferences, and printed reports were useless if unsupported by action on the campuses where the real work is done. All agreed that improvements between professional education and liberal arts departments would be achieved only as staff people at each teacher-training institution talked together in a professional manner over an extended period. In the view of the Commission, this called for the same kind of collaboration on the local campus that had proved so successful statewide.

The strategy was clear. The Commission urged, by public declaration and written communication, that an all-college committee on the education of teachers—a kind of joint commission in miniature—be organized on the campus of every institution in California accredited for teacher education. As the Commission saw it, this required the formation of interdepartmental committees which were something more than an exercise in diplomacy dedicated to togetherness. Their object, rather, was to create a new kind of working unit on each campus that would view the total program of teacher education from an interdisciplinary perspective, assess and balance the various components, and define a set of learning experiences with a clear purpose. Making use of the specific strengths of the particular institution, such a program would have implications far beyond its point of origin.

PROGRESS

The response to this call for campus-wide teacher education committees pleased both the Commission and its sponsors. Forty-seven of the fifty institutions in California accredited for teacher education have now organized some type of all-college committee on campus.

Ranging in size from six to fifteen members, the campus committees at most institutions were appointed by a chief administrative officer, either the president or dean. On some campuses, each academic department selected its own representative; a few institutions chose the new committee members by a vote of the general faculty.

The power assigned to these all-college committees varied from place to place. On nine campuses, the newly formed unit was given broad authority in matters of teacher preparation, but in most instances committee power was limited to a policy-recommending or advisory role only.

As anticipated, not everyone welcomed this innovation. Men do not give up the old for the new easily. At a few institutions, hostility, apathy, or confusion blocked the effort to form an all-college committee. Others failed in their effort to execute the plan simply because busy men from many departments could not find time to get together.

But the greatest barrier to the whole idea was fear—fear that the college-wide approach to the education of teachers would violate long-standing departmental autonomy and limit authority and power. The project sought to meet this concern head on. Time and again commissioners insisted that cooperative planning was intended to enhance rather than destroy departmental effort. They stressed that the goal was to provide machinery for effective cooperation among departments without invading any specialized field or seeking to rob it of the freedom required to do its work. But for some the argument did not impress, and at the schools where fear and suspicion persisted, the moves toward increased cooperation were more symbolic than substantial.

While some colleges did meet roadblocks too high to hurdle, most institutions took giant strides forward. One California college reported that "this cooperative venture has increased campus understanding of the complexity of teacher preparation" another testified that the all-college committee stirred a new spirit of cooperation on campus. A large private institution told of "increased interest in teacher education on the part of the entire faculty," and still another predicted that "the campus-wide committee will play a major role in adjusting our teacher education to new credential requirements in the state."

Several institutions reported even more substantial gains. One campus-wide committee designed a new major for elementary teachers; another developed a unique internship program; and a third committee has led the way in constructing an imaginative new sequence for the in-service education of teachers.

These were the achievements reviewed by the Joint Commission at its final luncheon meeting in Santa Barbara. While there was a consensus that no miracles had occurred, there was also a feeling that the effort had not gone unrewarded. On many campuses, the statewide move to provide a framework for mutual discussion did indeed create a greater respect between professional educators and members of "the academy." A host of faculty members from a variety of disciplines now are prepared to agree that the training of teachers is in fact the responsibility of the college or university as a whole. Communication has led to a united quest for better ways to prepare better teachers—teachers equipped to mobilize the heritage of the past for the conquest of the future in a time of ceaseless change and challenge.

As a result of the venture, one may reasonably conclude two things: first, traditional barriers to better practice are not insurmountable; and second, when men of diverse purpose are collectively asked to put reason to work in an unreasonable situation, good can come. Much as the academicians and educationists were able to improve the preparation of teachers in the instance described, other collaborators can take on other issues as long as they are committed to a willingness to tolerate the necessary anxiety involved, to meet the critical reactions head on, and to recognize that innovations must be nurtured with painstaking slowness and that a little progress is not to be scorned.

A total of seventeen California educators served on the Joint Commission. Replacements were necessary from time to time to accommodate personal schedules. The Commissioners and their fields are:

Harold M. Bacon, Stanford University (Mathematics)
Mitchell P. Briggs, Secretary-Treasurer, Western College Association.
William A. Brownell, University of California, Berkeley (Education), Chairman of the Joint Commission, 1958–1962.
Wendell E. Cannon, University of Southern California (Education)
Sister Elizabeth Ann, Immaculate Heart College (Education)
Darrell F. X. Finnegan, S.J., Loyola University (Education)
William B. Fretter, University of California, Berkeley (Physics)
Barbara M. Garcia, Mills College (Spanish)
Lloyd G. Ingles, Fresno State College (Biology)
L. L. Jones, Superintendent of Schools, Ventura (Administration)
Lelia Taggart Ormsby, Sacramento State College (Education)
Thomas F. Parkinson, University of California, Berkeley (English)
D. W. Rowland, University of Southern California (History)
Hallet D. Smith, California Institute of Technology (English)
Tracy E. Strevey, University of Southern California (Administration)
Procter Thomson, Claremont Men's Colleges (Economics)
Fred T. Wilhelms, San Francisco State College (Education)

ANNOTATED BIBLIOGRAPHY

BOOKS

Bibliographical Data	Annotation
American Association of Colleges for Teacher Education, *Freedom with Responsibility in Teacher Education,* American Association of Colleges for Teacher Education, 1964. 217 pp.	Proceedings of the 1964 Annual Meeting. Pages 43–49 give the results of an opinionaire on the Conant report issued to 310 members of AACTE. Takes Conant recommendations, and asks for reactions to them. There is a speech by Conant and other reactions to the report in form of papers. All articles pertinent. Good discussion of the need for empirical research in teacher education.
American Association of Colleges for Teacher Education, *Liberal Arts Colleges and Teacher Education,* American Association of Colleges for Teacher Education, 1963. 58 pp.	Excellent for statistics. Points out the role of the liberal arts college in training teachers.
Barzun, Jacques, *Teacher in America,* Doubleday, 1954. 280 pp.	Entertaining and vital. A discussion of what is taught, how it is taught, and why it is taught. Particularly good on the teaching of science and of woman's place in the university.
Beggs, David W., *Decatur-Lakeview High School: A Practical Application of the Trump Plan,* Prentice-Hall, 1964. 266 pp.	A case history of what happened in Lakeview H.S., Decatur, Illinois, in an effort to improve instruction. Stressed team teaching, large and small group instruction with independent study, multimedia teaching aids, and flexible scheduling. Sections on Programmed Learning, Teacher Clerical Aids, and a Lay Advisory Committee.
Beggs, Walter K., *The Education of Teachers,* The Center for Applied Research, 1965. 110 pp.	Good historical review. Largely concerned with pre-service education. Chapters dealing with certification, accreditation, and the growing interest in teacher education.
Bereday, George Z., et al., *The Changing Soviet School: The Comparative Education Society Field Study in the U.S.S.R.,* Houghton Mifflin, 1960. 514 pp.	A description of a visit made by 70 members of the Comparative Education Society to the U.S.S.R. in 1958. The chapters on Pre-School Education, Primary Education, and Secondary Education reflect how the teachers are trained. Chapter 12 is on Teacher Education.

BOOKS (continued)

Bibliographical Data	Annotation
Bestor, Arthur E., *Restoration of Learning: A Program for Redeeming the Unfulfilled Promise of American Education*, Knopf, 1955. 459 pp.	Similar to his *Educational Wastelands*, 1953; four parts. Describes what education is necessary, criticizes existing policies, discusses solutions.
Biddle, Bruce J., and W. J. Ellena (eds.), *Contemporary Research on Teacher Effectiveness*, Holt, Rinehart and Winston, 1964. 315 pp.*	A symposium of nine chapters, all on teacher effectiveness. Discusses past methods of evaluating results of teaching, and research now in the field.
Boles, Donald E., *The Bible, Religion, and the Public Schools*, Iowa State University, 1963. 313 pp.*	Good survey of the entire problem.
Combs, Arthur W., *The Professional Education of Teachers*, Allyn and Bacon, 1965. 130 pp.	Centers on noncurricular considerations in teacher training, such as personality, beliefs. Chapter on Organizing the Professional Aspects of a Teacher Preparation Program.
Conant, James B., *The American High School Today*, Signet, 1964. 140 pp.	More on the composition of the high school curriculum than on teacher education, but still applicable. Section III, Recommendations for Improving Public Secondary Education, has 21 specific recommendations.
Conant, James B., *The Education of American Teachers*, McGraw-Hill, 1963. 275 pp.	Entire volume highly applicable, particularly the chapters on Who Guards the Gates?, The Academic Preparation of Teachers, and The Education of Secondary School Teachers. Makes numerous specific recommendations.
Conant, James B., *A Memorandum to School Boards: Recommendations in the Junior High School Years*, Educational Testing Service, 1960. 46 pp.	A 14-point thorough but brief examination of what the junior high school should be like.
Conant, James B., *Slums and Suburbs*, Signet, 1964. 147 pp.	An excellent summary of the slums and suburbs of the U.S. Discusses personnel problems for slum schools.
Crow, Alice, and Lester D. Crow, eds., *Vital Issues in American Education*, Bantam Books, 1964. 305 pp.*	A collection of essays by Gilbert Highet, W. B. Reiner, R. N. Bush, and L. J. Rubin.
Diekhoff, John Siemon, *Tomorrow's Professors: A Report of the College Faculty Internship Program*, Fund for	Chapters on Teachers Born or Made?, Supervised Teaching: The Hard School of Experience. Recommended

* Indicates bibliography.

BOOKS (continued)

Bibliographical Data	Annotation
Advancement of Education [1959 or 1960]. 91 pp.	for advice to new college teachers. Eighteen campuses participated.
Herzog, John D. (ed.), *Preparing College Graduates to Teach in Schools,* American Council on Education, 1960. 49 pp.	A survey of where qualified graduates may go to qualify to teach by a fifth year of work.
Hodenfield, G. K., and T. M. Stinnett, *The Education of Teachers: Conflict and Consensus,* Prentice-Hall, 1961. 177 pp.	Written in popular style. Tells of a confrontation of liberal arts professors with education professors at three conferences. Sections on student teaching, certification, liberty without license. Interesting and provocative.
Jamer, T. Margaret, *School Volunteers: Creating a New Dimension in Education Through Lay Participation,* Public Education Association, 1961. 200 pp.	New York City Program for school volunteers. Excellent survey of the entire problem of using volunteers.
Jeffreys, Montagu V. C., *Revolution in Teacher Training,* Pitman, 1961. 85 pp.	An exposition of teacher training in England.
Kershaw, Joseph A., and Roland N. McKean, *Teacher Shortages and Salary Schedules,* McGraw-Hill, 1962. 198 pp.	A highly documented account, particularly strong on teacher salaries. A good chapter on The Shortages in Relation to Salaries. Pithy.
Koerner, J. D. (ed.), *The Case for Basic Education: A Program of Aims for Public Schools,* Little, Brown, 1959. 256 pp.	Sixteen scholars provide a discussion of what secondary education could be like if the American high school did what it should. Chapter on speech by Bower Aly.
Koerner, J. D., *The Miseducation of American Teachers,* Houghton Mifflin, 1963. 360 pp.	One of the controversial books in the field. Discussion of the Carleton College case with NCATE. Chapters on The Conduct of Education Courses and The Masters and Doctors of Education. Discusses the quality of textbooks and attitudes of students toward education courses and points out that a poor quality of student is attracted to education. Good graphs and case histories.
Lindsey, Margaret (ed.), *New Horizons for the Teaching Profession,* National Commission on Teacher Ed-	Good overall viewpoint. An excellent chapter is A License to Teach.

BOOKS (*continued*)

Bibliographical Data	Annotation
ucation and Professional Standards, National Education Association, 1961. 243 pp.	
Lynd, Albert, *Quackery in the Public Schools*, Little, Brown, 1953. 282 pp.	Chapter 10, What to Do about It?, suggests some practical remedies which are applicable to teaching.
Mayer, Martin, *Where, When, and Why: Social Studies in American Schools*, Harper & Row, 1962. 206 pp.	A research project sponsored by the American Council of Learned Societies. Describes the activity of the Physical Sciences Study Committee in improving instruction in physics in high schools. Discusses training in social sciences, anthropology, psychology, sociology, math, and science.
McGrath, Earl James, and Charles H. Russell, *Are School Teachers Illiberally Educated?*, Bureau of Publications, Teachers College, Columbia, 1961. 28 pp.	A study to determine how much pedagogy is required of teachers, how broadly the teacher is educated, and how his specialized instruction compares with other fields. Tables. Good brief coverage.
Moffitt, John C., *In-Service Education for Teachers*, Center for Applied Research in Education, 1963. 243 pp.	Discusses summer schools, institutes, mathematics as an example of curriculum change, the workshop as a means of in-service education.
National Commission on Teacher Education and Professional Standards, *Axioms and Goals, Selected Recommendations, Questions and Issues, A Position Paper*, National Education Association, 1963. 31 pp.	A terse report of objectives, proposals for change, and implications of the changing picture in American education.
Richardson, Cyril Albert, et al., *The Education of Teachers in England, France, and the U.S.A.*, UNESCO, 1953. 340 pp.	Somewhat dated, but excellent for background on the three countries.
Rickover, Hyman G., *American Education—A National Failure*, Dutton, 1963. 502 pp.	The report to the House Appropriations Committee in May, 1962, plus a preface, Fact and Fiction in American Education, and a conclusion, A National Standard for Education.
Rickover, Hyman G., *Education and Freedom*, Dutton, 1959. 256 pp.	Chapter 11, Demonstration High Schools and National Standards, asks schools to show that a broad liberal arts education can be obtained in about 14 years, rather than 16. Notes on Dutch and Russian education.

BOOKS (continued)

Bibliographical Data	Annotation
Robbins, Glaydon D., *Teacher Education and Professional Standards in England and Wales*, Ohio State University, 1963. 116 pp.	A concise study of teacher training in England and Wales.
Sarason, Seymour B., K. S. Davidson, and Burton Blatt, *The Preparation of Teachers—An Unstudied Problem in Education*, Wiley, 1962. 121 pp.*	A thought-provoking summary of the problem of how to train teachers— the debate between "the scholar" and "the educationist." Good coverage of the value of observing to teacher education.
Sebaly, Avis Leo (ed.), *Teacher Education and Religion*, American Association of Colleges for Teacher Education, 1959. 281 pp.*	Chapters on Teacher Education and Religion, Religion and the Humanities in Teacher Education, Teaching about Religion in the Social Sciences, and Teaching Reciprocal Relations between Natural Science and Religion.
Smith, Mortimer B., *The Diminished Mind: A Study of Planned Mediocrity in Our Public Schools*, Regnery, 1954. 150 pp.	Chapters on The Decline in Learning; Adjustment Replaces Education; Education Brainwashing, Democratic Style; and Putting Parents in Their Place, or, The Customer Is Always Wrong. Particularly applicable is chapter 5, The Stranglehold of the Educationists.
Smith, Mortimer B., *Public Schools in Crisis*, Regnery, 1956. 164 pp.	A series of very entertaining essays, some of which have appeared elsewhere, biased toward an emphasis on liberal arts training. Stimulating and entertaining.
Stabler, Ernest (ed.), *The Education of the Secondary School Teacher*, Wesleyan University, 1962. 239 pp.	Good chapters on Teacher Training in England and France, and on training teachers in specific subjects, such as English, history, modern languages, and mathematics.
Stiles, Lindley Joseph, et al., *Teacher Education in the U.S.*, Ronald, 1960. 512 pp.	Chapters on Student Teaching, Internship, General Education of Teachers. Recommended for survey of area.
Strom, Robert D., *Teaching in the Slum School*, Merrill, 1965. 116 pp.	Chapter 3 discusses Preparation and Recruitment of Teachers, with subheadings of Staffing the Difficult Schools, Collegiate Training, Discipline in the Classroom, and Inservice Programs.

BOOKS (continued)

Bibliographical Data	Annotation
Strom, Robert D., *The Tragic Migration: School Dropouts*, National Education Association, 1964. 38 pp.*	Speaks of the teacher's part in dropouts. An excellent survey of the problem.
Thut, I. N., and Don Adams, *Educational Patterns in Contemporary Societies*, McGraw-Hill, 1964. 494 pp.	Sixteen excellent chapters on education in Western and Asian countries. Good graphics.
Trace, Arthur S., *Reading Without Dick and Jane*, Regnery, 1965. 186 pp.	An examination of how reading is being taught, with regrets about the lack of excellence of the programs.
Trace, Arthur S., *What Ivan Knows That Johnny Doesn't*, Random House, 1961. 211 pp.	By an associate professor at John Carroll University. Compares textbooks and curricula of U.S. and U.S.S.R. on reading, literature, foreign languages, history, and geography. Makes recommendations for improvement.
Walcutt, Charles Child (ed.), *Tomorrow's Illiterates: The State of Reading Instruction Today*, Little, Brown, 1961. 168 pp.	A release of the Council for Basic Education. Discusses phonics, reading retardation, and reading readiness. Six English and American authors discuss the various problems of reading.
Wales, John N., *Schools of Democracy: An Englishman's Impressions of Secondary Education in the American Middle West*, Michigan State University, 1962. 161 pp.	Chapters on The Idea of Educational Democracy, The Mental Pablum, and The Inherent Contradiction. American schools tend to follow and not lead. Urgent need for leadership and scholarship.
Wiggins, Samuel P., *Battlefields in Teacher Education*, Peabody College Book Store, 1964. 109 pp.	Good, controversial. Interesting chapters on Conant vs. State Teacher Licensing, Desegregation: As a Man Thinketh, and Philanthropic Angels: Horns vs. Halos.
Woodring, Paul, *New Directions in Teacher Education: An Interim Report of the Work of the Fund for the Advancement of Education in the Areas of Teacher Education and Recruitment*, Fund for the Advancement of Education, 1957. 142 pp.	Short and to the point. Discusses The Two Traditions of Teacher Education in the United States, Programs for Older College Graduates, The Master of Arts in Teaching, and The Problem of Evaluation. A synopsis of 25 teacher-education programs receiving Fund support. Excellent on the new ideas that are being tried.

Periodical	Author	Title, Date	Annotation
American Association of Colleges for Teacher Education Yearbook		Basic rationale for the education of teachers: three views; symposium. 16:13–49; 63.	Koerner, Woodring, and Stinnett offer three excellent articles summarizing some of the issues of conflict in teacher education.
	H. S. Broudy	Can we save teacher education from its enemies and friends? 16: 85–91; 63.	In favor of methods courses. An attempt to "organize, systematize, and stabilize" training for education.
	E. O. Melby	Teacher education for a changing society. 17:68–76; 64.	Why teacher education is totally divorced from the needs of society and what to do about it.
		The Conant opinionaire. 17:43–49; 64.	Of 191 forms returned, 178 showed that changes were not planned as a result of the Conant report.
	H. Taylor	Future implications and repercussions of the report; Conant report. 17:26–35; 64.	Points to the narrow framework of Conant's report and the need to adapt teacher education to the society teachers live in, not the society that teachers' teachers live in.

PERIODICALS (continued)

Periodical	Author	Title, Date	Annotation
American Educator	C. P. Williams	Fifth year makes the difference. 1: 6–8; May, 65.	A detailed report of the intern program established by the University of Pittsburgh.
American School Board Journal	R. W. Elliot	Team teaching: effective in-service training. 144:19; Feb., 62.	A widespread system of off-campus team teaching will serve to introduce the new teacher to his profession.
Atlantic Monthly	J. D. Koerner	How not to teach teachers. 211:59–63. Feb., 63.	Proposes that the intellectual caliber of the education faculty is the fundamental limitation of the field.
Better Homes and Gardens	R. H. Beck	How well are our teachers being taught? Never better! 36:51–54; May, 58.	A forceful support of the excellence of teacher education. Good supporting materials.
	John Keats	How well are our teachers being taught? Never worse! 36:51–52; May, 58.	Depicts a fictitious college in New York State called "Fairly Normal." Proposes that the college is more interested in methods than in subject matter.
Bulletin of the California State Department of Education	C. Robinson, et al.	The place of internship programs in teacher educacation. 29:31 pp.; Sep., 60.	An excellent, specific account of how persons who had not taken education

PERIODICALS (continued)

Periodical	Author	Title, Date	Annotation
			courses during their college career were prepared to teach. Statistics. Take student teaching and then teach under supervision.
Business Education World	J. Lahey	Methods courses don't have to be busy work. 42: 28–30; Feb., 62.	Suggests what needs to be included in a methods course.
Catholic Education Review	M. Kinnane	Second look at five-year plan for teacher education. 61:608–611; Dec., 63.	Questions the validity of changing to the five-year plan when the four-year plan has not been proven unsuccessful.
Changing Times		How good are our teachers? 17:25–31; June, 63.	Discusses four topics: Teacher Preparation: Is It a Boondoggle; Who Is Qualified to Teach; Where Do Teachers Come From; and How Well Do Teachers Teach. Four-step solution offered.
Clearing House	E. Brainard	JHS. teacher: has the training been adequate? 38:179–181; Nov., 63.	Junior high school teachers need specific training and should not be recruited from senior high teachers.
	E. R. Fagan	Conant on	Discusses the

PERIODICALS (continued)

Periodical	Author	Title, Date	Annotation
		teacher education. 39:461–466; Apr., 65.	colleges that are testing Conant's plan.
	E. B. Weisse	Five steps to quality education. 38:158–160; Nov., 63.	The answer to better education is better teachers. A five-step plan for improving teacher quality.
College English	G. W. Stone	Five years since the basic issues report; reflections and predictions. 26:585–591; May, 65.	Points to the establishment of teacher institutes as a result of recent federal appropriations for the purpose of upgrading the teaching of English.
Economist		Teacher training: crabbed colleges. 213:1332+; Dec. 19, 64.	Britain's problems with teacher education. Lord Robbins proposes that training colleges be affiliated with university faculties of education.
Education Digest	I. N. Berlin	Unrealities in teacher education. 30:23–26; March, 65.	Teachers taught to cope with the ideal, and not the realistic, classroom and community situation.
Educational Forum	L. J. Stiles	Role of liberal arts colleges in teacher education. 28:171–177; Jan., 64.	The liberal arts college is responsible for the knowledge of the teacher, but there is more to it than that.

PERIODICALS (continued)

Periodical	Author	Title, Date	Annotation
Graduate Comment, Wayne State University		Education in the U.S.S.R. and in the U.S.A. 3:1–16; Feb., 60.	Excerpts from Rickover's testimony on Russia, followed by comments by four professors.
High School Journal	W. J. Popham	Individual differentiation in teacher education. 48:364–367; Feb., 65.	An experiment to test how individuals who enter a professional education course with mastery of subject matter can complete the course in an abbreviated manner.
Journal of Secondary Education	D. L. Knapp	Deemphasizing professional education. 40:110–112; Mar., 65.	Reasons why the number of required education courses should be cut down.
	Sterling McMurrin	The education of teachers. *41, no.* 2:81–85; Feb., 66.	Speech before California "Governor's Conference on Education." Discusses teacher education in light of school's responsibility for social reform.
	A. C. Ornstein	Teacher training for "difficult" schools. 39:172–173; Apr., 64.	A plan to educate teachers who are willing to teach in the difficult schools.
Journal of Teacher Education	R. B. Brown	Dangers in the misuse of NCATE accreditation. *14:* 326–332; Dec., 63.	How NCATE might abuse powers, how they have been abused, and suggestions for improvement.

PERIODICALS (continued)

Periodical	Author	Title, Date	Annotation
	D. D. Darland (ed.)	The education of teachers in America. 16, no. 4: 389–481; Dec., 65.	Symposium issue. Sixteen articles, all of direct interest.
	A. S. Fischler	The methods course, why? 12: 201–204; June, 61.	A recommendation for revising the present methods courses, using science as an example.
	A. M. Kazamias	Education of good teachers and the Oberlin Master of Arts in Teaching Program. 12: 205–208; June, 61.	A description of the program at Oberlin.
	R. M. Magee	Admission-retention in teacher education. 12:81–85; Mar., 61.	Admission to and retention in the teacher-education program.
	J. B. Whitelaw, C. B. Lindquist	Continuing challenge of Soviet teacher education 1963. 14:119–127; June, 63.	A comprehensive report of the differences between teacher training in the U.S. and the U.S.S.R.
	F. T. Wilson	Motivation of the gifted and teacher education. 12: 179–184; June, 61.	Suggests a special program to train teachers of the gifted.
		James Bryant Conant's The Education of American Teachers; symposium. 15:5–49; Mar., 64.	Ten authorities discuss Conant's report, both agreeing and disagreeing.
Liberal Education	P. C. Reinert	Liberal arts and teacher education. 51:20–28; Mar., 65.	A plea against state control of practice teaching, as proposed by Conant.

PERIODICALS (continued)

Periodical	Author	Title, Date	Annotation
	W. K. Selden	Basic issues in accreditation of teacher education. 47:536–546; Dec., 61.	Excellent for an understanding of who and what NCATE is and how it operates.
Music Educators Journal	W. Kuhn	Experimental program for training secondary teachers. 49:57–58+; Feb., 63.	A comparison of the traditional and experimental approaches to teacher education at Stanford University. Detailed, with statistical support.
National Association of Secondary School Principals Bulletin	J. B. Conant	Teacher education and the preparation of secondary school teachers. 48:192–208; Apr., 64.	Conant's plan for a five-year teacher-training program. Mentions NCATE objections.
	L. D. Haskew	Evaluation of teacher education in land-grant institutions. 46:29–50; Mar., 62.	An appraisal of the state of teacher education in land-grant colleges.
	L. S. Standlee, W. J. Popham	Too much pedagogy in teacher education. 45:80–81; Dec., 61.	Research study shows no relationship between formal teacher preparation and (1) principals' ratings of teachers and (2) teachers' Minnesota Teacher Attitude Inventory scores.
National Commission on Teacher Education and Professional Standards:	G. W. Denemark, et al.	Encouraging expertness through extending the period of professional preparation beyond four years;	A good coverage of the five-year program and its difficulties. Several programs studied.

PERIODICALS (continued)

Periodical	Author	Title, Date	Annotation
Official Report		with discussion. 163–199; 62.	
	W. B. Spalding	Evaluation of proposals for change in teacher education. 37–49; 63.	Criteria for the evaluation of several changes in teacher education.
National Education Association Journal	A. W. Combs, H. E. Mitzel	Can we measure good teaching objectively? 53:34–36+; Jan., 64.	Combs says objective measurement is impossible. Mitzel says recent research holds promise.
	J. H. Kleinmann	Merit pay; the big question. 52:42–44; May, 63.	Attempts to prove that merit raises are less effective and more painful than others. Suggests other solutions.
	S. M. Lambert	Angry young men in teaching. 52:17–20; Feb., 63. Discussion. 52:8–10; May, 63.	Low salaries cause departure from teaching.
The National Elementary Principal	H. H. Long	What price parent participation? 37:132–138; Sep., 57.	Describes parent participation in the Mamaroneck, N.Y., elementary school system.
The Nation's Schools	A. H. Rice	What administrators can do to improve teacher education. 74:26; July, 64.	How administrators can improve the training of elementary and secondary school teachers.
Negro History Bulletin	R. W. Hatch	American Teachers Association pushes activity in two vital areas;	A program to improve teacher competency in predominantly

PERIODICALS (continued)

Periodical	Author	Title, Date	Annotation
		commission for improvement of teacher competency initiated. 27:149–152; Mar., 64.	Negro schools.
Phi Delta Kappan	K. Winetrout	In defense of the four-year program in teacher education. 44:183–184; Jan., 63.	A plea for flexibility so than no one plan dominates teacher education.
The Reading Teacher	V. F. Haubrich	The culturally disadvantaged and teacher education. 18:499–505; Mar., 65.	What can be done to prepare teachers for disadvantaged areas.
Reporter	M. Pines	Little extra push: school volunteer program. 24:37–38; Mar. 16, 61.	A discussion of the school volunteer program in New York City.
Saturday Evening Post	E. Hill	Have our teachers colleges failed? 234:30–31+; Nov. 11, 61.	Well documented. Do teachers trained in teachers colleges know as much as their students?
	J. D. Koerner	Speaking out; teachers get the worst education. 236:8+; June 1, 63.	Statistics comparing education majors with other graduates.
Saturday Review	M. Bennett	Teaching is better with! 46:82–83; Feb. 16, 63.	An elementary teacher who was glad she had had methods courses.
	G. K. Hodenfield	Nobody asked me, but . . . 45:51–52; Jan. 20, 62.	A detailed plan for teacher education. Seven years for certification.

Periodical	Author	Title, Date	Annotation
	J. D. Koerner	Teacher education: who makes the rules? 45:78–80+; Oct. 20, 62. Discussion. 45:53+; Nov. 17, 62. 45:43+; Dec. 15, 62.	Accreditation and how it works in teacher education.
	J. S. LeSure	Teacher certification: is overhaul enough? 46:72–73+; Jan. 19, 63.	An attack on teacher certification by an employee of the state department in Connecticut who wants to eliminate his position.
	B. F. Skinner	Why teachers fail. 48:80–81, 98–102; Oct. 16, 65.	Article by professor of psychology at Harvard. Research is needed to test teaching methods. Learning and teaching must be analyzed to realize improvement.
	T. M. Stinnett	Vast overhaul of teacher certification. 45:87–88; Mar. 17, 62.	Data to show that the evolution in teacher certification is healthy and will reach fruition.
		How should teachers be educated? Symposium. 44:68–69; June 17, 61.	Seven authorities questioned about minimum teacher education requirements, curriculum needs, student teaching, and certification.

PERIODICALS (continued)

Periodical	Author	Title, Date	Annotation
School and Society	C. C. Anderson	Canadian critic on teacher education in Western U.S.A. 88:204–207; Apr. 23, 60. Reply. J. D. McAulay. 88: 472; Dec. 3, 60.	Believes teacher education in U.S. deplorable, partially because we insist upon giving university educations to unqualified persons.
	H. K. Hutton	Compulsory professional teacher training in England. 92:358–359; Nov. 28, 64.	An excellent rebuttal of those who want a plan modeled on the British "no compulsory standards" system.
	B. Mehl	Standards in teacher education and the new image makers. 93: 81–82; Feb. 6, 65.	Public bias toward the teacher and what to do about it.
	R. C. Preston	Education graduates view education and academic courses. 92:233–237; Summer, 64.	A survey of attitudes toward education courses by graduates of a school of education at an eastern university.
	L. J. Stiles	University of Wisconsin plan for teacher education. 90:189–191; Apr. 21, 62.	An excellent description of the Wisconsin plan, which approaches Conant's recommendations.
	C. C. Travelstead	New and better teacher education. 91:332–334; Nov. 2, 63.	The University of New Mexico plan of cooperation between the liberal arts and education.

PERIODICALS (continued)

Periodical	Author	Title, Date	Annotation
			Housing provisions interesting.
School Life	S. E. Dean	Team teaching: a review. 44:5–8; Sep., 61.	History and description of team teaching.
Science Digest	R. E. Packer	Tomorrow: automated schools. 53:34–38; May, 63.	Short, but stimulating. Needs supplementation.
Science News Letter		Grants of $26.4 million to 475 summer institutes. 80:414; Dec. 23, 61.	N.S.F. aid to 20,500 high school and 2000 college science and engineering teachers.
		Married women teachers urged to stem shortage. 80:304; Nov. 4, 61.	Urges use of married women to combat the teacher shortage.
		Teacher training liberal. 79:342; June 3, 61.	Proposes that the average school teacher is more "liberally" educated than are persons in any other profession.
Senior Scholastic	R. Marsh	Phase programming; sophomore English at Central High School, Columbus, Ohio. 83:7+; Nov. 15, 63.	A good explanation of phase programming, resulting from a year's experimentation.
Teachers College Journal	W. V. Hicks	Working together in preparing capable teachers. 34:82–90; Dec., 62.	What is the good teacher, and whose responsibility is it to train him? Discusses teacher preparation in many areas, including speech.
	R. H. Jerry	Cooperative	Four Indiana

PERIODICALS (continued)

Periodical	Author	Title, Date	Annotation
		program for teacher education. 36:181–182; Jan., 65.	universities work together to improve further work toward master's degrees for teachers.
Teachers College Record	L. Elvin	Education and training of teachers in Elgland. 66:153–161; Nov., 64.	A discussion of the Robbins recommendations and a description of English teacher education.
	M. Smith	Where angels fear to tread. 64:367–373; Feb., 63.	A distaste for methods courses and for the government bureaucracy in education. The best training ground is the liberal arts college.
	W. W. Wattenberg	Evidence and the problems of teacher education. 64:374–380; Feb., 63.	Points to the lag between research and changes in teacher education.
U.S. News		Drive to unionize school teachers. 53:76–77; July 16, 62.	How to unionize a half million teachers in a large metropolitan area.
Yearbook of Education	G. Baron	Training of teachers in England and Wales. 137–155; 63.	A detailed description of teacher education in England.
	W. H. Cartwright	Post-war revisions in teacher education in the United States. 499–506; 63.	Points to the progress that has been made in teacher education since the war.

PERIODICALS (continued)

Periodical	Author	Title, Date	Annotation
	J. Katz	Education and training of teachers in Canada. 213–227; 63.	A description of teacher training in Canada.
	L. W. Shears	Training of teachers in Australia. 201–212; 63.	A comparison of the Australian, U.S., British, and Canadian systems.
	R. Thabault	Professional training of teachers in France. 244–255; 63.	Historical development and present structure and problems of teacher education in France.

ANNOTATED BIBLIOGRAPHY

DOCUMENTS[1]

Source	Annotation
Hearings before the Subcommittee on Research and Development, Joint Committee on Atomic Energy of the United States, 84th Congress, 2nd session, "Shortage of Scientific and Engineering Man Power," Apr. 17, 18, 19, 25, 26, May 1, 1956. 487 pp.	A shocking indictment. Compares the U.S. with the Soviet Union. Rickover testimony on pp. 99–117. Sarnoff testified for R.C.A.
Hearings before the Appropriations Committee, U.S. House of Representatives, 86th Congress, 1st session, "Report on Russia," Aug. 18, 1959. 82 pp.	Testimony by Hyman G. Rickover following his return from Russia as a member of Vice President Nixon's party.
John F. Kennedy, "Special Message to the Congress on Education," Feb. 20, 1961, *Public Papers of the Presidents: John F. Kennedy, 1961,* U.S. Government Printing Office, 1962. pp. 107–111.	Concerns assistance to public elementary and secondary schools, construction of college facilities, and aid to college students.
Hearings before the General Subcommittee on Education of the Committee on Education and Labor, U.S. House of Representatives, 87th Congress, 1st session, on H.R. 4970 and related bills. Part I: Mar. 13, 14, 15, 16, 17, 20, 1961. 603 pp.; Part II: Mar. 21, 22, 24, 27, 28, 29, 1961. 447 pp.	Principal proponent of the bill was the N.E.A.; principal opponent, the U.S. Chamber of Commerce. H.R. 4970 would provide federal assistance to public elementary and secondary schools, in support of President Kennedy's address of Feb. 20, 1961.
John F. Kennedy, "Special Message to the Congress on Education," Feb. 6, 1962, *Public Papers of the Presidents: John F. Kennedy, 1962,* U.S. Government Printing Office, 1963. pp. 110–117.	Excellent general survey of the problem. The role of the federal government, assistance to higher education, and special education and training programs.
Hearings before the Committee on Appropriations, U.S. House of Representatives, 87th Congress, 2nd session, "Education for All Children: What We Can Learn from England," May 16, 1962. 333 pp.	A thorough if somewhat redundant report by Rickover on education in England.

[1] Chronologically arranged.

DOCUMENTS *(continued)*

Source	Annotation
Hearings before the Special Subcommittee on Labor of the Committee on Education and Labor, U.S. House of Representatives, 88th Congress, 1st session, on H.R. 6013 and H.R. 6025, "Improvement of Educational Quality," May 7, 8, 1963. 107 pp.	H.R. 6013 proposed advanced study for elementary school teachers through institutes; H.R. 6025 broadened the scope of the Cooperative Research Act of July 26, 1954.
Lionel Charles Robbins (Lord), "Higher Education"; report of the Committee appointed by the Prime Minister, under the chairmanship of Lord Robbins, 1961–1963. London, H.M. Stationery Office, 1963. 335 pp.	This controversial report on British higher education has five appendixes. See articles in the London *Times*, Oct. 24, 63; 8–9, and the New York *Times*, Oct. 24, 63; 1, 4; Oct. 25, 63; 12.

American Association of Colleges for Teacher Education, 1201 16th St., N.W., Washington, D.C. 20036

> Action for Improvement of Teacher Education, 18th Yearbook, 1965. $5
>
> Teacher Education for the Future, 12th Yearbook, 1959. $2.50
>
> The Certification of Teachers: The Restricted State Approved Program Approach, 1964. free
>
> Liberal Arts Colleges and Teacher Education, 1963. $1.25
>
> Revolution—In Instruction, 1961. free
>
> Focus on Religion in Teacher Education, 1955. $1
>
> Teacher Education and Media—1964. A Selective Annotated Bibliography. 50¢
>
> Opinions on NCATE: Preliminary Report, 1963. 50¢

American Council on Education, 1785 Massachusetts Ave., N.W., Washington, D.C. 20036

> The Positive Values in the American Educational System, 1959. $2
>
> American Degree Mills, 1959. $1

American Teachers Association, 145 Ashby St., N.W., Atlanta, Ga. 30314 (Composed of 35,000 Negro educators.)

Association for Supervision and Curriculum Development, 1201 16th St., N.W., Washington, D.C. 20036

> Extending the School Year (summer in-service for teachers). $1.25
>
> The Three R's in the Elementary School. $1.50

The Carnegie Foundation for the Advancement of Teaching, 589 Fifth Ave., New York, N.Y. 10017

> The Flight from Teaching, 1963–1964 Annual Report.
>
> Education of the Academically Talented, 1958–1959 Annual Report.
>
> Liberal Education, 1955–1956 Annual Report.

Council for Basic Education, 725 15th St., N. W., Washington, D.C. 20005

> Teaching the Third R: A Comparative Study of American and European Textbooks in Arithmetic. $1
>
> Reprint series, from the CBE Bulletin (10¢ each): CBE: What It Is and What It Is Not; The Decline of English; The Aural-Oral Approach in Foreign Language Teaching.
>
> Occasional papers (25¢ each): Teacher Education: Who Holds the Power; How One Citizens' Group Helped Improve the Public Schools: The East Greenbush Story.
>
> Basic Education in French Secondary Schools. 10¢
>
> Bulletin. 10 issues per year; 20¢ each; $1.25 per year to students

National Commission on Accrediting, 1785 Massachusetts Ave., N.W., Washington, D.C. 20036

> Accreditation in Teacher Education—Its Influence on Higher Education. $3

---

[1] Only representative items are listed, to demonstrate what materials are available (materials of this nature go out of print quickly). Students are urged to write for lists of releases.

National Council for Accreditation of Teacher Education, 1750 Pennsylvania Ave., N.W., Washington, D.C. 20006

> Accredits teacher training institutions. Twenty-seven states grant reciprocity in teacher certification to NCATE accredited institutions. Some releases.

National Education Association, 1201 16th St., N.W., Washington, D.C. 20036

> *A Position Paper on Teacher Education and Professional Standards* (381-11624). 25¢
>
> *This Is TEPS.* free
>
> *Milestones in Teacher Education and Professional Standards.* free
>
> *Directory of Innovations in Teacher Education.* free
>
> *Teaching: A Second Career* (for retiring military personnel). free
>
> *Student NEA Constitution and Bylaws.* free

SUGGESTED SPEECH SUBJECTS

Informative Speeches: Round One: Organizations and Personalities

1. John Dewey
2. James Bryant Conant
3. Hyman G. Rickover
4. Mortimer B. Smith
5. William Heard Kilpatrick
6. Lord Lionel Charles Robbins and His British Report
7. James D. Koerner
8. Edward L. Thorndike
9. Johann Heinrich Pestalozzi
10. Nicholas Murray Butler
11. National Commission on Teacher Education and Professional Standards (NCTEPS)
12. Future Teachers of America
13. National Education Association (NEA): National Committee on Teacher Education and Professional Standards
14. Council for Basic Education
15. The American Teachers Association
16. The National Commission on Accrediting
17. The Department of Education of the State of ———
18. The Carnegie Foundation for the Advancement of Teaching
19. The Association for Supervision and Curriculum Development
20. The American Council on Education
21. The American Association of Colleges for Teacher Education
22. The American Federation of Teachers
23. The Office of Education of the U.S. Department of Health, Education and Welfare
24. The Summer Institute Program of the National Science Foundation (NSF)
25. The School (or Department) of Education of ——— University (or College)

Informative Speeches: Round Two: New Trends in Teaching

26. The Nonthesis Program for the Master's Degree for Teachers
27. The Oregon Master of Arts in Teaching as Sponsored by the Ford Foundation
28. How Teachers Are Being Taught the New Mathematics
29. Learning to Teach by Television
30. Training Laywomen As Helpers for the Teacher
31. Team-Teaching
32. Teaching Machines
33. The Lay Advisory Committee as an Adjunct to the School Board
34. Teaching the Teacher to Teach the Gifted Child
35. The Fifth-year Program in Teacher Education
36. The Internship in Teacher Education

37. The Reaction of Schools of Education to the Conant Report
38. Teacher Institutes in the Sciences
39. Teacher Institutes in the Liberal Arts
40. Teaching the Teacher to Teach in the Difficult or Problem School
41. The Master of Arts in Teaching
42. Phase Programming
43. NCATE vs. the University of Wisconsin
44. The University of Wisconsin Plan for Teacher Education
45. The University of New Mexico Cooperative Program for Teacher Education
46. The Type of Teacher Training Acquired by the College Graduate Assistant
47. The National Defense Education Act of 1958
48. The Shortage of Ph.D.'s for College Teaching
49. The Role of Experimentation in Teacher Education
50. The Student Rates the Teacher: A New Way of Insuring Teacher Proficiency

Informative Speeches: Round Three: General

51. Carleton College vs. NCATE (1960–1962)
52. The Academic Excellence of Students in Schools of Education in Comparison with Students in Liberal Arts Colleges
53. Teaching Teachers to Teach Reading
54. The Training of Modern Language Teachers for the Elementary School
55. Teacher Unions
56. Teaching Classroom Discipline in Student Teaching
57. The General Certificate of Education (GCE) Examination in England
58. Teacher Education in the U.S.S.R.
59. Teacher Education in England
60. Methods of Evaluating Successful Teaching
61. Parent Participation in Evaluating the Teacher
62. The History of the Teachers College
63. The Attitudes Toward Education Courses Held by College Students
64. Teacher Education in Canada
65. Teacher Education in Australia
66. Teacher Education in France
67. The Particular Problems of the Junior High School Teacher
68. The Slum Environment: How Can the Teacher Be Trained to Cope with It?
69. The Language Requirement for the Ph.D. Degree
70. The Course in Student Teaching at ———— College (University)
71. College Textbooks in Educational Psychology
72. The Course in Adolescent Psychology
73. The Content of the Initial Course in Education for Undergraduates
74. The Methods Course in the Subject Area of Social Studies (or English or Mathematics or Language Arts, etc.)
75. The Critic Teacher for the Course in Student Teaching

Persuasive Speeches: Round One

1. Instruction in how to teach should be limited to a fifth-year program which would follow the receipt of an undergraduate degree.
2. The teacher shortage can be substantially alleviated by a major recruiting program to attract retiring military personnel into teaching.
3. Master's theses should be abolished for M.A. candidates who plan to make the degree terminal.
4. There is no accurate or just way to evaluate teaching ability.
5. Teachers should be required to attend a summer institute in their major academic area once every five years.
6. Student teachers should be supervised only by highly paid, highly specialized, highly experienced high school teachers.
7. Internship is the answer to how to raise teacher training excellence.
8. Schools (or departments) of education should be abolished and teachers should be trained in academic colleges plus an intensive course in student teaching.
9. The junior high school teacher should be a highly trained specialist.
10. All student teaching should be taken off-campus, where the student is in full residence.
11. The teacher exchange program with foreign countries is one of the chief ways to improve teacher excellence.
12. The number of high school dropouts cannot be blamed on the quality of teacher excellence.
13. The layman, such as Admiral Rickover, has a right and an obligation to speak out on teacher education.
14. The establishment of special high schools for the gifted, such as the English grammar school, would be undemocratic.
15. An examination of five textbooks in educational psychology shows that much worthwhile material is offered in such an education course.
16. Federal funds to improve teacher training will result in federal control of teacher instruction.
17. The change by which the former "teachers college" has become a state university is a healthy thing for teacher education.
18. Improvement in teacher training can only be of minimal value until the prestige of the teacher is improved so that a higher caliber of candidate is attracted into teaching.
19. Schools (or departments) of education are busier preserving their vested interests than they are in improving teacher education.
20. Teacher certification requirements should be nationally standardized.
21. No lifetime teaching certificates should be issued.
22. A national advertising campaign to recruit teachers should be started.
23. Only by a federal subsidy of teacher salaries can teacher training be improved.
24. In order to broaden the spectrum of high school administrators, a concerted effort should be made to attract to teacher training a larger proportion of men who are majoring in the sciences and the arts, so that others

than physical education majors will be principals and superintendents.

25. Teachers should be permitted to teach only in areas for which they have been certified by their schools.

Persuasive Speeches: Round Two

26. Standardized tests should not be used to determine teacher certification because the ultimate test should be how the teacher performs in the classroom.

27. Certification should not be based on specific required courses because the excellent teacher may well vary widely in his proficiencies in these courses.

28. The "approved program" approach to certification is the solution to teacher certification.

29. State education authorities should make certain that teachers are not assigned to subjects for which they are not properly prepared.

30. NCATE and regional associations should include the lay public and representatives of the scholarly disciplines other than education in their governing boards.

31. Beginning teachers in slum areas should be given special training and extra compensation.

32. The "liberal arts" college is no better equipped to train teachers than is the "teachers college."

33. Teachers should be recruited largely from the upper one-third of high school graduating classes.

34. Conant is correct when he says: "Graduate schools of education should cease trying to train professors of the philosophy of education without the active and responsible participation of the departments of philosophy."

35. The "clinical professor" who is to supervise practice teaching should be analogous to the clinical professor in medical schools.

36. Schools that cannot afford to employ two or three professors to work in the area of elementary education should not try to train elementary teachers.

37. In order to achieve a passing grade, student teachers should be in full charge of the classroom for four hours per day for a four-week period.

38. All secondary school teachers should be prepared to teach in at least two subjects.

39. The "bribing" of teachers to continue their education by relating their salaries to course work is of questionable value.

40. Summer school instruction for teachers is much superior to afternoon or evening instruction during the school year.

41. School boards should contract with an institution of higher learning to provide short term seminars during the school year so that all teachers can participate in continuing education without extra cost to the teacher.

42. Any teacher certified by one state should be accepted for certification by another state.

43. States should establish loan funds aimed at attracting higher caliber persons into the teaching profession.

44. Each college should be permitted to develop its own policy for preparing

teachers, provided that it includes student teaching and provided that the college endorses its candidates.

45. The interdepartmental approach to the training of teachers is superior to the stratified school (or department) of education approach.

46. Teachers should be able to complete an M.A. degree in four summer sessions.

47. The Congress should establish a National Standards Committee, such as was recommended by Admiral Rickover, to act as a watchdog on education and to formulate a national scholastic standard.

48. A teacher can be effectively trained in four years of college, and the fifth year should be reserved for graduate work.

49. Teachers' unions are the best answer to improving teacher status and therefore teacher training.

50. If teachers at the college level do not need methods courses to qualify them to teach, neither should high school teachers.

Debate Propositions

1. *Resolved:* that merit pay will improve teacher training by attracting more qualified personnel into the profession.

2. *Resolved:* that a seven-year program (four years of academic training, one year of education courses, one year of internship, and one year of graduate work) should be required for teacher certification.

3. *Resolved:* that the social studies teacher should be trained to discuss religion in the secondary school classroom.

4. *Resolved:* that all courses in education should be taken as postgraduate work.

5. *Resolved:* that undergraduate education courses are of an acceptable academic standard.

6. *Resolved:* that NCATE is having a bad influence on teacher education.

7. *Resolved:* that student teaching should be the only required course for teacher certification.

8. *Resolved:* that small liberal arts colleges are probably not equipped to prepare teachers and should be carefully screened before permitting to do so.

9. *Resolved:* that schools (or departments) of education should be abolished.

10. *Resolved:* that teachers are born and not made.

Discussion Subjects

1. Who is the good teacher?

2. What should be taught in the methods courses in education?

3. Should the high school teacher be trained to discuss religion in the classroom?

4. How should sex education be taught and how should the teacher be trained to teach it?

5. Can the superior teacher help to reduce the problem of high school dropouts?

6. Should students be permitted to evaluate teachers?

7. How can the prestige of the high school teacher be raised?
8. Should college teachers be required to supplement their education periodically, just as many states require high school teachers to do?
9. Should graduate assistants without teaching experience be permitted to teach freshman courses in college?
10. What should be the role of teacher certification agencies in certifying teachers?

IV

THE REVOLT ON THE CAMPUS

SELECTED READINGS

OF THE FOUR UNITS in this research manual, this one may be the most interesting to the college student, but it will also be the most difficult to research. So much of the material is so recent that libraries may not have acquired the latest books, and periodicals may be at the bindery. Also, there is no practical way of limiting the subject, because revolts are taking place in all phases of campus life. Furthermore, there has not been time for the proper perspective to develop on the movement, and therefore materials tend to be fragmentary.

The editors have chosen to limit their materials to those areas of the revolt that most directly concern the student—his academic environment and his social affairs. These specific suggestions are offered:

1. Although students may wish to contribute their own experiences to their speeches, they should not make the mistake of leaning too much on what they themselves have seen. Nor should they offer a point of view limited to their own campus. The problems are national and deserve adequate research to demonstrate their universality.

2. Students speaking on areas of social relationships should avoid indulging in radical departures simply to be controversial. If a speaker wishes to present an unorthodox point of view, he should recognize his responsibility to justify his point of view on pragmatic bases.

3. Students should supplement this unit carefully by consulting the guides in their library. This area is changing more rapidly than the other three, and the sources used must be up to date.

Naturally, there are many sources of information on the revolt on the campus that the researcher can contact personally. The offices of the personnel deans may contain magazines that are not in the main library. The keeping of a newspaper file would be helpful—students may wish to subscribe to a leading daily. Leaders of campus movements should be interviewed. Administrators can be contacted for their opinions. The university faculty senate may have a committee that is vitally concerned with the problem. The researcher should hold himself responsible for casting down his buckets where he is and making the most of local sources.

Only by diligent research and careful presentation of viewpoints does the individual student deserve to become a part of the revolt on the campus.

ACADEMIC FREEDOM AND CIVIL LIBERTIES OF STUDENTS IN COLLEGES AND UNIVERSITIES

INTRODUCTION

American students, like students in other countries, are participating increasingly in the political affairs of their society and are also seeking a larger voice in the determination of college policy. It is therefore appropriate for the American Civil Liberties Union to re-examine the various issues raised by this growing demand, and to state its own views regarding the proper freedom and responsibility of university and college students.[1]

The relationship between the educational institution and its students must be viewed in the light of the function of the college or university: to transmit to the student the civilization of the past, to enable him to take part in the civilization of the present and to make the civilization of the future.[2] In this great pursuit, the student must be viewed as an individual who is most likely to attain maturity if left free to make personal decisions and to exercise the rights, as well as shoulder the responsibilities, of citizenship on and off the campus.

I. THE COLLEGE, THE COMMUNITY AND THE EDUCATIONAL PROCESS

Like all complex human enterprises, the American college is made up of many groups—students, faculty, several levels of administration, and boards

American Civil Liberties Union, November, 1961; revised edition, March, 1965 (10 cents per copy). Reprinted by permission.

[1] As used in this pamphlet the word "college" refers to all institutions of higher education, including the university. The relevance of the principles and practices discussed, for students in secondary schools, is briefly set forth in Section VI.

[2] Ralph Barton Perry, *Realms of Value*, Harvard University Press, 1954, p. 411.

of trustees—which will at times disagree on means as well as goals. The college also exists in a network of human relations with many other organizations and constituencies, including alumni, parents, legislatures and various governmental agencies, which may desire to influence its policies.

The healthy, strong college asserts its autonomy, its necessary right to decide for itself, even though it is aware that many people constantly scrutinize its policies and can help or harm it by granting or withholding support. The truly independent college will meet criticism not by modifying its policy, but by redoubling its efforts to persuade its constituencies that freedom is an important means toward its educational goal.

It is understandable that Boards of Trustees and Boards of Higher Education, to say nothing of college administrators themselves, should be acutely sensitive to public as well as private criticism. Yet it is clear that the *public* interest is not served when the *academic* community is fearful of experimentation, controversy and dissent.

The college which wishes to set an example of open-minded inquiry in its classrooms will defeat its purpose if it denies the same right of inquiry to its students outside the classroom—or if it imposes rules which deny them the freedom to make their own choices, wise or unwise. Limitations on the freedom of students are not then to be seen as simple administrative decisions which adjust the school to the prevailing climate of public opinion. The college's policy vis-à-vis its students goes to the heart of the condition necessary for adequate personal growth and thus determines whether an institution of higher education turns out merely graduates or the indispensable human material for a continuing democracy.

II. BASIC PRINCIPLES

A. FREEDOM OF EXPRESSION

The student government, student organizations, and individual students should be free to discuss, pass resolutions upon, distribute leaflets, circulate petitions, and take other lawful action respecting any matter which directly or indirectly concerns or affects them.

Students should take responsibility for helping to maintain a free academic community. They should respect and defend not only their fellow students' freedom; but also their teachers' right to the free expression of views based on their own pursuit of the truth and their right to function as citizens, independently of the college or university.

B. FREEDOM FROM DISCRIMINATION

Just as the college should not discriminate on grounds of race, religion, color, or national origin in its admission policies, so should it not permit discrimination in any area of student life, such as housing on or off the campus, athletics, fraternities, social clubs, or other organizations.

C. GOVERNMENT BY LAW

Students should live under a government of law, created, where appropriate, by joint action of students, faculty and administration. The United States National Student Association has properly said:

> The functioning of the educational community requires an awareness of mutual responsibility, understanding, trust, and respect in order that all its members actively contribute to the development of policies and programs; this purpose can best be achieved only through the continuous cooperation within the educational community. . . . These policies and procedures should in no case be subject to change without notice under the pressure of a particular situation, and the groups affected should participate at all times in their application.[3]

III. STUDENTS AS CAMPUS CITIZENS

A. STUDENT GOVERNMENT

The primary purpose of student government is to provide students with the means to regulate student-sponsored activities, organizations, publications and any other matters properly subject to their jurisdiction. The electorate of such a government should consist of the entire student body and should not be defined in terms of membership in clubs or organizations. Designation of delegates, officers, committees and boards should be by student vote only, should be non-discriminatory and should not be subject to administrative or faculty approval. Academic authorities may, however, set up a uniform and reasonable system of scholastic eligibility requirements for major student offices.

B. STUDENT CLUBS

1. *Freedom of Student Association:* Students should be free to organize and join associations for educational, political, social, religious or cultural purposes. The fact of affiliation with any extramural association or national organization or political party, so long as it is an open affiliation, should not of itself bar a group from recognition. Any campus group which plans political discussion or action within legal bounds should be allowed to organize in any educational institution. The administration should not discriminate against a student because of membership in any such organization.

2. *Registration and Disclosures:* A procedure for official recognition and registration of student organizations should be established by the student

[3] *Codification of Policy,* United States National Student Association, 1960–1961, p. 25.

government. The organization applying for recognition should submit a constitution and provide information about its purposes, affiliations, officers and activities. Such information should be available to all within the college community and should be subject to publication on the campus. If a faculty-student committee has reason to believe that any organization has concealed, misrepresented, or otherwise failed to disclose its purposes or affiliations, it may require the organization to state or clarify them. Should such explanation not be forthcoming, the committee's findings may properly be publicized to the educational institution at large. Such a procedure has proved to be more effective from the educational standpoint than withdrawal of recognition or any other disciplinary action.

3. *Membership Lists:* Organizations should not be required to file a list of members, but, if number of students is a condition of chartering or financial aid, the club's officers and the faculty adviser may be required to attest to the fact of such numerically sufficient membership. The names of officers and members should not, without the consent of the individuals involved, be disclosed to any non-college person or organization or to any college persons having no direct and legitimate interest therein.

4. *Social clubs and fraternities* may be permitted to function provided they do not discriminate on grounds of race, religion, color, or national origin. For non-members, the college should provide living and eating facilities of as good a quality as those offered by fraternities or clubs.

5. *Use of Campus Facilities:* Meeting rooms and other campus facilities should be made available, as far as their primary use for educational purposes permits, on a non-discriminatory basis, to registered student organizations. Bulletin boards should be provided for the use of student organizations; school-wide circulation of all notices and leaflets which meet uniform and non-discriminatory standards should be permitted.

6. *Advisers for Organizations:* A student organization should be free to choose its own faculty adviser. No organization should be forbidden to function when, after reasonable effort, it has failed to obtain a faculty adviser. An adviser should consult with and advise the organization but should have no authority or responsibility to regulate or control its activities.

C. STUDENT-SPONSORED FORUMS

Students should be accorded the right to assemble, to select speakers and to discuss issues of their choice. When a student organization wishes to invite an outside speaker it should give sufficient notice to the college administration. The latter may properly inform the group's leaders of its views in the matter but should leave the final decision to them. Permission should not be withheld because the speaker is a controversial figure. It can

be made clear to the public that an invitation to a speaker does not necessarily imply approval of his views by either the student group or the college
administration. Students should enjoy the same right as other citizens to
hear different points of view and draw their own conclusions. At the same
time, faculty members and college administrators may if they wish acquaint
students with the nature of organizations and causes that seek to enlist student support.

D. PAMPHLETS, PETITIONS AND DEMONSTRATIONS

Student organizations and individual students should be allowed, and no
special permission should be required, to distribute pamphlets, except in
classrooms and study halls, or collect names for petitions concerning either
campus or off-campus issues. Orderly demonstrations on campus should
not be prohibited.

E. STUDENT PUBLICATIONS

All student publications—college newspapers, literary and humor magazines, academic periodicals and yearbooks—should enjoy full freedom of
the press. They are too often denied it by college administrations which
fear public criticism. Except for the relatively few university dailies which
are independent financially, college publications in general are dependent
on the administration's favor in that they use campus facilities and are
subsidized either directly by the college or indirectly by a tax on student
funds.

The College Newspaper: Whether a daily or a weekly, the campus paper
should report news of student interest on and off campus, should provide
an outlet for student and faculty opinion through letters to the editor, and
make its own editorial comments on college and other matters. While
these comments need not necessarily represent the view of the majority of
students, fair space should be given to dissenting opinion.

The advisory board of the college newspaper, or college publications
board which supervises all student publications, should be composed of at
least a majority of students, selected by the student government or council
or by some other democratic method. Other members might include a
member of the faculty of the School of Journalism in universities with such
schools, an alumnus, a local newspaper editor, or other qualified citizen,
and such representation from the liberal arts faculty and/or Dean's office
as may be mutually agreed upon.

One of the main duties of the publications or advisory board may be the
interviewing of qualified candidates and the selection of the editor-in-chief
and possibly of all the major staff writers on the campus newspaper. In

colleges where this is not the practice, some other method of selection appropriate to the institution, should be devised by the student government to ensure that competent responsible editors are put in charge and that the college newspaper does not fall into the hands of a self-perpetuating clique.

The editor-in-chief should be left free to exercise his own best judgment in the selection of material to be published. The adults on the board (or the faculty adviser if the paper has a single consultant) should counsel the editors in the ethics and responsibilities of journalism, but neither a faculty member nor an administrator should exercise veto power over what may be printed. Should the board as a whole, after publication, consider that the paper's editor has exercised excessively poor judgment, in one or a number of instances, it may take steps to impeach and remove him from office, after holding hearings and according him due process rights.

Literary and Humor Magazines: Since the literary magazine, in common with other student academic periodicals in such fields as the social sciences, the humanities, the natural sciences, economics, etc., is an extension of classroom activity, students should be as free in writing for and editing such a magazine as in submitting papers to their instructors or in making comments in class. The same freedom of expression should be accorded the college humor magazines. Whether such magazines are responsible to a college publications board or have a single faculty adviser, chosen by the editors, they should be accorded the same freedom to print as the college newspaper. While adult sensibilities may at times be offended by youthful humor and lack of taste, a policy of encouraging the editors to use their best judgment places the responsibility where it belongs, on the editor and not on the college administration. In the long run the editor's product will be accepted or rejected by student readers.

In summary, the college administration which takes no step to control the content of a student publication, and refrains, in a controversial situation, from suspending or discontinuing publication or penalizing one or more student editors, testifies to its belief in the principles of academic freedom and freedom of the press. The student governing body, for its part, should encourage a sufficiently large number of able, responsible and interested students to seek editorial and writing positions, and should devise appropriate selection procedures if they do not already exist.[4]

---

[4] In summarizing replies to a questionnaire on *Supervision and Control of Student Publications*, sent to 127 colleges and answered by 105, John E. Hocutt, Dean of Students at the University of Delaware, writes, "The three points made most often by those commenting are the difficulty of finding interested, qualified faculty to serve as advisers to student publications; the need to improve the fiscal operation of student publications; and the scarcity of interested, able students who seek top editorial positions." University of Delaware, Office of the Dean of Students, Newark, Delaware, March, 1961, mimeo. 15 pp.

F. RADIO AND TELEVISION

College radio and TV stations whose signal goes beyond the campus operate under a license granted by the Federal Communications Commission and are therefore responsible to the government as well as to the college administration which provides the facilities. Since the law requires that "the public interest, convenience and necessity" be served, all radio and TV stations are obligated to present all sides of controversial issues. Also, under an FCC ruling of 1949, all stations are free to editorialize in the name of the station provided they make answering time available to responsible opponents. While campus, like other radio and TV stations, accordingly enjoy under the law broad freedom of speech, they are forbidden by the Federal Communications Act to broadcast "profane or obscene words, language, or meaning." Inasmuch as radio and TV are a family medium, literary or humorous material which student editors may think suitable to print might be considered an infringement on the FCC law.

On campuses where the radio or TV station is used as a closely-linked teaching adjunct by such departments as drama, speech and communications, faculty direction becomes necessary.

Student directors of campus communications stations which are not used primarily for instruction, after being counselled by the college administration in their responsibility to the FCC and to the public, should thereafter be granted, within legal limits, the same freedom of judgment and action as should editors of college publications. The same freedom should be accorded to student directors of closed-circuit stations which reach only campus listeners and are not used primarily for instruction.

IV. REGULATIONS CONCERNING STUDENT LIFE AND DISCIPLINE

A. ENACTMENT AND PROMULGATION OF REGULATIONS

Responsibility for regulations on academic matters naturally rests with the faculty and administration. Regulations governing the conduct of students should be enacted by a committee composed of students, administrators and faculty members if desired.

Regulations governing the behavior of students should be fully and clearly formulated, published, and made available to the whole academic community. They should be reasonable and realistic. Over-elaborate rules that seek to govern student conduct in every detail tend either to be respected in the breach, or to hinder the development of mature attitudes. As a rule, specific definitions are preferable to such general criteria as "conduct unbecoming to a student" or "against the best interests of the institution," which allow for a wide latitude of interpretation.

B. DUE PROCESS IN DISCIPLINARY CASES

In most institutions the faculty joins the administration in making and enforcing the regulations for the disciplining of students for academic derelictions including cheating. Failure to meet academic standards is patently a ground for probation or dismissal. But since a student expelled for cheating may find it difficult or impossible to continue his academic career, he should be protected by every procedural safeguard. This is particularly necessary since the courts have rarely granted the student legal review or redress; they have assumed that the academic institution itself is in the best position to judge culpability. This places the college in the unique position of being prosecutor and judge and having at the same time the moral obligation to serve as a trustee of the student's welfare.

No student should be expelled or suffer major disciplinary action for any offense, other than failure to meet the required academic standards, without having been advised explicitly of the charges against him, which at his request should be in writing. He should be free to seek the counsel of a faculty member of his choice or other adviser. Should he admit guilt but consider the penalty excessive, or should he claim to be innocent, he may ask for a hearing by a review committee. After ample notice, such a hearing should be held by a faculty-student committee, or if the student prefers, by a faculty committee. The hearing committee should examine the evidence, hear witnesses as to the facts and the student's character, and weigh extenuating circumstances. The student should be allowed to call witnesses on his own behalf and confront and cross-examine those who appear against him. If the review committee's decision as to the student's innocence or guilt and in the latter case, appropriate punishment, is not acceptable to the college administration, a final appeal to the board of trustees should be allowed.

V. STUDENTS AS PRIVATE CITIZENS

A. NON-ACADEMIC ACTIVITIES

In their non-academic life, private or public, students should be free from college control. On the other hand, the college should not be held responsible for the non-academic activities of its individual students.

The student, like the teacher, is a member not only of an academic community, but of the community at large and of other specific communities. His college must regard him as both a student and a private individual. It must recognize that his being a student is sometimes irrelevant to his private status. In this private status he should not be subject to punitive measures by the college, unless the college can prove (in the course of a hearing with due process safeguards as specified in IV) that he has acted in a way which adversely affects or seriously interferes with its normal educational function, or which injures or endangers the welfare of any of its other members.

B. OFF-CAMPUS ACTIVITIES

No disciplinary action should be taken by a college against a student for engaging in such off-campus activities as political campaigns, picketing, or participating in public demonstrations, provided the student does not claim without authorization to speak or act in the name of the college or one of its student organizations. Students should observe the same kind of self-discipline that their teachers accept when they speak as citizens and not as representatives of their educational institution.

When students choose to participate in activities that result in police action, such as demonstrations against segregation, the civilian defense program or nuclear tests, it is an infringement of their liberty for the college to punish such activity. Students who violate a local ordinance or any law which they consider to be morally wrong, risk the legal penalties prescribed by the civilian authorities. Since not every conviction under law is for an offense with which an educational institution must concern itself, it is incumbent on the college to refrain from administrative decisions which would violate the student's academic freedom.

In this connection, it is important to make clear that our discussion here concerns convictions. A record of mere arrest, not followed by conviction, should not be used by any educational institution to penalize a student in any way. As is any other citizen, a student is presumed to be innocent until proven otherwise.

And even in the case of conviction of a student for civil rights and other political activities such as those listed in paragraph B above, this should be distinguished by the college from convictions for criminal offenses not involving First Amendment considerations. In screening candidates for admission, college officials should take the position that the existence of an arrest and conviction record for civil rights and other political activities is irrelevant to the question of admission. However, even where the practice is to take cognizance of such records, this inclusion should not be permitted to affect adversely the student's chances of admission.

When students run into police difficulties off the campus in connection with what they regard as their political rights—as, for example, taking part in sit-ins, picket lines, demonstrations, riding on freedom buses—the college authorities should take every practical step to assure themselves that such students are protected in their full legal rights, to wit: That they are given fair trials in a court of law where they are defended by counsel. That they are not abused by the police and that charges are brought against the police if the latter act wrongfully. That bail be sought and furnished. That they have speedy trials and that appeals be taken when necessary. Ideally, the college itself should provide such assistance. If this is not feasible, then the administration should permit and encourage individual faculty, student or alumni groups to render the help required.

In order to protect the interests of students convicted for civil rights and other political activities, a college should separate the records of such convictions from other student records. In other words, such records ought to be given a restricted status in order to obviate intentional or unintentional abuse. In order further to protect the interests of students, an institution should not make the records in question available to prospective employers, graduate and professional schools, or government agencies, without the consent of students involved.

Unless college authorities act in behalf of students, there is the very real danger of alienation: of the weakening of confidence in the university as a community and the resort by students to outside agencies—some of which may very well be self-serving—for support and defense. College authorities have as much responsibility for maintaining that community—based upon mutual trust, respect, and forbearance—as do teachers and students.

Both the United States Civil Service Commission and all similar state commissions require applicants to answer a question regarding arrests or convictions for any offense other that minor traffic violations. Although we believe mere arrest records should not be used to penalize applicants, a student should answer such a question fully and accurately. Where the interrogation, arrest or conviction occurs as the result of civil rights and civil liberties activities, he should make it a point to specify in detail the circumstances, including the kind of court before which such a hearing took place. In this connection, the philosophy of the United States Civil Service Commission, as expressed in a letter to the ACLU from Chairman John W. Macy, Jr., dated May 12, 1964, is commended for the consideration of state and local commissions, although we continue to believe that all references to "arrest" should be replaced by "conviction."

When the information furnished indicates that the arrest was in connection with a peaceful demonstration for civil rights or similar purposes, the arrest is not used by the Commission as a basis for disqualifying the applicant. When the arrest was for a more serious offense than peaceful demonstration for civil rights or similar purposes, it is considered on its individual merits in terms of the specific circumstances involved.

The Commission has a sincere concern that civil rights arrests not be used arbitrarily to disqualify applicants. Accordingly we have instructed our regional offices to submit to us for approval any cases in which they consider the circumstances so serious as to warrant adverse action. Our purpose in doing this is to assure review of these cases at the highest level of responsibility.

C. TEACHER DISCLOSURE[5]

Teachers who are asked to supply information to employers or prospective employers, governmental or private, about students or former students should be aware of the dangers to academic freedom inherent in this proliferating practice. Since the best education calls for probing, sharing and hypothesizing, and for uninhibited expression and thinking out loud by the student, disclosure by the teacher to a source outside the college community of a student's expressed opinion, or the making of a statement based on such an opinion, becomes a threat to the educational process.

The teacher-student relation is a privileged one. The student does not normally expect that either his utterances in the classroom, or his discussions with teachers outside the classroom, or his written views, will be reported beyond the walls of the college community. If he knew that anything he said or wrote might be revealed indiscriminately, the kind of relation in which he originally felt free to voice his thoughts, would cease to exist. While no detailed prescription can be set down for teachers, who must remain free to use their own judgment, the following standards, with the reasons therefore, are recommended:

When interrogated directly by prospective employers of any kind, public or private, or indirectly by the institution's administrative officers in behalf of prospective employers, a teacher can safely answer questions which he finds clearly concerned with the student's competence and fitness for the job. There is always the chance that even questions of this kind will covertly require the teacher to violate academic privacy. Questions and answers in written form make it easier to avoid pitfalls, but the teacher's alertness is always essential. Ordinarily, questions relating to what the student has demonstrated as a student—for example, the ability to write in a certain way, to solve problems of a certain kind, to reason consistently, to direct personnel or other projects—pose no threat to educational privacy. But, questions relating to the student's loyalty and patriotism, his political or religious or moral or social beliefs and attitudes, his general outlook, his private life, may if answered jeopardize the teacher-student relation.

As a safeguard against the danger of putting the student in an unfavorable light with government representatives or employers of any category, simply as a result of the fact that some questions are answerable and others are not, teachers can preface each questionnaire with a brief pro forma statement that the academic policy to which they subscribe makes it inad-

[5] Reprint available from the ACLU of full statement on "Teacher Disclosure," adopted by the Academic Freedom Committee and printed in School and Society, October 7, 1961 (5 cents per copy).

visable to answer certain types of questions. Once this academic policy becomes widespread, presumptive inferences about individual students will no longer be made by employers.

Whether or not the student wishes his teacher in a given instance to disclose details which adherence to general academic principles would leave undisclosed, is irrelevant. Personal expediency of this kind has uncertain consequences and does not seem justifiable as an exception to warranted policy. This choice again involves a balancing of risks. An individual student might benefit from having his teacher answer questions about him fully; yet a satisfactory principle would not admit *ad hoc* violations of academic sanctuary.

It is to be hoped that faculty senates or other representative faculty bodies will take cognizance of the teacher disclosure problem, and will recommend action which would leave intact the teacher-student relationship.

D. HOUSING

Wherever numbers of students are obliged to live off-campus because of insufficient dormitory space, or because they are married, the college administration should ensure that private rentals are on a non-discriminatory basis.[6]

VI. STUDENTS IN SCHOOLS BELOW
THE COLLEGE LEVEL

Considerable progress has been made in extending the principles of free student expression and association to American secondary schools. A good secondary school usually has a student government democratically organized, with a clear budget of power. In the secondary school, student publications should provide as much opportunity as possible for the sincere expression of all shades of student opinion. Traditionally, principals have a legal veto over student activities, but the wise principal in an enlightened community uses this veto seldom and with great reluctance, and explains his reasons carefully. Most American schools include among their educational objectives the development of civic competence, and an acceptance of a responsibility for active participation in the civic affairs of a free society. The imposition of loyalty oaths, arbitrary punishment for editorials on controversial issues, or for participation in orderly demonstrations supporting such causes as integration or nuclear disarmament or in protest against the civilian defense program, will tend to make the objecting students at

[6] A study published in 1961 by the New York State Commission Against Discrimination revealed that only 19 out of more than 100 colleges and universities surveyed across the country in 1959 reported having regulations which forbid bias in renting to students. *Housing Bias in the College Community*, N.Y. State Commission Against Discrimination, New York, N.Y. 10007, 1961, mimeo. 10 pp.

once cynical and resentful, and the student body as a whole conformist. In rating students for college admission, principals and teachers should not down-grade those who have shown independence of spirit in promoting such activities. It is further recommended that in supplying information about former students to government investigators and private employers, high school principals and faculty members answer no "questions relating to the student's loyalty and patriotism, his political or religious or moral or social beliefs and attitudes, his general outlook and his private life."[7]

SUMMARY

The principles set forth in this pamphlet on *Academic Freedom and Civil Liberties of Students in Colleges and Universities* are consistent with those expressed by many leading educators. President James F. Dixon of Antioch College, after a group of students had staged an off-campus demonstration against a governmental action, commented as follows in the May 1961 edition of *Antioch Notes:*

> . . . the college as a total community does not take positions on political matters that are local or international. Our business is education, not politics. But this does not mean that we restrict the positions that members of the faculty or members of the student body may take on social and political concerns.
>
> As a matter of fact we believe that academic freedom is as important to the student as it is for the faculty member. We recognize that these kinds of activities by students are widely interpreted and, we believe, sometimes misinterpreted in the community. They are misinterpreted because they are not understood to be part of an educational process. They are misinterpreted because, not understood as part of an educational process, they are regarded as irresponsible kinds of actions.
>
> But I think it is important to recognize that these activities are part of the total educational process that we have in our colleges, and that these are the young people who are going to be deeply involved in the political and social affairs of the next decade; that wise people believe that the problems of the next decade require us to develop leadership with sufficient courage to take positions, that one of the ways in which one learns how to do this is by doing it, and that there should be an opportunity in the educational situation to do this in a fashion that is, shall I say, somewhat experimental. . . .

Delineating the university's over-all function, Dean Erwin N. Griswold of the Harvard Law School wrote in 1961:

> A university is the place where students learn not merely from the past but also through developing the capacity for and habit of independent thought. If they are well taught, they learn to do their own thinking. There is no "party line" in any American university worthy of the name.

[7] See page 281.

Great ideas can rarely be developed in an atmosphere of constraint and oppression. The university has a unique function not merely in systematizing the orthodox, but also in providing the soil in which may be nourished the speculative, the unfashionable, and the unorthodox. . . .[8]

In common with these educators and others of their persuasion, the American Civil Liberties Union and its Academic Freedom Committee believe that today's young people, who will be responsible in the not too distant future for the conduct of the Nation's political and social affairs, will have been ill-prepared unless they have as students developed "the capacity for and habit of independent thought."

[8] Griswold, Hesburgh, Sachar, and Everett, *The Challenge to American Education,* Anti-Defamation League, 515 Madison Avenue, New York, N.Y. 10022, 1961, p. 15.

FREEDOM AND THE UNIVERSITY

STEPHEN WEISSMAN AND DOUG TUTHILL

Many commentators have drawn the obvious connections between Berkeley's free speech controversy and the emergence of the civil rights "sit-in generation." It was local opponents of civil rights pickets and sit-ins, such as ex-Senator Knowland, who provided the pressure which led to the curtailment of student liberties. Due note has also been taken of the Mississippi and Northern civil rights experience of Free Speech Movement (FSM) leaders, of the singing of freedom songs at noon rallies, of the use of the sit-in tactic in Sproul Hall. Discoverers of the New Left have, I believe correctly, seen in the southern field worker of the Student Non-violent Co-ordinating Committee (SNCC) one prototype of the more political of Berkeley's rebels. And educational reformers—often more faithful to their own battles than to that of the students—have at least mentioned civil rights in their analyses of Berkeley. But they have located *the cause* of the Berkeley uproar in the impersonality and student alienation inherent in the factory-like Multiversity which University of California President Clark Kerr poses as the future of American higher education.

Fortunately we need not here agree upon *the cause:* neither the political disputes over free speech and civil rights nor any other single set of factors can explain the Berkeley of FSM—or that of Clark Kerr. And even those of us most publicly wedded to a predominantly civil rights explanation of the Free Speech Movement can agree on this: What began as a battle auxiliary to the Negro movement had become in the faces of those thousands carrying picket signs in the student strike and in the faces of those eight hundred returning from Santa Rita prison after the Sproul Hall arrests, a struggle for the right to set the conditions in which they themselves lived and worked. Berkeley students, unlike so many of the white faces in

Motive Magazine, 26:4–13; October, 1965. Reprinted by permission. Copyright ©
1965 by the Division of Higher Education of the Methodist Church.

civil rights marches, had carried the freedom struggle beyond a compelling abstraction to a fight for a change in their own community.

The present protest against the Vietnam war, at Berkeley and elsewhere, and the increased efforts at organizing the poor have again taken students beyond the campus community. Meanwhile the movement for administrative and educational reform in the impersonal university, which without specific provocations has been unable to draw widespread support, barely continues to hobble along. Without arguing for a change in priorities (the elimination of poverty and the end of the Vietnam war are more immediate concerns to me than a revamping of the multiversity) I would urge that we not continually make stepchildren of our alma maters. Such neglect will be impossible if on-campus reform is animated by those concerns for freedom and democratic control which have denied student activity off-campus during the past few years.

FROM PATERNALISM TO THE BENEVOLENT BUREAUCRACY

The "Silent Generation" of the 1950s did, at schools such as Berkeley, now and then emerge from its apathy. However, the real lifting of the McCarthy era silence can conveniently be dated from the Greensboro, North Carolina, sit-ins of February, 1960. The Greensboro movement led to the formation of the Student Non-violent Co-ordinating Committee, which through Friends of SNCC groups on Northern and Western campuses brought students from across the nation into permanent contact with the Southern movement.

From this beginning the question of on-campus rights has been important, if auxiliary. Student demonstrators have often been harassed with suspension from college for "conduct unbecoming a student." This *in loco parentis* power of a university administration was exercised in the expulsions from Louisiana's all-Negro Southern University. More recently, the power was misused in the obscenity row at Berkeley and in the unsuccessful attempt by the administration there to ban on-campus sales of a student magazine. Similarly, battles over speaker prohibitions usually revolve around the "right" of a university administration to protect its students, as well as its right to regulate the use of its facilities.

Student activists have staged numerous protests against specific arbitrary uses of the *in loco parentis* power (a power generally defended for its usefulness in protecting student inebriates from over-zealous sheriffs). More recently, the on-campus emphasis has been shifted from protests of particular infringements of political rights to a wholesale condemnation of the power of the college dean to act in the place of parents. This condemnation has been especially strong in the area of First Amendment liberties, but there have also been demands for the abolishment of *in loco parentis* power over "beer, sex, and cheating." The most wholesale challenge to the parietal power of administrators has been Berkeley's Free Student Union, an off-spring of the FSM, which openly demands that any rules concerning a student's nonacademic life be made and enforced by the students themselves.

The full-scale on-campus attack against administrative power is not a necessary part of civil rights or other off-campus politics. Nonetheless it clearly stems from the off-campus involvements of the present student generation. The most indefensible abuses of arbitrary power have been aimed at curtailing this involvement. More important, the emphasis upon freedom and participatory democracy by groups such as SNCC and the Students for a Democratic Society (SDS) has led those students to a redefinition of those concepts in their own lives. The insistence upon the right of Mississippi sharecroppers to govern themselves and the refusal to accept token integration into a basically unfree white society has subverted the ivory tower. Many of the new Campus Freedom Parties draw their inspiration from the example of the Mississippi Freedom Democratic Party.

In loco parentis control of personal life is less pervasive at Berkeley and other of the big-name schools than at smaller universities and colleges. Compulsory chapel, strict regimentation of women's dormitories, class attendance requirements, and puritanical dress regulations are still too frequently encountered. But they are giving way to free "cuts," the careful nonenforcement of lax dorm and dress rules, and dorm keys for senior women. Fewer and fewer speakers are denied access to campus, although Malcolm X, were he alive, would still have trouble speaking at most "liberal" schools. Students are coming to find that the most serious challenge to their freedom is the subtle "liberal" manipulation which passes for a democratic student personnel program.

Sophisticated administrators, such as Minnesota's Dean Williamson (whose observations at a recent conference support many of the above generalizations), have themselves led the fight against custodial implementation of the *in loco parentis* doctrine. These benevolent bureaucrats recognize the absurdity as well as the rebellion-provoking nature of many university restrictions. Thus they have brought "student leaders" onto the rule-making and rule-enforcing committees. This practice has been called shared responsibility by some, co-optation or Uncle Tomism by others; it has also been called student freedom.

Many analysts of the Berkeley conflict, including now-pessimistic student radicals, maintain that the velvet glove application of just such freedom could have stifled the Free Speech Movement. Serious errors were certainly made by both the Berkeley administration and the FSM leaders. But one is hard-pressed to imagine velvet soft enough to mask the iron fist inherent in any attempt to deny campus facilities to those advocating off-campus civil disobedience. The administration could have reversed the intent of their new policy and permitted the courts to determine the legality of on-campus advocacy. Short of this, the administration might have avoided a mass confrontation only by ignoring the premeditated guerilla campaign of FSM to violate clamorously and massively *all* university restrictions of political activity. Nor was this situation changed by the much-discussed split within the FSM after the "liberalization" of rules by the Regents on November 22. Far from an indication of the acceptance of the new rules by the moderates, the "split" was merely a tactical dispute. On one side were the moderates who wanted to await further disciplinary action which they felt would inevitably follow. On the other were the militants who wanted a sit-in without waiting for any cause other than the "liberalization."

The specifics of Berkeley aside, educational authorities have responded to the jangling echos of Berkeley with just such prescriptions as "shared responsibility." More personal attention for student personnel, better psychiatric and career counselling services, liberalized dorm rules, liberalized rhetoric and a more cosmopolitan attitude toward political activity—these and similar nostrums are changing the face of *in loco parentis* to resemble the bureaucratic paternalism that awaits the college graduate in the world of industry. Perhaps these measures will succeed in minimizing the extent of student eruptions. There is, however, the great danger that administrators and graduates alike will accept this paternalism as the definition of freedom.

"Freedom" in America, on or off-campus, too often means a choice between predetermined alternatives rather than participation in forming those alternatives, acting within a context fixed and manipulated by others rather than taking a hand in the definition of that context. Does a student committee on curfews have freedom when limits are implicit in the possibility of an administrative veto; Does student government have freedom to disburse student funds when student leaders know that the administration will permit donations to the Red Cross but not to SNCC? Such administered democracy should be avoided by all who would establish alternatives to the Dick and Jane student governments which mar the campus landscape.

AUTOMATED LEARNING

A restricted sense of freedom is found not only in the Dean of Women's office, but in the classroom as well. For many, *this* restriction or absence of freedom is normal, even commendable. To quote a comment on the Free Student Union in a Baton Rouge newspaper:

> Education is impossible without authority and the recognition of authority. Management has to manage. That this affects one's place in life—

and throughout life—is elementary. If a university can't teach that to its students, it'll never be able to teach them anything.

Every institution—families, schools, enterprises, government, our armed forces, everything—falls apart on any other basis. And the future of American youth falls apart with it.

I would suspect that an equation of education with discipline and a resistance to classroom freedom marks the thought of people with far less authoritarian sentiments. There is even resistance among those unafraid of the very unradical proposition that, as in most European universities, the nonacademic life of the student be no concern of the administration.

The classroom is the holy of holies, an AAUP-(American Association of University Professors) protected inner sanctum where professors are free (usually) to pass on the wisdom of the ages according to their own lights. But what of the student? "At Berkeley," report Professors Sheldon Wolin and John Schaar, "the educational environment of the undergraduate is bleak. He is confronted throughout his entire first two years with indifferent advising, endless bureaucratic routines, gigantic lecture courses, and a deadening succession of textbook assignments and bluebook examinations testing his grasp of bits and pieces of knowledge."

In this "mass producing of men into machines" freedom is the loser. Although he is usually free to choose between various course offerings, the student has little freedom to determine what will be offered. Once enrolled in a class, the student must yield to the professor much of the decision-making power over the course and over the nature of that process through which learning is scheduled to take place. The student's recognition and acceptance of his subordinate status stem not from his knowledge and respect for his professor's intellect, but, simply stated, from an acquiescence to authority. This same pattern, plus the "necessities" of grading exams and essays, provides for the development of production schedules long before even initial personal contact between student and professor.

God forbid that the student challenge the schedule by getting "hung-up" on Dostoevsky the week in which the syllabus requires that he produce an exam on Tolstoy. Any personal involvement in the learning process, any unleashing of curiosity, might well result in intellectual *coitus interruptus*.

Fortunately, the curiosity of childhood is usually disconnected in the public schools. In college the motivation to learn is not supposed to be found in personal satisfactions arising from the work itself. The intellectual assembly line is not designed to produce such satisfactions, except as a by-product. Learning is a means to grades, to careers; the important questions are those which will appear on the next test. Even the persistent find that over-sized classes, ritualized papers, and too-frequent examinations make of one's own questions an extra-curricular activity.

Of course students do learn something. Unfortunately, much of what they learn, from the point of view of developing men and women who are willing to determine the course of their own lives, is negative; blind accept-ance of hierarchical authority, intellectual indifference, a willingness to do meaningless work, to produce according to schedule, to do without internal gratification in their work. Or to quote from a study by Christopher Jencks and David Riesman, "It is difficult to say to what extent colleges, along with the rest of the educational system, train students to respond with a disciplined attitude toward work not of their own devising (and therefore provide employers and professional schools with a good yardstick for de-termining who will do well in a highly organized and authoritarian setting) and to what extent colleges help inculcate a distaste for work precisely be-cause of its frequently imposed and alienated quality."

ALIENATION IN THE MULTIVERSITY

This state of affairs finds its ultimate expression in the large multiver-sities or federal grant universities such as Berkeley. "The production, dis-tribution and consumption of knowledge," Clark Kerr tells us, is now a major industry and a major proportion of America's Gross National Prod-uct. As the university begins "to merge its activities with industry as never before," it increasingly becomes a knowledge-factory. But what of the teaching "activity"? "There seems to be a 'point of no return,'" Kerr re-ports, "after which research, consulting and graduate instruction become so absorbing that faculty efforts can no longer be concentrated on the un-dergraduate instruction as they once were."

The now-entreprenurial professor takes on the style and attitudes of in-dustry. He considers his product—knowledge—to be more important than the students to whom he is transmitting that knowledge. Even that knowl-edge itself is changed. For the nature of the product is determined not by the student consumers, but by the federal agencies, foundations, and in-dustries who are the true purchasers of knowledge in our society.

The knowledge-factory also produces graduates. Here, too, teaching and learning are secondary concerns in preparing college graduates for the un-free society and alienated work awaiting them in the world to which they are graduating. That world is also increasingly defined by the same federal agencies, foundations and large industries which define the multiversity. Real preparation for "life" comes from the administrative paternalism and alienated learning which the student is "free" to undergo at the multiver-sity of his choice.

"Alienation," "alienated learning," "alienated work"—unfortunately, journalistic popularization and uncritical repetition have depleted these once-rich concepts of their meaning. But perhaps we can reach beyond the level of cliche to an understanding of that malaise mirrored in the faces of a generation of student rebels. Alienation, according to a noted 19th-cen-tury sociologist, is that condition in which the individual worker has lost any say over the conditions of his work. ". . . the work is external to the worker, . . . consequently he does not fulfill himself in his work but denies himself, . . . has a feeling of misery, not of well-being." Given this description, we can more easily see how a definition of freedom born of the movement in Mississippi could become meaningful to a generation deprived of little except the right to control their own lives and work.

When at Berkeley we sought to use our campus for the exercise of our constitutionally guaranteed rights, we learned that our campus was "the property of the Regents of the University of California." And our rights had to be yielded at the gates of *their* university before they would allow us to become educated for jobs in *their* society. In point of fact, the State of California is to a large extent a society belonging to the Regents. Among their number are the state's major owners of banking, communications, transportation, mining, philanthropy, agriculture and industry, plus its chief political figures. Such a group is consecrated to the task of education in a democratic society only by their worldly success and their appointment to the Board of Regents by an elected governor.

But even if the Board were elected as in Michigan, even if its membership included civil rights leaders and artistic geniuses, the problem of student alienation would remain. If alienation stems from the nature of work, then the student will be alienated from the work of learning until he is free to shape the process in which he learns. And the general university environment will remain hostile to the student as long as the administration of that environment is geared to preparing him for the administered world of work off the campus. Wolin and Schaar have defined the alienation of students as "a sense of not being valued members of a genuine intellectual and moral community." If that alienation is to be overcome, students must regain control over their own lives, their own work. They must fight for the freedom of students and faculty to run their universities.

Student freedom is meaningless, however, without the freely-given and freely-accepted instruction, guidance, and friendship of the faculty. Yet paradoxically, faculty members are often responsible for the most alienating features of the university. Responsible? Are the professors to blame if society does not supply sufficient rewards for teaching students rather than subjects? Are they responsible if there are not sufficient resources allocated to provide the small classes necessary for the kind of teaching which is its own reward? At Berkeley, professors were held responsible by students until, through student pressure, they fought against the curtailment of student political activity. It is now time that professors everywhere fight to change the educational alternatives offered by society. They must unlearn the lessons taught by McCarthy and learn from their students. It is never enough to make the best of one's conditions—one must always fight for the freedom to shape those conditions.

But the problem goes still deeper. As William Appleman Williams explains, the professor "has become accepted as a full member of the system in direct proportion as he has become an expert or advisor concerned to rationalize and to sustain the system." Even when he does teach students, he is often happy to be "a servant of established power." And it doesn't matter if that power be the giants on the California Board of Regents or the merchants who run Osh Gosh U. Certainly most professors deplore the grosser prejudices of this middle-class society, but how many make criticisms and suggest alternatives outside the "realities" posed by the conventional wisdom? How many go beyond "refining established revelation"?

Too often university intellectuals become "yes men" for society even when they say "no": evidence the academic debate over American action in Vietnam. The vast majority have argued that present American policy is wrong because it is not the best way to stop communism or block Chinese aggression. Few are the academics who have challenged root and branch America's underlying assumptions about present-day communism, Chinese foreign policy, our role in the world, and revolutions and economic development in the underdeveloped countries.

A NEW ACADEMIC FREEDOM

Not unexpectedly this impersonal, unfree assembly-line learning is producing its own opposition. Kerr himself points to "an incipient revolt against the faculty." At Berkeley the revolt was specifically against the administration, but great strength was drawn from generalized grievances against the Multiversity and the society which it so faithfully mirrors. In that revolt the students took their desire for personal authenticity in learning and in life to the point of on-campus action only when the advocacy of off-campus action was denied them. But Kerr is correct: the revolt was there in the alienated condition of student life.

Today's students demand a personal relevance to knowledge which is the direct opposite of the Multiversity's alienated process of learning. They demand a relationship between learning and their own moral concerns. Such a demand seems singularly appropriate to the existential attitudes of the post-nuclear generation and to the almost arrogant posture which permits so many members of that generation to feel guilty for the condition of *their* world and personally responsible for changing it. But to demand that the learning process be focused on personal involvement is to demand freedom in the classroom, to demand "a situation in which there would be questioning, release from rigid squelching of initiative and expression."

Far removed from any discussion of university reform, this definition of academic freedom has already impressed itself upon the present student generation. It comes from a prospectus for the Mississippi Freedom Schools, in which so many northern volunteers served during the summer of 1964. The Freedom School idea has now spread, and there is continuous experimentation in the development of free and creative educational environments. Such an environment is vital to give underprivileged children a sense of their own worth.

But are underprivileged children the only ones to ask, "Why are we not taken seriously?" Are they the only students who would benefit from determining the course of their own learning? Would children of the middle class become less free or less educated if their teachers refrained from both the exercise of dictatorial authority or the more subtle, indirect manipulation inherent in the grading process? Could not students learn more (and remember more of that "learning" beyond the exam) if their courses answered questions which they themselves phrased? Should we not prefer the self-discipline which comes with problem-solving to the blind acceptance of external authority? Can an automated society endure without citizens who study because they are curious, who work because their work brings them pleasure?

Of course the Freedom School cannot totally replace the Multiversity. It can, however, demonstrate the validity of a new kind of academic freedom. In the humanities and social sciences the need for intuitive involvement is already preached, though present-day universities make the practice extracurricular. But even in math and the sciences, there is increased recognition that the teaching of facts is insufficient. Free universities, like Freedom Schools, must provide personal confrontation with the concepts of science as well as of history, and encourage personal responsibility for the application of those concepts.

It is not, however, any inappropriateness of freedom to learning which blocks the growth of the free university. Rather it is the very definition of Clark Kerr's multiversity, a definition which leaves as little room for free, personalized teaching and learning as Senator Eastland's plantation leaves for Negro freedom.

A FREE UNIVERSITY

From their experience in civil rights students have come to value highly their own freedom and the democratic control of the institutions which shape their lives. In their struggle to defeat the multiversity they have recognized that their own campus community presents an environment hostile both to freedom and to learning. Thus they must fight for an end to administrative paternalism and unfree learning. They must make a revolution to share with the faculty in the government of their universities.

But, imperatives and a vision are not sufficient. It is, perhaps, impossible to build a free university without a free society. Nonetheless, we must start to define alternatives wherever we can. Several on-campus alternatives are presently available to the student movement. First is the possibility for an organized campaign of nonparticipation in sandbox student government.

One vehicle for such a campaign is the Campus Freedom Party. With a platform expressing the need for student democracy "rather than student government," Campus Freedom Parties have little chance of winning elections. But they can help to build movements on campus which can provide the nucleus for action when direct provocation occurs. They also provide a forum for a self-education in freedom and a reserve for off-campus political activity. If the party does elect its candidates, there are many opportunities for organizing students around shadow freedom governments and other forms of creative nonparticipation.

The area of learning provides greater difficulties. Counter-curricula have shown little success in competition with the grade hunger which drives even free students back into their regular courses. But efforts should continue especially in the direction of utilizing freedom school concepts in the counter courses. Equally important is the need for students, especially graduate students, to define areas of radical research in which they can pose alternatives to the conventional wisdom. The Vietnam protest offers many such opportunities, as do the questions of automation, political sociology, and the social responsibility of the sciences. The Vietnam protest also offers opportunities for creating learning environment with maximum participation.

Finally there is the need to become more explicit in our aims and attitudes. If we honestly feel that on-campus freedom is impossible without student-faculty control, we must say so. New alternatives are impossible unless we make clear our opposition to the present alternatives. And for our generation there must be no alternative to a redefining of freedom, on-campus and off.

STATEMENT ON THE ACADEMIC FREEDOM OF STUDENTS

Upon the recommendation of Committee A on Academic Freedom and Tenure in October, 1960, the Association's Council authorized appointment of a new standing committee, designated as Committee S on Faculty Responsibility for the Academic Freedom of Students. Dr. Philip Monypenny, Professor of Political Science at the University of Illinois, was appointed to serve as Chairman of the new committee. Once established, Committee S gave primary attention to the task of formulating a statement on the academic freedom of students. Several drafts were prepared, one of which was published with the consent of the Council in the Autumn, 1964, issue of the AAUP Bulletin for the express purpose of inviting reaction and comments from members, chapters, conferences, and other interested persons and organizations.

The preliminary Committee S statement stimulated considerable interest and response. Committee S therefore directed most of its attention during 1965 to refining the tentative statement published in 1964. The statement which follows has been approved by the Council in principle but remains a tentative, rather than a fixed, statement of Association policy. The Council has also authorized Committee S to initiate discussions with representatives of other interested national organizations in the hope that these efforts might result in the formulation of a joint statement on student rights and responsibilities. These discussions will commence this winter.

The Members of Committee S who prepared the following statement are:
Philip Monypenny (Political Science) University of Illinois (Chairman)
Philip Appleman (English) Indiana University
Frederick H. Hartmann (Political Science) University of Florida
Beatrice G. Konheim (Physiology) Hunter College
John J. Reed (History) Muhlenberg College
Tom J. Truss Jr. (English) University of Mississippi
William Van Alstyne (Law) Duke University
Robert Van Waes (History) Washington Office

American Association of University Professors Bulletin, 51:447–449; December, 1965. Reprinted by permission.

PREAMBLE

Free inquiry and free expression are essential attributes of the community of scholars. As members of that community, students should be encouraged to develop the capacity for critical judgment and to engage in a sustained and independent search for truth. The freedom to learn depends upon appropriate opportunities and conditions in the classroom, on the campus, and in the larger community. The responsibility to secure and to respect general conditions conducive to the freedom to learn is shared by all members of the academic community. Students should endeavor to exercise their freedom with maturity and responsibility.

I. IN THE CLASSROOM

The professor in the classroom and in conference should encourage free discussion, inquiry, and expression. Students should be evaluated solely on the basis of their academic performance, not on their opinions or conduct in matters unrelated to academic standards.

A. *Protection of Freedom of Expression.* Students are responsible for learning thoroughly the content of any course of study, but they should be free to take reasoned exception to the data or views offered, and to reserve judgment about matters of opinion.

B. *Protection Against Improper Academic Evaluation.* Students are responsible for maintaining standards of academic performance established by their professors, but they should have protection through orderly procedures against prejudiced or capricious academic evaluation.

C. *Protection Against Improper Disclosure.* Information about student views, beliefs, and political associations which professors acquire in the course of their work as instructors, advisers, and counselors should be considered confidential. Protection against improper disclosure is a serious professional obligation. Judgments of ability and character may be provided under appropriate circumstances.

II. STUDENT RECORDS

Institutions should have a carefully considered policy as to the information which should be part of a student's permanent educational record and as to the conditions of its disclosure. To minimize the risk of improper disclosure, academic and disciplinary records should be separate, and the conditions of access to each should be set forth in an explicit policy statement. Transcripts of academic records should contain only information about academic status. Data from disciplinary and counseling files should not be available to unauthorized persons on campus or to any person off campus except for the most compelling reasons. No records should be kept which reflect the political activities or beliefs of students. Provision should also be made for periodic routine destruction of noncurrent disciplinary records. Administrative staff and student personnel officers should respect confidential information about students which they acquire in the course of their work.

III. STUDENT AFFAIRS

In student affairs, certain standards must be maintained if the academic freedom of students is to be preserved.

A. *Freedom from Arbitrary Discrimination.* Colleges and universities should be open to all students who are academically qualified. While sectarian institutions may give admission preference to students of their own persuasion, such a preference should be clearly and publicly stated. College facilities and services should be open to all students, and institutions should use their influence to secure equal access for all students to public facilities in the local community.

B. *Freedom of Association.* Students bring to the campus a variety of interests previously acquired and develop many new interests as members of the academic community. They should be free to organize and join associations to promote their common interests.

1. Affiliation with an extramural organization should not of itself affect recognition of a student organization.

2. Each organization should be free to choose its own campus adviser, and institutional recognition should not be withheld or withdrawn solely because of the inability of a student organization to secure an adviser. Members of the faculty serve the college community when they accept the responsibility to advise and consult with student organizations; they should not have the authority to control the policy of such organizations.

3. Student organizations may be required to submit a current list of officers, but they should not be required to submit a membership list as a condition of institutional recognition.

4. Campus organizations should be open to all students without respect to race, religion, creed, or national origin, except for religious qualifications which may be required by sectarian organizations.

5. Students and student organizations should be free to examine and to discuss all questions of interest to them, and to express opinions publicly or privately. They should also be free to support causes by any orderly means which do not disrupt the regular and essential operation of the institution.

6. Students should be allowed to invite and to hear any person of their own choosing. While the orderly scheduling of facilities may require the

observance of routine procedures before a guest speaker is invited to appear on campus, institutional control of campus facilities should never be used as a device of censorship. It should be made clear to the academic and larger community that sponsorship of guest speakers does not necessarily imply approval or endorsement of the views expressed, either by the sponsoring group or the institution.

C. *Student Participation in Institutional Government.* As constituents of the academic community, students should be free, individually and collectively, to express their views on issues of institutional policy and on matters of general interest to the student body. The student body should have clearly defined means to participate in the formulation and application of regulations affecting student affairs. Student governments should be protected from arbitrary intervention.

D. *Student Publications.* Student publications and the student press are a valuable aid in establishing and maintaining an atmosphere of free and responsible discussion and of intellectual exploration on the campus. They are a means of bringing student concerns to the attention of the faculty and the institutional authorities and of formulating student opinion on various issues on the campus and in the world at large.

1. The student press should be free of censorship and advance approval of copy, and its editors and managers should be free to develop their own editorial policies and news coverage.

2. The integrity and responsibility of student publications should be encouraged by arrangements which permit financial autonomy or, ideally, complete financial independence.

3. Editors and managers should subscribe to canons of responsible journalism. At the same time, they should be protected from arbitrary suspension and removal because of student, faculty, administrative, or public disapproval of editorial policy or content. Only for proper and stated causes should editors and managers be subject to removal and then by orderly and prescribed procedures.

IV. OFF-CAMPUS FREEDOM OF STUDENTS

A. *Exercise of Rights of Citizenship.* As citizens, students should enjoy the same freedom of speech, peaceful assembly, and right of petition that other citizens enjoy. Faculty members and administrative officials should insure that institutional powers are not employed to inhibit such intellectual and personal development of students as is often promoted by their off-campus activities and their exercise of the rights of citizenship.

B. *Institutional Authority and Civil Penalties.* Activities of students may upon occasion result in violation of law. In such cases, institutional officials should apprise students of their legal rights and may offer other assistance. Students who violate the law may incur penalties prescribed by civil authorities, but institutional authority should never be used merely to dupli-cate the function of general laws. Only where the institution's interests as an academic community are distinct from those of the general community should the special authority of the institution be asserted. The student who incidentally violates institutional regulations in the course of his off-campus activity, such as those relating to class attendance, should be subject to no greater penalty than would normally be imposed. Institutional action should be independent of community pressure.

V. PROCEDURAL STANDARDS IN DISCIPLINARY PROCEEDINGS

The disciplinary powers of educational institutions are inherent in their responsibility to protect their educational purpose through the regulation of the use of their facilities and through the setting of standards of conduct and scholarship for the students who attend them. In developing responsi-ble student conduct, disciplinary proceedings play a role substantially sec-ondary to counseling, guidance, admonition, and example. In the excep-tional circumstances when these preferred means fail to resolve problems of student conduct, proper procedural safeguards should be observed to protect the student from the unfair imposition of serious penalties. The following are recommended as proper safeguards in such proceedings.[1]

A. *Notice of Standards of Conduct Expected of Students.* Disciplinary proceedings should be instituted only for violation of standards of conduct defined in advance and published through such means as a student hand-book or a generally available body of university regulations. Offenses should be as clearly defined as possible, and such vague phrases as "undesirable conduct" or "conduct injurious to the best interests of the institution" should be avoided. Conceptions of misconduct particular to the institution need clear and explicit definition.

B. *Investigation of Student Conduct.*

1. Except under emergency circumstances, premises occupied by stu-dents and the personal possessions of students should not be searched un-less appropriate authorization has been obtained. For premises such as dormitories controlled by the institution, an appropriate and responsible authority should be designated to whom application should be made be-fore a search is conducted. The application should specify the reasons for the search and the objects or information sought. The student should be present, if possible, during the search. For premises not controlled by the institution, the ordinary requirements for lawful search should be followed.

2. Students detected or arrested in the course of serious violations of institutional regulations, or infractions of ordinary law, should be informed

---

[1] Honor codes offering comparable guarantees may be an acceptable substitute for the procedural standards set forth in this section.

of their rights. No form of harassment should be used by institutional representatives to coerce admissions of guilt or information about conduct of other suspected persons.

C. *Status of Student Pending Final Action.* Pending action on the charges, the status of a student should not be altered, or his right to be present on the campus and to attend classes suspended, except for reasons relating to his physical or emotional safety and well-being, or for reasons relating to the safety of students, faculty, or university property.

D. *Hearing Committee Procedures.* The formality of the procedure to which a student is entitled in disciplinary cases should be proportionate to the gravity of the offense and the sanctions which may be imposed. Minor penalties may be assessed informally under prescribed procedures. When misconduct may result in serious penalties, the student should have the right to a hearing before a regularly constituted hearing committee.

1. The hearing committee should include faculty members or, if regularly included or requested by the accused, both faculty and student members. No member of the hearing committee who is otherwise interested in the particular case should sit in judgment during the proceeding.

2. The student should be informed, in writing, of the reasons for the proposed disciplinary action with sufficient particularity, and in sufficient time, to ensure opportunity to prepare for the hearing.

3. The student appearing before the hearing committee should have the right to be assisted in his defense by an adviser of his choice.

4. The burden of proof should rest upon the officials bringing the charge.

5. The student should be given an opportunity to testify and to present evidence and witnesses. He should have an opportunity to hear and question adverse witnesses. In no case should the committee consider statements against him unless he has been advised of their content and of the name of those who made them, and unless he has been given an opportunity to rebut unfavorable inferences which might otherwise be drawn.

6. All matters upon which the decision may be based must be introduced into evidence at the proceeding before the hearing committee. The decision should be based solely upon such matter. Improperly acquired evidence should not be admitted.

7. In the absence of a transcript, there should be both a digest and a verbatim record, such as a tape recording, of the hearing.

8. The decision of the hearing committee should be final, subject to the student's right of appeal to the governing board of the institution.

STUDENTS SPEAK FOR ACTION

―――――――――・◄●►◄――――――――――

Many words have been written in recent months about student activism and the attitudes that engender it. But few interpretations have come from those who are closest to the action—the students themselves. Here SR presents excerpts from two commencement addresses given last spring by students at opposite ends of the country. Mr. Wagner was graduated magna cum laude from Harvard University. Mrs. Gatlin was graduated summa cum laude from San Francisco State College and is now a graduate student in American Civilization at the University of Pennsylvania.

1. THE DIMENSION OF COMMITMENT

ROBERT F. WAGNER, JR.

Countless commencement addresses have focused on the problem of student unrest, and almost without exception they have concentrated on the more radical outbursts—particularly the picketing over faculty appointments at Yale, the teach-ins across the country, and the rioting at Berkeley. All of these are forms, concrete and substantial, of student dissatisfaction. They are symbols of ferment, of a refusal to accept traditions as absolutes, the tried as the best.

But student unrest is much broader, if less strident, than most commencement speakers admit. What is significant about Berkeley, in my opinion, is not that 10 percent of the students rebelled, but that the majority supported their rebellion. Indeed, according to a Harris survey, two-thirds of all college students sympathized not only with their cause but with their tactics as well.

To be sure, student unrest has no single credo, no one goal. Yet in it there is one unifying theme: a search for adventure that too often seems lacking in both education and society. By adventure I do not mean that

Saturday Review, 48:82–83+; October 16, 1965. Reprinted by permission of the publisher and the authors.

students are looking for a joy-ride or a lark, but a sense of excitement that is constant and purposeful.

They fear stagnation that comes from two directions: one in the present, the other in the future. At some point in college, usually toward the end, many students find formal education increasingly removed from their real concerns. An exam becomes little more than gamesmanship; a paper, an exercise in technique.

A general sense of helplessness reinforces the pattern of frustration. Students feel helpless because of anxiety about their future and their society. Certainly opportunity abounds, but opportunity for security, not adventure. To many of us the world seems bureaucratized, a kind of massive civil service. I do not mean to toll the bell of doom. But this helplessness is there, and its existence helps explain the increased popularity of politics, journalism, and, especially, civil rights—all fields in which an individual can assert himself and in which the restrictions on adventure are more the result of self-will than the system.

And it is in this context, against this background, that student unrest has led to student activity in the 1960s. Action—above all, political action—came partially as a result of the excitement conveyed by President Kennedy's example and his ideas. It was also the crystallization of discontent that remained inchoate but real, under a blanket of apathy, in the 1950s.

The rise of involvement, which has been the most significant development in our four years at Harvard, is both natural and healthy. It has brought to the surface discontent that had long existed below. It has made students aware of problems of education and society, and has provided the added dimension of commitment.

At their best, protests and demonstrations can lead to more penetrating thinking about issues of deep concern, as the teach-ins on Vietnam have done. Even at their worst, they can compel people who have not thought before to think, to clarify, to form opinions.

But action for the sake of action should not become the motto of student unrest. Doubtless, though, in the years ahead, at Harvard and elsewhere, there will be outbursts that defy reason and countermand good sense. There will be outbursts that lack constructive ends and well-defined aims.

In such cases, authority should display all the tolerance and forbearance it can muster. Of course, there are bounds beyond which disrespect cannot go, but these should be bounds of law, not of taste or personal judgment.

And those who are dissatisfied or actively rebel should remember that theirs ought not to be an attack to destroy the machine, as Mario Savio said, but an attempt by man to assert himself over the machine. Theirs should not be a battle between individuals and society, but an attempt by individuals to overcome all that is stultifying and dehumanizing in society.

Unless based on such beliefs, student unrest will become only a negative force. Its protests will present a shrill, irritating dissonance rather than a critical voice that can be heard and hopefully heeded. Without genuine commitment to reason and understanding, student activists will alienate their sympathizers and at the same time justify their critics.

But despite some doubts about the future of student unrest, I do not envision an inevitable process of degeneration and deterioration, as some educators and writers have suggested. I do not believe that anarchy will become its philosophy or irresponsibility its hallmark. The vast majority of us who are dissatisfied shun ideology. Instead, we seek to find honest alternatives that permit adventure without destroying principle. Ours is not an unrest to be feared or suppressed. Rather, it should be accepted, tolerated, and encouraged, for from it can come fresh thoughts and new directions, as America examines and questions the quality of its life.

2. A RADICAL FRAME OF MIND

ROCHELLE GATLIN

College students of the 1960s are different from those of ten years ago. Specific issues in which questions of ethics are sharply defined have impelled them to reject the beat-style withdrawal of the 1950s. To paraphrase Crane Brinton, "Many of the new generation have thrown themselves into movements like the Peace Corps, civil rights, disarmament, and international government. They do this often to the accompaniment of words of despair and anger, but their deeds belie their words." Many of the same students who heroically went to Mississippi last summer were carried out of Sproul Hall last winter. Although the Berkeley Free Speech Movement contained a few hipsters and revolutionary zealots, there was a surprisingly large proportion of what U.C. graduate Michael Miller calls the most intellectually serious and morally alert students on campus, who demand the most from the university, who are concerned with putting knowledge of the past to work in the present and who believe that the educational process should provide a continuum between ideas and social action.

Fortunately demonstrations, sit-ins, and arrests are not the only ways to affect university and social reform. The Free Speech Movement was a dramatic event that occasioned sensational headlines, but at other institutions less publicized programs have been initiated. For example, the Committee for an Ideal Campus at Brandeis University in Massachusetts is an officially recognized organization, which receives a budget from the associated student body. Some of the programs of this committee include: compiling a critique of professors and courses, tabulating a student-faculty poll intended to ascertain what issues concern the campus community, making plans for a national convention of similar student groups, and initiating the Spinoza

Institute—which will offer non-graded courses and seminars next fall in the Modern Cinema, Eastern Thought, Psychedelic Stimulants, and the History of Peace Movements.

In its first Statement of Purpose, the Committee for an Ideal Campus summed up principles which are advanced by student reformers and university critics all over the country. This statement says in part:

> We believe that the ideal university is an intellectual community of teachers and students. . . . knowledge is advanced as a force which is personally relevant and meaningful, not as a commodity which is produced and marketed. . . .
> By virtue of its intellectual freedom, the university can serve society as a center of independent thought and criticism. The members of the university may challenge undesirable customs and values, offer suggestions for their improvement, and exercise their rights as citizens to participate in social and political action.

Obviously the constant scrutiny of university and social practices found in the above declaration may lead to unrest, but I do not believe that unrest is something that can or should be "remedied" by suppression. To state this positively, the effect of current student unrest may be a critical analysis—even exposé—of hypocritical practices in relation to traditional American values of peace, equality, and individual freedom. For example, it took the Freedom Riders and the registering of disenfranchised Southern Negroes—and unfortunately the murder of a few white Northerners—to focus the country's attention on the wide discrepancy between the ideal and the practice of equality.

One characteristic of socially alert students is their dissatisfaction with and even discarding of the liberalism of Woodrow Wilson, Franklin Roosevelt, and Clark Kerr. Stanley Kauffmann has expressed the growing irrelevance of liberalism with its optimistic belief in progress by saying that although liberal sentiments are unimpeachable, they are almost irresponsible in the light of existing conditions—the contemporary equivalent of a hundred Hail Marys to avert the Black Plague. To many students, there is something ineffectual about the liberal bureaucrat with his tools of mediation and compromise. Furthermore (as Michael Miller has said in a recent article in *Dissent*),"the more militant students regard liberalism with something less than satisfaction. They believe it to be somehow implicated, if only by default, in the heritage of nightmares that compose modern history—Auschwitz, Hiroshima, the Cold War, McCarthyism."

But student radicals do not look to bureaucratic, puritanical Russia or to unindustrialized, overpopulated, and poverty-ridden China as models. Not Marx, but Gandhi and Thoreau are their mentors. Their goal is to eliminate the divorce between the political and the personal; no definite programs, no slogans, only a direct emotional response to hypocrisy and injustice.

This graduating class joins with others throughout the country in facing tasks that require a radical and experimental frame of mind, guided by generous social impulses. We must find workable ideas to replace the myths that have been outrun by technology and social upheaval; we must develop a social vision less shallow than the duty to spend money to keep the economy going; and we must emphasize that although education might *sometimes* produce practical innovations beneficial to our health and material comfort, it should *always* produce greater understanding of the human condition and promise.

STUDENT ACTION

FRED M. HECHINGER

Spring is around the corner, but college students thus far have given up panty raids for more serious mass action—support of their teachers. Dissatisfaction has been fermenting for some time. Dr. Logan Wilson, President of the American Council on Education, last week traced it all to the fact that the undergraduate has become the "forgotten man."

Thousands of undergraduates last week reminded the academic world that they intend to be remembered.

At Yale, students protested vigorously when Dr. Richard J. Bernstein, a 32-year-old associate professor of philosophy, was denied tenure—the lifelong appointment which can be terminated by the professor but not by the university.

At St. Johns University in Jamaica, N.Y., students booed the administration when hundreds of faculty members charged that they had too little to say in policy-making. There were some hints that the administration had put excessive stress on rapid expansion of the Roman Catholic institution in direct competition with other Catholic universities.

At Brooklyn College, students demonstrated against the dismissal of Professor Leonard Altman of the music department, for his failure to engage in music activities, even though he is a former concert pianist and remains active in concert administration.

In other places—among them Kansas (over discrimination in fraternities) and New Hampshire (over a proposed bill to prohibit alleged subversives from speaking on state campuses)—student protests erupted. As in the earlier student rebellion at Berkeley, a general sense of unhappiness began to forge a new alliance between undergraduates and those faculty members who see their mission as primarily one of teaching.

The issues are more complicated than is suggested by the popular slogans of "publish or perish" or even of administration versus scholars. The fascination of the Yale episode is that it opened to laymen's eyes the inner workings of the academia, with its protocol and intrigue—as well as a high sense of mission.

Scene and actors seemed straight from one of the novels of C. P. Snow or Mary McCarthy. When Dr. Bernstein was turned down by the Committee on Tenure more than a week ago, the students cited as their strongest pro-Bernstein argument that the philosophy department had unanimously recommended him for tenure.

At this point, the department did nothing to dispel the general feeling that the fault was entirely with the big, bad tenure committee. However, when Kingman Brewster, Jr., Yale's president, asked the tenure committee to reconsider the case, the philosophy department's senior professors voted 5 to 2 to withdraw their support of Dr. Bernstein.

What the students had not been told was that the philosophy department, along with its unanimous recommendation for tenure, had withheld its promise to promote Dr. Bernstein to full professor. This omission was crucial. Mr. Brewster, in earlier guidelines, has insisted that anyone worthy of tenure must also be eligible for the top academic rank.

In this light, the unanimous vote was an evasion—passing the buck to the tenure committee which thus became the villain.

In the next round, the veneer of protocol cracked. The polite fiction that Dr. Bernstein unfortunately had not published—or published enough —gave way to growing suspicion that some of the dominant men in the inner circle might not like his views.

In addition to having written two books, Dr. Bernstein is editor of the *Review of Metaphysics*, an international philosophy journal founded by Professor Paul Weiss, a noted teacher and Dr. Bernstein's strongest supporter on the faculty.

Now the battle produced some of the choice invective of the tradition of academic infighting. Professor Norwood Russell Hanson, former Marine fighter pilot, amateur boxer and musician, specialist in the philosophy of science (physics), who had originally voted for Dr. Bernstein's tenure, now proclaimed his work "clever, urbane and never unreasonable . . . pleasant, but featureless . . . distinctly undistinguished."

Such language is familiar only to those who read the book reviews in scholarly journals where professors knife each other in grand style. It is in shocking contrast to the bland agreeability of television panelists.

Even the lay observer can grasp the academic one-upmanship in Professon Hanson's excuse of not having read his colleague's books before first judging him. "Intense pressure from publishers allowed me little opportunity to read widely in Bernstein's written work," he said.

He called the students' protest "the Pavlovian response of woefully uninformed enthusiasts . . . against the carefully deliberated verdict of seasoned judges possessed of data wholly unknown to the chanting, protesting, bellicose demonstrator." (In a subsequent letter to the New York *Times*, Erich Segal [Harvard '58], visiting lecturer at Yale, pointed out that "Yale undergraduates are not dogs.")

From this unusual exhibition match emerge these key observations:

(1) The professional promotion system, with clearly discernible ranks, makes the academic community more readily comparable to a military, rank-conscious post than scholars care to admit or the public realizes.

(2) Although academic men often stand in the forefront of the battle for freedom of expression for all views in society at large, they are frequently not nearly as liberal about granting free range of expression to rival opinions or divergent schools of thought within their own domain.

(3) The "publish or perish" threat, while unquestionably serious, is not necessarily imposed as exclusively by college administrators as the academic folklore implies. Faculty departments must at least share the blame, as the Yale episode shows.

In one of the most basic issues—rescue of the student from the limbo of "forgotten man" or "Pavlovian dog"—Mr. Brewster, as Yale's chief administrator, appears to have made the most pointed contribution.

He praised the students' zeal, goodwill and responsibility. He asked for the appointment of a faculty committee, to include junior as well as senior ranks, to review promotion procedures. And he added: "I would hope that students would be able to present any constructive ideas to this committee."

The students may be losing a war over a favorite professor, but they appear to have won a major battle over their place in the academic society.

THE LESSON OF BERKELEY

SEYMOUR MARTIN LIPSET AND PAUL SEABURY

Improbable as it may have seemed to outsiders, events at the Berkeley campus of the University af California during the last three months of 1964 constituted a small-scale but genuine revolution. Through continuous violation of university regulations, sit-ins, almost daily mass demonstrations, and finally a strike by students and teaching assistants, the authority of both the administration and the faculty had become virtually nonexistent at Berkeley by December.

The immediate cause was the withdrawal of a privilege. In mid-September, political groups and civil-rights organizations were barred from a twenty-six-foot-long strip of pavement at the entrance to the campus that traditionally had been used as a site for informal debate. More recently, it had been used for fund raising and recruiting for off-campus activities, both forbidden on university property.

Much of the intensity of student reaction to this ruling is directly attributable to a change of attitude on the part of young people all over the country—a change brought about by their participation in the civil-rights movement. Moreover, both students and faculty members at Berkeley, as at other large universities, are unhappy about changes taking place in American higher education today. In protesting the university administration's political restrictions, they were also voicing a discontent with the nonpolitical aspects of university policy. American students today are more concerned with ultimate moral ends than with responsibility or consequences. The civil-rights movement has provided them with a moral cause, and the example of civil disobedience with a tactic.

In the last two or three years, a civil-rights movement emanating from colleges in the San Francisco Bay Area has conducted sit-ins in hotels, restaurants, banks, supermarkets, and newspapers to demand the hiring of Negroes. Of the students arrested in these demonstrations, many were strongly influenced by various leftist groups that are currently stronger in the Bay Area than anywhere else in the United States.

STEERING LEFT

The campus protests crystallized in the organization of the Free Speech Movement (FSM) early in October, with Mario Savio, a twenty-two-year-old philosophy major, as its leading figure. Savio spent last summer in Mississippi and was arrested during a sit-in demonstration in San Francisco last spring. He is an emotional, effective speaker and calls himself a "democrat with a small d." Membership in the FSM was open to any individual or organization that chose to affiliate. Hard-core support was estimated at around five hundred; by December as many as three or four thousand students were committed to all-out support, and according to FSM claims three thousand nonstudents from the university community were supporting the movement. The executive committee was composed of delegates from affiliated groups, elected representatives of graduate-student organizations, unaffiliated students meeting in assembly, and elected spokesmen for the nonstudents in the university community. But the real leadership of the movement was provided by a steering committee (appointed by the executive committee) of less than a dozen members who were considerably to the left of the executive committee. The political convictions of the steering committee notwithstanding, the overwhelming majority of student followers of the FSM, including those who have engaged in the sit-ins, were moderates whose politics are limited to the civil-rights cause. A minority within the FSM attempted to restrain the more extreme elements and included at various times two democratic socialist organizations, the Young Democrats, and a variety of conservative groups, including Youth for Goldwater.

The growth of FSM must be ascribed to a series of blunders caused to some degree by the fact that various crucial decisions were made at different levels of the local campus administration as well as by the president, the regents, and the governor. Repeatedly, the university took an uncompromising position on a variety of matters, and then, under FSM pressure, backed down and accepted conditions it had previously rejected out of hand. Naturally, this behavior encouraged the FSM to increase its demands.

In mid-September, the students were demanding only the return of the "right" to carry on political activity on the twenty-six-foot strip; gradually this demand grew into an insistence on the elimination of all university restriction of political activity on campus. The FSM's position was that there should be no restrictions besides those imposed by the civil authority for any public place, and that the only enforcement agency should be the police—the reverse of the one usually taken by leftist student movements abroad and people concerned with academic freedom in this country. These groups have maintained that universities should govern their own affairs, and that public authority is a greater threat to academic freedom than univrsity administration. Indeed, in much of Latin America, students are legally protected from arrest within university precincts. Some who opposed the FSM on this position pointed to the fact that the city and county police, summoned when a campus police car was held captive for thirty-six hours on October 1 and 2, were not sent into action against the students by President Kerr, who had authority over them. By the time of the second major sit-in on December 3, Governor Edmund G. "Pat" Brown took over control of law enforcement on campus and, against the explicit advice of the university administration, ordered police to arrest students sitting in at Sproul Hall.

The most important reason for the weak position of the university administration during the past four months was that there were few on campus, among either students or faculty, who supported its original position on the political-rights issues: that a university should restrict the collection of funds for, or the advocacy of, off-campus political activities. The administration, in fact, modified its original position by early November and agreed to all the major student demands except the right to advocate and plan unlawful actions—chiefly the sit-ins. This position was ratified by the regents, and though the FSM continued to denounce university policy, it seemed at the time that it had lost the bulk of its support. The university returned the moral advantage and mass backing to the FSM by bringing charges over the Thanksgiving weekend against Savio and three other leaders for having organized the original sit-ins and capturing the campus police car almost two months earlier. To many, this seemed an implicit violation of the signed agreement between the university and the student leaders that had brought the police-car episode to an end. The December sit-in and strike were a result of this action.

But it should be noted that Steve Weissman, leader of the FSM graduate students and, after Savio, the most influential, told a *New Yorker* writer, "that if the university had not broken the thing open again . . . by its disciplinary action against four of the FSM leaders, they would have acquired a print of . . . a Genet film that had been banned as obscene from a student film series that week—set up a portable projector and loudspeaker, and shown the film on the wall of Sproul Hall."

KERR AS PROPHET

The opposition to the FSM among faculty members and students was based on antagonism to the use of illegal means, such as campus sit-ins and deliberate violations of university regulations, to attain political ends that might have been gained through conventional channels of redress. But these critics, many of whom felt that the use of illegal tactics was part of a conscious effort by extremists to undermine faith in the democratic system, were constrained to silence by their belief that the university's position was morally indefensible.

The meaning of these events cannot be understood by limiting the discussion to an analysis of the right of on-campus advocacy, or of the use of illegal and extremist methods. Despite the FSM's name, free speech was never the central issue—Savio admitted as much. The revolt was not just against the injustices of society at large but also against the university as a microcosm of that society. To fully understand the student and faculty response, one much recognize that many educators believe that the American university community is becoming increasingly restive as a result of changes in our system of higher education. Ironically, a vivid description of these changes can be found in The Uses of the University, by the president of the University of California, Clark Kerr.

Kerr warns that major universities have become predominantly research institutions; that teaching, particularly on the undergraduate level, holds little interest for many on the faculty; that administrators tend to become preoccupied with raising funds and gaining influence; that faculties have little institutional loyalty, with many professors choosing their universities on a careerist basis. These circumstances should produce considerable resentment among students, and Kerr, in fact, predicted a sharp increase in tensions and conflicts between students and instructors.

The large degree of political free speech long enjoyed at Berkeley, the size and eminence of the university, and the high caliber of its students and teachers are the very reasons why a mass student uprising took place there. Berkeley students have always made more use of their political rights to meet and speak freely on campus than American students elsewhere. Every sort of extreme-left group is represented—the DuBois Club (Communist), the Young Socialist Alliance (Trotskyist), the Independent Socialist Club (Revolutionary Marxist Socialist), and the Progressive Labor Movement (Maoist)—and so are various rightist groups. Even the American Nazi Party has been presenting speakers on campus and has announced that it will open headquarters nearby. The new student revolt began precisely where students were most free to organize.

For years, Berkeley has been evolving into a research center perched precariously on a mountain of somewhat neglected undergraduates. Many on the faculty came to support the FSM in the hope that the revolt will help to establish better contact between students and faculty and to increase autonomy of the Berkeley campus within the vast machinery of the "multiversity"—nine campuses of the statewide university system geared into a cumbersome synchronization.

Although faculty recommendations are accepted by the administration on most matters of educational policy, it is the multiversity faculty, represented on an all-state representative body, that speaks for the professors of the university. This arrangement leaves Berkeley representatives in a definite minority. Many important decisions have been made by the statewide Academic Senate or by the president's office. While these decisions may be defended as necessary for the advancement of higher education in California, they are apt to be resented by Berkeley faculty members who, rightly or wrongly, feel that their interests and academic eminence are being sacrificed to the system. Many feel that it was a mistake to increase the student body to 27,500 and that the concept of an all-state university has taken from Berkeley the right of deciding which applicants may be admitted there. But perhaps the most burdensome decision forced on Berkeley by the need for a co-ordinated statewide approach is the establishment of the year-round four-quarter system. In the eyes of many professors, this creates an academic production line that processes larger and larger numbers of students through already overburdened facilities.

The FSM leadership has denounced all efforts to analyze the sources of the Berkeley revolt in any but its manifest civil-liberties context. Yet Mario Savio explained the student protest to a meeting of the Trotskyist Young Socialist Alliance in these terms: "The most important concept for understanding the student movement is Marx's notion of alienation. Its basic meaning is that the worker is alienated from his product, but the concept is applicable to students too. . . . The students are frustrated; they can find no place in society where alienation doesn't exist, where they can do meaningful work. Despair sets in, a volatile political agent. The students revolt against the apparatus of the university. This is the motive power of the student movement."

Though the ideology of the movement was directed mainly against the university, the idea of alienation became the intellectual rallying point for a rejection of all power centers. The tragedy is that many within the university community who had diverse grievances against aspects of the university were drawn into support of a movement many of whose leaders saw every crisis as an opportunity to humiliate the university administration and to demonstrate the hollowness of authority.

Following the arrest on December 3 of about eight hundred students for occupying the university administration building, Sproul Hall, many faculty members who had previously ignored the struggle came to the support of the few professors who had defended the FSM, in principle at least, almost from the start. Graduate students and teaching assistants went on strike. Growing faculty support for the FSM resulted not only in the passage of resolutions backing much of the FSM position by the Berkeley Academic Senate (assistant professors and above), but also in the emergence of a variety of faculty grievances against the multiversity system. This accumulation of grievances naturally gravitated to the aggressive leadership of the FSM protest. In early December, dozens of new student organizations, closely linked to the FSM leadership, sprang up to advance special causes.

Perhaps the most destructive part of this affair was the extent to which civil disobedience and its consequences pushed the external community and the university in two opposite directions. The community at large reacted to events by moving to the right as far as its attitude toward the university was concerned; within the university, the sight of eight hundred young persons being dragged off to jail brought many previously apathetic students and teachers into the FSM camp. Most of these newcomers to the struggle saw it as a fight to defend students against oppressive authority. They were ignorant of the political forces at work within the steering committee of the FSM, and of its highly developed organization.

By the time the Berkeley revolt reached its crest, from December 3 to 6, the steering committee had a highly efficient organization at its disposal. FSM members, in touch with a central command post, covered the campus from one end to the other with walkie-talkies, and were able to learn of speeches and actions taken at closed faculty meetings as they occurred. The steering committee systematically rounded up the "right" faculty members to attend meetings and vote.

The strike, which closed down close to half the university, convinced many that peace was worth any price. A number of conservatives on the faculty who disagree in principle with the FSM reluctantly agreed that the university had to give up its power to regulate political activities on campus, and on December 8 voted in the Academic Senate for a motion that incorporated almost all FSM demands. While many voted on principle, others voted for it as a strike settlement by the weaker party.

The faculty voted for the right of free speech on all issues and the right to organize for off-campus political action, including civil-rights demonstrations. The regents accepted all but two points. First, they refused to yield to a committee of the Academic Senate their authority over matters of student discipline for infractions of rules governing political matters. (They did provide, however, that the faculty could take part in local campus administration judgment of such infractions.) Second, while affirming the rights of students and their organizations to advocate anything on campus that is lawful under the provisions of the First and Fourteenth Amendments, the regents continued to insist on the university's right to prohibit organized efforts to prepare illegal off-campus activities—a restriction aimed primarily at the organization of civil-rights sit-ins. A special emergency faculty committee, which had been elected on December 14 to represent the Academic Senate and which had discussed these issues with the regents before they met, concluded that the new regulations granted almost all that the faculty and the FSM had demanded in the area of free speech.

The new year brought an uneasy peace. During the holidays, the faculty emergency committee worked hard to obtain a broad consensus for reasonable regulations governing "time, place, and manner" of political activity acceptable to faculty, students, and regents. On January 2, just before classes resumed, the regents appointed a new acting chancellor, Martin Meyerson, the forty-two-year-old dean of the School of Environmental Design. Meyerson has shown strength and sophistication in dealing with the crisis, and he commands wide support from all major groups within what has continued to be a badly divided Academic Senate.

THE AFTERMATH

During the spring semester, the conflict between the university and various student groups continued apace, although since the arrests of the 800 there has been no further effort at massive civil disobedience. The most eventful crisis arose around the issue of "obscenity." Seeking to test the widest limits of the commitment to no restrictions on speech, various individuals, many of whom were non-students and some of whom were Maoists, carried signs of, or chanted, the word "fuck" in Sproul Plaza. Nine were ultimately arrested by campus police over a five-day period beginning March 3. Some of the FSM leadership, including Art Goldberg, former Slate leader and self-described "Maoist," who led the picket line that interrupted a university meeting addressed by the Chancellor in September, conducted protest meetings. As a result of language used at one of these meetings, Goldberg and others were subjected to university charges. Few students, however, showed interest in defending the "filthy speech movement."

The furor occasioned by the "obscenity" issue led a number of Regents and legislators to demand that the university take immediate punitive action. President Kerr and Acting Chancellor Meyerson suddenly resigned on March 10, in protest against being ordered by some Regents to expel the students involved at once. After considerable agitation by the faculty in support of Kerr and Meyerson, the Regents requested them to withdraw their resignations. Four students, including Goldberg, were later convicted by a faculty trial committee. Goldberg was dismissed from the university, while the three others were suspended for five months. A second "obscenity" crisis involved the suspension of two publications, *Spider* and *For Unlawful Carnal Knowledge*, by the Chancellor on March 19. After a faculty committee hearing, the Chancellor lifted the suspension of the first, but kept the one on the second permanently. Meyerson also issued regulations defining the conditions under which student groups might post announcements, locate tables to distribute materials and collect monies, and sell literature, which denied non-students the right to engage in such activities. Suggestions that these actions be met by civil disobedience did not receive much support, possibly because the two-month-long trial of the students arrested in Sproul Hall was then going on less than ten blocks from the campus. Some radical groups have followed the tactic of deliberate violations of minor regulations seeking to provoke the Administration into imposing severe penalties as in September. Thus far the Administration has refused to co-operate.

The punishments for obscenity led to bitter attacks on Chancellor Meyerson by the FSM. The conflict between them was also joined over the rights of student self-government. Slate had won all the seats up for election for the student council in December, almost half the Student Senate. Slate hoped to gain a majority by bringing the graduate students into the ASUC. Although a majority of both graduates and undergraduates who balloted endorsed compulsory graduate membership, the Regents, acting on a recommendation from Kerr and Meyerson, refused to authorize their admission on the grounds that not enough graduates had voted for it. (They wanted two thirds of half or more.) The Graduate Coordinating Committee, an FSM affiliate, protested with many mass meetings and petitions. This issue declined in early May when close to two thirds of the undergraduates chose moderate opponents of Slate in the ASUC elections, and a majority of graduates, voting in a second referendum, opted against membership.

Following these continued crises, the FSM decided to dissolve its crisis-born structure, and to form a new more permanent membership organization, the FSU (Free Student Union). The FSU is designed to carry on indefinitely, representing its members on various items of politics and educational policy. It claims three thousand dues-paying members. The Teaching Assistants Union, affiliated with the American Federation of Teachers, which was formed earlier in the conflict, spent much of the semester seeking to negotiate with various departments concerning the working conditions and job rights of graduate-student assistants.

As important as the institutionalization of conflict organizations among the students has been a somewhat comparable development among the faculty. Two and a half formal political factions have appeared within the Academic Senate. These are: the Committee of Two Hundred, formed in the late fall by faculty somewhat sympathetic to the FSM; the Faculty Forum, organized in January by others who, though voicing their support for maximum political freedom on campus, indicated their concern with the increasing politicization of the campus, and their disapproval of FSM tactics as inappropriate to a university campus in a democratic society; and a third smaller and less formally organized conservative grouping, which felt that liberalization of regulations had gone too far. The Chancellor and the Faculty Executive Committee have sought to reduce friction by consulting the leaders of the three "parties" on all controversial decisions. Such efforts, however, have not prevented sharp intrafaculty controversy.

Spring Senate meetings have witnessed bitter debate and close votes. And as the term ended, it appeared that the three-party system, as well as FSU-Administration conflict, would carry on into the fall.

The Regents also became targets of attack. Many students and faculty criticized them for their interference with local campus matters. The effort of the Regents to impose new rules concerning student political behavior in April and May met with rather aggressive criticism from the "Two Hundred," less violent criticism from the Faculty Forum, and approval from the conservative group. A study commission employed by a Regental Committee to look into the causes of the Berkeley uprising reported in May, and, to the surprise of the Regents, placed much of the blame for the university's inability to meet the problems of student political activity on over-centralization of university authority, and Regental interference with the actual administration of local campuses. A structural reorganization of the university and the Berkeley campus seems the order of the day. And at this point the legislature decided to take a hand in the proceedings. Speaker of the Assembly Unruh and Senate Majority Leader Burns announced at the end of May that there would be an investigation of the problems of higher education in California, with special reference to the Berkeley crisis. The legislature also enacted a law giving university authorities power to order any non-student to leave the campus or suffer arrest.

To restore the Berkeley campus to the normal life of a first-rate American university is still an immensely difficult task. It requires a high and rare level of administrative leadership and intelligence, qualities which fortunately Martin Meyerson seems to have. (Whether the Regents will appoint him the permanent Chancellor is still unsettled at this writing.[1]) It requires a faculty which is as sophisticated politically as it is intelligent academically, and which understands how a few extremists can exploit genuine grievances to make the large majority of moderates do their bidding.

Most shaken by this sudden crisis, however, has been the human trust that is the ethical basis of any university—or, for that matter, of any community. This delicate though often impersonal confidence between teachers and students, professors and professors, students and students, was severely breached. The wounds left by suspicion and resentment over apparent betrayals of trust will remain for a long time. This is a poignant future problem for the teacher and his students. Once classrooms have been bitterly divided with covert and overt defamation of faculty members as "stooges of the administration" or "tools of the FSM Steering Committee," the community of scholarship is clearly endangered.

The FSM leadership was first responsible for spreading this atmosphere,

[1] Martin Meyerson has since returned to his duties as Dean of the Environmental Studies College. R. W. Heyns of the University of Michigan was appointed Chancellor as of October 1, 1965. (P.D.B.)

but everyone has become somehow involved. A divided faculty can not long command respect from its students, and extremists can be counted upon to make the most of such divisions if they continue.

The Berkeley Revolt is not just another California curiosity. This new style of campus political action may affect other campuses, and eventually our national political life. The new student generation is brilliant and aggressively serious. The number of graduate students who spend years at a university increases steadily. The student leftist movements are growing and probably will continue to grow as they demand totally moral solutions to issues of racial discrimination, and foreign policy. The indifference to legality shown by serious students can threaten the foundations of democratic order if it becomes a model for student political action. Extremism in the pursuit of liberty was quite recently a favorite slogan of the radical right. Berkeley has shown that anyone can play this game. The danger now exists that students at other universities will have learned how easily a great university can be brought to its knees if but two or three per cent of the student body are willing to engage in actions which may force the police on campus. Universities are probably more vulnerable to civil disobedience tactics than any other institution in the country precisely because those in authority, whether administration or faculty, are liberal. They are reluctant to see force invoked against their students regardless of what the students do. Now that this secret is out, it may be difficult to restrain students from having their way on many university issues much as occurs on Latin-American campuses.

ANNOTATED BIBLIOGRAPHY

Bibliographical Data	*Annotation*
Anderson, Albert (ed.), *Focus on Rebellion*, Chandler, 1962. 238 pp.	A controlled research manual, including 27 articles. Part I: The San Francisco Affair. Part II: A Student Renaissance, with subdivisions on Focus on San Francisco, Focus on the National Scene, Focus on the Counter Rebellion, Focus on Values and Attitudes.
Baskin, Samuel (ed.), *Higher Education: Some Newer Developments*, McGraw-Hill, 1965. 342 pp.	Pages 304–317 on The Campus Climate: A Reminder are challenging. Providing the Conditions for Learning: The "New" Media, pp. 128–152, gives an excellent survey of new teaching devices.
Bell, Norman T., *Introduction to College Life*, Houghton Mifflin, 1962. 142 pp.	Twenty-five essays ranging in topic from College Student Government to Blueprint for an Ideal College.
Boroff, David, *Campus, USA*, Harper & Row, 1961. 210 pp.	Not statistical but introspective. Harvard, Wisconsin, Claremont, Swarthmore, Brooklyn, Parsons, Birmingham–Southern, Smith, Sarah Lawrence, and Michigan are analyzed. Interesting and entertaining.
Buckley, William F., Jr., *God and Man at Yale: The Superstitions of Academic Freedom*, Regnery, 1951. 240 pp.	Through personal experience, the author examined religion and economics at Yale and found them too liberal.
Butz, Otto (ed.), *The Unsilent Generation*, Holt, 1958. 189 pp.	Eleven essays written by Princeton Seniors who graduated in 1958. Essays were chosen at random. Not a flattering picture, but an interesting one.
Cain, Edward, *They'd Rather Be Right*, Macmillan, 1963. 327 pp.	The impact of conservatism on youth. Gives a history of conservatism on the college campuses in the 1930s, 1940s and 1950s. Brought up to date with interviews.
Douglas, William O., *Freedom of the Mind*, Doubleday, 1964. 37.*	A provocative short essay covering such subjects as loyalty oaths, censorship, and challenging the status quo.

* Indicates bibliography.

BOOKS (*continued*)

Bibliographical Data	Author
Draper, Hal, *Berkeley: The New Student Revolt*, Grove Press, 1965. 246 pp.	Author is librarian at Berkeley. Anti-administration. Intro. by Mario Savio.
Eble, Kenneth Eugene, *The Profane Comedy*, Macmillan, 1962. 234 pp.	Chapters on The Fourth R, concerning "dumbbell" or "bonehead" remedial college courses and student life. A chapter on Paradise discusses the role of the professor at the exclusive college.
Eddy, Edward D., Jr., et al., *The College Influence on Student Character*, American Council on Education, 1959. 185 pp.	The authors visited 20 college campuses. The book is sensitive to the views of students. Many good thoughts and ideas.
Evans, Medford Stanton, *Revolt on the Campus*, Regnery, 1961. 248 pp.	A documented account of the rise of conservatism on the college campus. Discusses Intercollegiate Society of Individualists, Young Americans for Freedom, William F. Buckley, Jr., the NSA and the Young Republicans.
Fellman, David, *The Constitutional Right of Association*, University of Chicago, 1963. 110 pp.	Chapters on Unlawful Assembly, Meetings in Streets and Other Public Places, The Problem of the Hostile Audience, and The Right to Associate.
Freedman, Morris, *Chaos in Our Colleges*, McKay, 1963. 241 pp.	An analysis of higher education, with some emphasis on graduate education. Sections on Breaking the Ph.D. Barrier; Large Classes, Small Classes, No Classes; Publishing, Perishing, Flourishing. Largely critical.
Goldsen, Rose K., et al., *What College Students Think*, Van Nostrand, 1960. 240 pp.	Chapters on The Fraternity System: A Style of Life, Men and Women, Political Apathy, Secular Religion, National and International Attitudes. Results of a research project financed by the Carnegie Corporation, out of Cornell. Excellent statistical coverage.
Gordon, Richard E., and Katherine Gordon, *Blight on the Ivy*, Prentice-Hall, 1963. 313 pp.	Twelve chapters, all highly applicable. Chapters on College Anti-Intellectualism, The Overachievers, Revolution and Evolution, Crisis on Campus, including subsections on fraternities,

BOOKS (continued)

Bibliographical Data	Author
	malarky peddlers, the faculty wife, and college hazing.
Greene, Gael, *Sex and the College Girl*, Dial, 1964. 256 pp.	Interviews with 614 coeds from 102 colleges. A sociological study with the findings cautiously reported. Individual and small group interviews. Also, 76 college men were interviewed.
Habein, Margaret L. (ed.), *Spotlight on the College Student*, American Council on Education, 1959. 89 pp.*	Papers on Student Culture and Faculty, Values, Student Capabilities for Liberal Education, and Knowledge of Students Through the Social Sciences. Excellent discussion of the changing values of college students, with comments by Killian, Kerr, and Pusey.
Hofstadter, Richard, and Walter P. Metzger, *The Development of Academic Freedom in the United States*, Columbia, 1955. 527 pp.	A history of academic freedom from the earliest stages through the establishment of the AAUP.
Hunt, Everett Lee, *The Revolt of the College Intellectual*, Human Relations Aid, 1963. 165 pp.*	A case history of what has transpired at Swarthmore College.
Husain, Zakir, *The Dynamic University*, Asia Publishing House, 1965. 119 pp.	A set of addresses by the Vice President of India, pointing out how the university should meet the needs of a developing country.
Jacob, Philip E., *Changing Values in College*, Harper & Row, 1958. 174 pp.	A study of what happens to the values of college students as a result of general education in the social sciences. The findings are mostly negative.
Johnson, Patrick, *Fraternity Row*, Brewster Publications, 1963. 172 pp.*	Part II on Why Fraternities? has sections on anti-fraternities and pro-fraternities.
Keats, John, *The Sheepskin Psychosis*, Lippincott, 1965. 120 pp.	Chapters on Desire Under the Elms, Who Is Grading the Graders?, Why Sophomores Slump. Theme is that a college education is oversold.
Kerber, August, and Wilfred L. Smith (eds.), *Educational Issues in a Changing Society*, Wayne State University, 1962. 477 pp.*	Chapters on Desegregation and Integration, Censorship and Loyalty Oaths in a Free Society, The Federal Aid Controversy, and the Separation of Church and State.

BOOKS (*continued*)

Bibliographical Data	Title, Date
Kirkendall, Lester Allen, *Premarital Intercourse and Interpersonal Relationships*, Julian Press, 1961. 302 pp.	The author is a professor of family life at Oregon State University. The book is based on a study of 200 college-level males.
Klopf, Gordon, *College Student Government*, Harper & Row, 1960. 108 pp.	Concerns student participation in student government. A fourth revised edition of a U.S. National Student Association publication, *Student Leadership and Government in Higher Education*.
Lipset, Seymour M., and Sheldon S. Wolin (eds.), *The Berkeley Student Revolt*, Doubleday-Anchor, 1965. 585 pp.	The seriousness of the events is not overlooked. The faculty senate seemed unable to prove a stabilizing influence.
Lunn, Harry H., Jr., *The Student's Role in College Policy-Making*, American Council on Education, 1957, 100 pp.	A description of the various ways in which students are involved in administration and policy formation.
Lunsford, T. F. (ed.), *The Study of Campus Cultures: The Papers Presented at the Fourth Annual Institute on College Self-Study, University of California, Berkeley, July 24–27, 1962*. Boulder, Colo., Western Interstate Commission for Higher Education, 1963. 190 pp.	A series of provocative papers on such subjects as Student Stress (by a psychiatrist); Interactions Among Academic, Administrative, and Student Subcultures; and Studying Students in Britain and America.
Mallery, David, *Ferment on the Campus*, Harper & Row, 1966. 147 pp.	An optimistic book based on interviews with students, deans, and teachers on a wide variety of campuses. Some interesting comparisons between the veterans of World War II and the veterans of civil rights and anti-poverty.
Mechanic, David, *Students Under Stress: A Study in the Social Psychology of Adaptation*, Macmillan, 1962. 231 pp.	Case histories of how 22 graduate students handled their Ph.D. examinations.
Miller, M. V., and S. Gilmore (eds), *Revolution at Berkeley: The Crisis in American Education*, Dial Press, 1965. 348 pp.	An anthology of articles about the Berkeley revolt, with considerable overlapping with Lipset-Wolin anthology.
Millett, John David, *The Academic*	Provocative chapters on Faculty, Stu-

BOOKS (continued)

Bibliographical Data	Title, Date
Community, McGraw-Hill, 1962. 265 pp.	dents, Alumni, and Administration. Entertainingly and forcefully written.
Moos, Malcolm, and Francis E. Rourke, *The Campus and the State*, Johns Hopkins, 1959. 414 pp.*	Chapters on The Statehouse and the Campus and Legislators and Legislative Committees. Appendixes on Michigan and on British Universities.
Pemberton, John de J., *Freedom Through Dissent*, Oceana Publications, 1963. 84 pp.	Forty-second annual report of the American Civil Liberties Union. Sections on Equality before the Law, Due Process of Law, and Freedom of Belief, Expression, and Association.
Remmers, H. H. (ed.), *Anti-Democratic Attitudes in American Schools*, Northwestern, 1963. 344 pp.	Includes several studies of the college and university population. Subjects respond to questions on civil liberties, rights, religion, and minorities. Results are very revealing.
Resnick, William C., and David H. Heller (eds.), *On Your Own in College*, Merrill, 1963. 275 pp.	Although aimed at the freshman, its sections on fraternities, scholarship, and the college of the future are highly applicable to this unit.
Rice, Charles E., *Freedom of Association*, New York University, 1962. 202 pp.	Section V on Freedom of Association and Political Parties and Pressure Groups gives the legal background of affiliation.
Riker, Harold C., and Frank G. Lopez, *College Students Live Here*, Educational Facilities Laboratories, 1961. 152 pp.	A pictorial and statistical report of how student housing can be provided satisfactorily.
Sanford, Nevitt (ed.), *The American College*, Wiley, 1962. 1084 pp.*	Chapter 23, Freedom and Authority on the Campus, by Harold Taylor, pp. 774–804. Most information for this chapter is based on surveys of Sarah Lawrence College. Ten other chapters based on research at Vassar. Good for both political and social views.
Sanford, Nevitt (ed.), *College and Character*, Wiley, 1964. 308 pp.	Includes sections on Student Peer Group Influence, Freedom and Authority on the Campus, Patterns of Residential Education: Reflections from a Case Study at Harvard, and Dropouts from College.

BOOKS (*continued*)

Bibliographical Data	Annotation
Simon, Yves, *A General Theory of Authority*, Notre Dame, 1962. 167 pp.	An excellent discussion of authority and its ramifications. Sections on Knowledge and Freedom and on Paternal Authority. Should help focus the position on authority on the college campus.
Warshaw, Stephen, *The Trouble in Berkeley*, Diablo Press, 1965. pp. not numbered.	A pictorial presentation with a running commentary. Sections on The Origins of Discontent, The Rules, The Needs, Direct Action Begins, The Effects of the Rebellion, and Epilogue.
Western Interstate Commission for Higher Education, *Research on College Students*, University of California, 1960. 188 pp.*	The WICHE is in Boulder, Colorado; the cosponsor of the publication is the Center for Higher Education, Berkeley, California. Good chapters on Exploiting Student Resources, Institutional Research on Retention and Withdrawal, and Student Values and Their Relationship to the College Environment.
Western Personnel Institute, *Rights and Responsibilities of College Students: An Annotated Bibliography*, Western Personnel Institute, Pasadena, Calif., 1962. 32 pp.	An excellent supplement to this bibliography. Lists of sources on Legal Bases, Self-Government, Misconduct, Student-Invited Speakers, Student Publications.
Wise, William Max, *They Come for the Best of Reasons—College Students Today*, American Council on Education, 1958. 65 pp.*	Distinguishes this college generation by data on age, marital status, socioeconomic background, and ability level. A new perspective on today's college student.
Zinn, Howard, *The New Abolitionists*, Beacon, 1964. 246 pp.	The author was a professor at Spelman College in Atlanta. This is the closest thing to a history of the Student Nonviolent Coordinating Committee.
Zweig, Ferdynand, *The Student in an Age of Anxiety*, Macmillan, 1964. 224 pp.	A sociological study of 205 randomly chosen students at Oxford and Manchester, England, stating their attitudes on parents, politics, religion, and sex. Describes the student in favorable terms.

ANNOTATED BIBLIOGRAPHY

Periodical	Author	Title, Date	Annotation
America	F. Canavan	Academic revolution at St. John's. 113:136–140; Aug. 7, 65.	The problems of free speech at St. John's and what they are doing about it.
American Association of University Professors Bulletin	American Civil Liberties Union Committee on Academic Freedom	Academic freedom and civil liberties of students in colleges and universities. 48:110–115; June, 62.	A manifesto on student rights, based on freedom of expression, freedom from discrimination, and government by law.
Atlantic Monthly	J. T. Rule	Must the colleges police sex? 213: 55–58; Apr., 64. Discussion, 213: 42+; June, 64.	Outlines a philosophy of not having rules and how no rules requires more, not less, responsibility by the student. Somewhat theoretical, as the letters say.
		The troubled campus. 216:107–160; Nov., 65.	Twelve separate articles, all excellent, by professors, students, administrators. Discusses Free Speech at Ohio State, So You Want to Be a Dropout, A Vote for Student Protest, etc.
	Jeffrey Goodman	How to be patriotic and live with	Urges a new universal national

PERIODICALS (continued)

Periodical	Author	Title, Date	Annotation
		yourself. 217:61–62; Feb., 66.	service requirement that would include "constructive alternatives to military service."
	Donald Graham	Taking a McNamara fellowship. 217: 59–60; Feb., 66.	Points up confusion and inequity in the Selective Service System. Urges careful consideration for proposals to reform the draft law.
The British Journal of Sociology	Philip Abrams, Alan Little	The young activist in British politics. 16, no. 4:315–333; Dec., 65.	An interesting contrast to American student activists in that young British activism is concentrated in and around the three regular parliamentary parties.
Catholic Educational Review	M. Kinnane	Catholic students' attitudes toward college authority. 61:294–301; May, 63.	Students at Boston College voted approval for university regulations of dress, speakers, etc.
College and University	E. G. Williamson	Do students have academic freedom? 39:466–487; Summer, 64.	Excellent discussion of philosophical implications of the rights of citizenship applied to college life.
College and University	Thomas E. Blackwell	Federal decision offers guidelines	Supreme Court declines to

PERIODICALS (continued)

Periodical	Author	Title, Date	Annotation
Business		on procedure for student discipline. 40:64; Jan., 66.	review a circuit court ruling that due process is violated in expelling students (in this case, at Alabama State College) unless notice and hearing are given.
	N. Glazer	Civil disobedience on campus: its methods, meaning and morality. 40: 47–52; Feb., 66.	A re-examination of Berkeley by an opponent of the student leaders at Berkeley.
	Archibald Cox	Can civil disobedience be legally justified? 40:53–58; Feb., 66.	By a professor of law at Harvard. Some "gray" areas in the law.
Commentary	N. Glazer	What happened at Berkeley. 39: 39–47; Feb., 65.	By sociology professor at Berkeley. Thoughtful analysis, made immediately after incident.
	P. Selznick, N. Glazer	Berkeley. 39:80–85; Mar., 65.	Selznick, sociology professor at Berkeley, says issue was "free speech." Glazer responds.
Comparative Education Review	B. B. Stretch, L. C. Pelaez	Autonomy and student cogovernment in the University of Uruguay. 7:166–172; Oct., 63.	Outlines the degree to which the students in Uruguay have control of the University.
Ebony	L. Bennett	SNCC: Rebels with a Cause. 20: 146–153; July, 65.	Informative article on the Student Nonviolent Coordinating Committee.

PERIODICALS (continued)

Periodical	Author	Title, Date	Annotation
Educational Record	E. G. Williamson	Students' academic freedom. 44:214–222; July, 63.	Students and administration must participate together to achieve academic freedom of students.
History of Education Quarterly	B. F. Cowart	Development of the idea of university autonomy. 2:259–264; Dec., 62.	History of the concept of university autonomy, results of instances of both authoritarian and student control.
Journal of Higher Education	B. C. Duke	Struggle for control of the Japanese university. 35:19–26; Jan., 64.	Description of student and government forces trying to control the traditionally autonomous Japanese university.
	A. H. Kiendl	Emancipation of students. 34:465–466; Nov., 63.	To what degree must the university exercise *in loco parentis?* Well documented.
	J. E. Watson	Place of controversy on the campus. 36:18–24; Jan., 65.	Presents the case for an open speaker's policy. Documented.
Life		Campus agitation v. education. 58: 4; Jan. 22, 65.	Deplores ability of a minority to interfere with education in a major university.
The Massachusetts Review	R. M. Abrams	The student rebellion at Berkeley—an interpretation. 6:	Disparages outside influences. Summarizes student thought of

PERIODICALS (continued)

Periodical	Author	Title, Date	Annotation
		353–365; Winter–Spring, 65.	1950s and 1960s. Must come to grips with changed student.
Nation	J. Newfield	The question of SNCC: 201:38–40; July 19, 65.	An exposition of SNCC.
	J. Newfield	The student left: revolt without dogma. 200:491–495; May 10, 65.	Traces the development of "a new generation of American radicals," their impact off the campus.
	H. S. Thompson	The nonstudent left. 201:154–158; Sep. 27, 65.	Concerns the left-activist nonstudent and the Free Speech Movement.
Nation's Business		Reds threaten U.S. youth. 48: 44–45+; Nov., 60.	Sees serious communist threat to American youth. Urges business to take positive action.
New Guard	J. Tuck	The Princeton popular front—a nostalgic testament. 6, no. 3:9–10, 22, Mar., 66.	Vietnam has supplanted Spain, and the left has changed its look, but nothing much is really different.
New Republic	G. A. Harrison	Berkeley: does that banner still wave? Free speech movement. 151: 7–8; Dec. 19, 64.	The author supports the student movement, says it was a genuine protest against impersonality.
	J. Neugeboren	Hoadley's test case in Indiana. 149: 14; Sep. 21, 63.	Members of Young Socialist Alliance subject to indictment

PERIODICALS (continued)

Periodical	Author	Title, Date	Annotation
			under Indiana's "non-communist law" for Cuban, civil rights protests.
New South Student	C. Jordan	A parable of no violence, some violence, and great violence. 3, no. 4:2–3; Apr., 66.	Published by Southern Student Organizing Committee, Nashville, Tennessee.
New Statesman	E. J. Hobsbawm	The campus rebellion. 60:371; Sep. 17, 60.	Points to resurgence of political involvement on the campus, is good antidote for conformity.
Newsweek		The demonstrators: why? how many? 66:25–34; Nov. 1, 65.	A survey of the problem, with excerpts from "Ways and Means of 'Beating' and Defeating the Draft."
		Uprising at Yale. 65:89; Mar. 15, 65.	Yale student protest for denial of tenure to Bernstein.
Ohio State University Monthly		The speaker's rule. 54:9–17; Dec., 62.	A series of small articles concerning the speaker's rule at Ohio State.
Quarterly[1] Monograph— University of South Florida	L. B. Mayhew (ed.)	Intellectual tone for a state university. 3, no. 4:28 pp.; 1961.	A new university examines what should be its intellectual tenor.
Saturday Review	A. Z. Bass	A platform for citizen-students. 48:84; Oct. 16, 65.	Report of the 18th Annual Congress of the NSA held in September at University of Wisconsin.

[1] Exact title of the quarterly is not clear.

PERIODICALS (continued)

Periodical	Author	Title, Date	Annotation
	J. Cass	What happened at Berkeley. 48:47–48+; Jan. 16, 65.	On causes and results at Berkeley. Relief that now student apathy is less.
	J. Ciardi	Manner of speaking. 48:45–73; Oct. 23, 65.	Contract written by faculty to student must be obeyed or student should withdraw.
	N. Cousins	Escalation in California. 48:20; Jan. 30, 65.	Points to lack of intellectual action by Berkeley authorities.
	D. A. Eldridge	More on campus mores. 47:57–59+; June 20, 64.	Student conference from eight Eastern colleges suggests college set tone for conduct, not regulations.
	J. L. Jarrett	College students —the new breed. 48:64–65+; Mar. 20, 65.	Education professor at Berkeley predicts that the revolt has only just begun.
	J. Katz, and N. Sanford	Causes of the student revolution. 48:64–66, 76, 79; Dec. 18, 65.	College authorities should welcome the student revolution as a unique opportunity.
	G. F. Lewis	"The new breed" —a dissenting view. 48:75–76; Sep. 11, 65.	Doubts that students have changed or that activists are likely to bring about any great changes.
School and Society	J. S. Brubacher	Off-beat speakers on the campus. 90:282–283; Sep. 22, 62.	Authorities justified in demanding notice ahead, but not in banning.

PERIODICALS (continued)

Periodical	Author	Title, Date	Annotation
	H. W. Stoke	Invitation of speakers to the college campus. 90:107–108; Mar. 10, 62.	Prerogative of college to decide what is fitting to its educational purposes.
United States News and World Report		Campus rules on sex: an ex-envoy joins the debate; excerpts from letter. 55:18; Nov. 25, 63.	Galbraith quoted as opposed to tighter rules for Harvard students.
		When students try to run a university: University of California, Berkeley. 57:43; Dec. 21, 64.	FBI warns college presidents of attempt to disrupt universities; 3% of student body can disrupt campus.
		More campus unrest: are reds to blame? Howard University; statements. 58:14; May 10, 65.	President of Howard University blames communists for lawlessness and disorder on campus.
	M. Rafferty	Cure for campus riots; interview. 58:70–72; May 17, 65.	California State Superintendent for Public Instruction fixes blame on beatniks, says university should get rid of them.
Vital Speeches of the Day	L. A. Kimpton	Unrest on the campus: which way to a better world. 32:302–305; Mar., 66.	An industrialist worries about student alienation from business careers. Suggests "crusade of our own" to communicate the challenge of our economic system.

ANNOTATED BIBLIOGRAPHY

NEWSPAPERS[1]

Author	Title, Date	Annotation

Christian Science Monitor

N. Abiko	Yale chaplain urges involvement. Apr. 24, 64; 18, 7–8.	Colleges should encourage student involvement.
	Faculty stirred by students. Feb. 12, 66; 7.	Student unrest has led to faculty and administration "stir over updating college policies and procedures."
L. Mouat	U.S. colleges stiffen curriculums. Feb. 24, 66; 1, 5.	Report of increasing academic pressure. Many freshman level courses now taught in high school.

The New York Times

	Freedom on campus. Oct. 12, 63; 22, 2.	Editorial opposes curbs on campus activities even if politically controversial.
	Colleges' free speech stand. Oct. 22, 63; 36, 5.	Letter by professor opposes curbs on speakers to campus groups.
	Aid for students in sit-ins urged. Feb. 10, 64; 24, 8.	ACLU issues revised publication on academic freedom.
S. Hook	Freedom to learn but not to riot. Jan. 3, 65; VI, 8–9+.	Excellent discussion of difference between civil rights and the right to an education, how they may conflict, where responsibility of the university lies.
D. Boroff	Protests added to campus scene. Jan. 13, 65; 75, 7+.	Compares recent student sit-ins and demonstrations with campus activities of the 1930s.
P. Bart	U.C.L.A. concedes signs of disquiet. Feb. 7, 65; 69, 1.	Restless student is discussed. Also the Free Speech Movement at U.C.L.A.
F. M. Hechinger	Student action. Mar. 14, 65; IV, 9, 1.	Comments about current student movements asserting role in academic community.

[1] Arranged chronologically.

Author	Title, Date	Annotation
F. Powledge	The student left; spurring reform: new activist intelligentsia is rising on campuses. Mar. 15, 65; 1, 3+.	Good review of student activist groups, including Northern Student Movement, Students for a Democratic Society, W. E. B. DuBois Clubs, and Student Nonviolent Coordinating Committee. Differentiates these from older student movements.
F. Powledge	Collegians adopt a bill of rights. Mar. 29, 65; 27, 3.	Students from 39 colleges, meeting at University of Pennsylvania, adopt student bill of rights.
	Professors decry curbs on politics. Apr. 11, 65; 53, 1.	AAUP defends right of students to engage in civil rights demonstrations and political activities.
	The university idea. Apr. 30, 65; 34, 2.	Editorial says "crass opportunism" and selfishness of many faculty aid student unrest.
F. M. Hechinger	Whys of the student revolts. May 2, 65; IV, 9, 1.	Outlines attitudes of college presidents from Howard and Hofstra on student revolts. Good criticism of use of civil disobedience without trying to use democratic processes available.
F. M. Hechinger	Activism on campus. June 6, 65; IV, 9, 1.	For years, commencement speakers have urged students to dissent. Now some are sounding note of caution.
	Pastor explores student revolt. Aug. 9, 65; 22, 3.	The Rev. Dr. C. B. Ketcham finds the revolts primarily positive, a search for the meaning of life.
F. M. Hechinger	Students at Yale to judge faculty: plan giving them voice on tenure would rec-	An effort to give proper emphasis to the good teacher by having selected students

NEWSPAPERS (*continued*)

Author	Title, Date	Annotation
	ognize the effective teacher. Oct. 15, 65; 1, 4⁺.	at Yale submit an evaluation of their education.
T. R. Brooks	Voice of the new campus "underclass." Nov. 7, 65; VI, 25–27.	A delineation of the Students for a Democratic Society.
I. M. Heyman	Tumult and shouting subside at Berkeley as restraints on students are eased. Jan. 12, 66; 29, 1.	Prof. Heyman of the Law School of the University of California was chairman of an important committee during the difficulties on the Berkeley campus.
A. H. Raskin	Yesterday's Berkeley rebel says: "I'm just here to study." Jan. 30, 66; VI, 12–13, 27–40.	A reflection on the leaders of the Berkeley revolt of 1964.
F. P. Graham	U.S. asks to have DuBois Clubs registered as communist front. Mar. 5, 66; 1, 6.	Justice Department petitions the Subversive Activities Control Board to require DuBois Clubs to register.
	U. of North Carolina forbids talk by Aptheker. Mar. 10, 66; 8, 4.	Leading American communist forced to speak to 2,000 students on edge of campus.
M. A. Farber	Faculty dispute haunts Duquesne. Mar. 13, 66; I, 39.	Students and faculty involved in dispute over a department chairmanship. Administrative "hands-off" policy is no guarantee of harmony.
	Are DuBois Clubs a danger? Mar. 13, 66; IV, 6.	Reflections on government motives in designating the clubs as Communist-front organizations.
N. Jaffe	Protests called aid to maturity. Apr. 16, 66; 30, 1.	Psychiatrists say mental health of protesters equal to others and maturity often greater

The Wall Street Journal

Author	Title, Date	Annotation
Claudio Segre	Berkeley's lesson. Dec. 23, 64; 164, 8.	Student unrest points up problem of big college, reaction against size and impersonality of Berkeley.

MATERIALS AVAILABLE FOR PURCHASE[1]

American Association of Colleges for Teacher Education, 1201 16th St., N.W., Washington, D.C. 20036
> *Student Participation in College Policy Determination and Administration*, 1959. $1.25

American Civil Liberties Union (ACLU), 156 Fifth Ave., New York, N.Y. 10010
> *Combatting Undemocratic Pressures on Schools and Libraries.* 10¢
> *What Is the ACLU?* 10¢
> *The Case against HUAC.* 35¢
> *Loyalty Oaths and Conscience.* 10¢
> *Teacher Disclosure of Information about Students to Prospective Employers.* 5¢

American Council on Education, 1785 Massachusetts Ave., N.W., Washington, D.C. 20036
> *The Student's Role in College Policy-Making,* 1957. $1

Campus Americans for Democratic Action (CADA), 156 Fifth Ave., New York, N.Y. 10010
> *The Free Speech Movement: University of California at Berkeley.* 14 pp. plus bibliography. mimeo
> *A Call to Student Action.* 8 pp. mimeo

Intercollegiate Society of Individualists (ISI), 629 Public Ledger Building, Philadelphia, Pa. 19106
> *The Intercollegiate Review.* 6 issues yearly; free to students and teachers
> *The Individualist.* bi-monthly
> *ISI Campus Report.* quarterly; free to students and teachers
> *The ISI Story in Brief.* free to students and teachers
> Monthly book and essay series.

Northern Student Movement (NSM), 514 West 126th St., New York, N.Y. 10027

Southern Student Organizing Committee, 1703 Portland Ave., Nashville, Tenn. 37212
> *Student Social Action.* 10¢
> *The University and the Cold War.* 10¢
> *"Call to Action."* free?
> *The Free University Movement.* 10¢

Students for a Democratic Society (SDA), 112 East 19th St., New York, N.Y. 10003
> Monthly bulletin.
> *The Activist.* quarterly
> *Common Sense.* 8 issues per year

---

[1] Students are urged to write each office for lists of releases, sample releases, or material on a specific subject (materials in this area change rapidly).

Student Nonviolent Coordinating Committee (SNCC), 360 Nelson St., S.W., Atlanta, Ga. 30313
> SNCC: Rebels with a Cause
> Barbour County (Alabama)

Student Peace Union, 5 Beekman St., New York, N.Y. 10038
> Can a Catholic Be a Conscientious Objector?
> SPU Organizers' Handbook. 25¢
> SPU Bibliography.
> Are You a Conscientious Objector to War?

United States National Student Association (USNSA), 2115 S St., N.W., Washington, D.C. 20008
> Campus Political Parties. $1.75
> Student Responsibility in Campus Affairs. $1.25
> Campus Justice: Principles, Practices, and the Law. $1.75
> Draft Statement on Faculty Responsibility for the Academic Freedom of Students. 50¢
> Multimistake: A Report on Berkeley. $1.25

United States Youth Council, 236 East 46th St., New York, N.Y. 10017

Young Americans for Freedom, Inc. (YAF), 514 C St., N.E., Washington, D.C. 20002
> The New Guard. monthly 35¢
> Report on the Left. 10 issues per year
> College News Service. free to college newspaper editors
> Spotlight on: The New Left. I. Return of the Campus Marxists; II. Rebellion at Berkeley; III. The Red Diaper Babies Grow Up. 25¢
> "Operation Greek": The Attempt to Destroy the American Fraternity System. free to fraternities and sororities
> The W. E. B. DuBois Clubs: Return of the Campus Marxists. free
> The NSA Myth.

Young Democratic Clubs of America (YDCA), c/o Democratic National Committee, 1730 K St., N.W., Washington, D.C. 20006
> The Democrat. every two weeks; $2 per year

Young Republican National Federation, College Republican National Committee, 1625 Eye St., N.W., Washington, D.C. 20006
> Young Republican Newsletter. bi-monthly
> Chairman's Report. bi-monthly
> Issue Paper. bi-monthly

SUGGESTED SPEECH SUBJECTS

Informative Speeches: Round One: Organizations and Personalities

1. American Civil Liberties Union
2. Americans for Democratic Action
3. Intercollegiate Society of Individualists
4. National Student Association
5. Students for a Democratic Society
6. Student Nonviolent Coordinating Committee
7. Student Peace Union
8. United States National Student Association
9. Young Americans for Freedom, Inc.
10. Young Democratic Clubs of America
11. Young Republican National Federation
12. Free Speech Movement
13. University of California President Clark Kerr
14. Mario Savio
15. W. E. B. DuBois Clubs
16. American Nazi Party
17. Young Socialist Alliance
18. J. Edgar Hoover and His Testimony before the Committee on Un-American Activities, March 26, 1947
19. Richard J. Bernstein, former Yale philosophy professor
20. AAUP, Committee S on Faculty Responsibility for the Academic Freedom of Students
21. American Association of University Women
22. Independent Socialist Club
23. Committee on Un-American Activities, U.S. House of Representatives
24. *Guide to Subversive Organizations and Publications* (1957) of the Committee on Un-American Activities, U.S. House of Representatives
25. War Resisters League

Informative Speeches: Round Two: General

26. Student Autonomy in Latin America
27. The Autonomous Status of the Japanese University
28. The Permissive Social Codes in Selected American Universities
29. The Role of the Non-Student[1] on the Campus
30. The Prosecution of the Young Socialist Alliance in Indiana
31. The Activities of Last Year's Annual Congress of the National Student Association
32. The History of the Student Revolt in the United States Before 1960
33. The College Fraternity
34. The College Sorority
35. The Role of the Faculty Senate in the Revolt on the Campus
36. The Relationship between Campus Housing Problems and the Revolt on the Campus

[1] The student who has dropped out but not left the campus, or who lives as a pseudo-student when he has never been enrolled.

37. The College Dropout
38. The Role of Authority on the Campus
39. The Role of the Campus Pastor during the Revolt on the Campus
40. The Northern Student Movement
41. The Concept *in loco parentis*
42. The "Teach-in" as an Instrument of Student Protest
43. The San Francisco "Operation Abolition" Demonstrations
44. The "Silent Generation" of the 1950s
45. The Free Speech Controversy at The Ohio State University
46. Draft Card Burning as an Instrument of Protest
47. The Use of Drugs by American Students
48. The Use of Alcohol by American Students

Persuasive Speeches

1. There is an organized movement by some American youths to "beat the draft."
2. A restrictive attitude toward sex on the campus is more benevolent toward the student than is a permissive attitude.
3. Students cannot ask for more freedom unless they are willing to accept more responsibility.
4. Federal aid to higher education will result in an end to university autonomy.
5. The signs of unrest on the campus are healthy, for they show that the student does care.
6. Administrators of universities should have the right to screen speakers who address student groups meeting on the campus.
7. Communist influence has played an important part in the recent unrest on the campus.
8. The impersonality of the large university is responsible for much of the present student unrest.
9. All university committees should have student representatives.
10. Liberal research grants to college professors, particularly in the sciences, are creating a "privileged" college professor who is no longer interested in teaching.
11. The Ph.D. must be streamlined in order to meet the demands of the growing college population.
12. The social fraternity will remain a vital influence on most college campuses.
13. The social sorority on the college campus is doomed to failure.
14. Much of the unrest can be traced to the ridiculous idea that everyone must go to college to achieve social status.
15. College students have been interested in going South with the integration-segregation controversy because they are looking for a new frontier.
16. Students from northern colleges have no business interfering in the socio-political affairs of the South.
17. The student unrest is due in part to the failure of college administrators to create effective student government.
18. The university should have no responsibility toward housing its students.
19. Students should organize sit-ins to ask for increased academic excellence

as well as to demand increased political responsibility.

20. The student revolts are caused in part by certain professors who seek publicity they could not otherwise achieve.
21. The college administration has the responsibility for controlling the use of alcohol on the campus.
22. Student protests are justified under the First Amendment.
23. The college administration has as its sole responsibility academic excellence and therefore should not hold itself responsible for regulating the social mores of its students.
24. "Civil disobedience" as an instrument of student protest is justified by the Constitution.

Debate Propositions

1. *Resolved:* that the *in loco parentis* role of college administrations is not justified.
2. *Resolved:* that students should play a more active role in the government of their college.
3. *Resolved:* that colleges are justified in enforcing moral codes for their students.
4. *Resolved:* that college faculties should actively encourage student participation in social and political reform movements.
5. *Resolved:* that colleges should permit speakers of all political persuasions to appear on their campuses.
6. *Resolved:* that student activists are rebels in search of a cause.
7. *Resolved:* that the student protest movement is communist inspired.
8. *Resolved:* that student protests against the role of the United States in Vietnam are un-American.
9. *Resolved:* that civil disobedience is justified as an instrument of social protest.
10. *Resolved:* that the social Greek-letter organization has a constructive influence on campus life.

Discussion Subjects

1. What should be the role of the college in prescribing and enforcing standards of student conduct?
2. What is the relationship between student activist movements and the radical political left?
3. What role should students play in university government?
4. Are college students justified in participating in civil rights reforms in the South?
5. What is the extent of communist influence upon student protest movements?
6. Are colleges justified in exercising *in loco parentis?*
7. Should faculty members encourage student activism?
8. What role has increasing institutional size played in fomenting the campus revolt?
9. Is student conduct today radically different from student conduct in the past?
10. Are students justified in using civil disobedience as an instrument of social protest?